Sovereign Attachments

Sovereign Attachments

MASCULINITY, MUSLIMNESS, AND
AFFECTIVE POLITICS IN PAKISTAN

Shenila Khoja-Moolji

UNIVERSITY OF CALIFORNIA PRESS

University of California Press
Oakland, California

© 2021 by Shenila Khoja-Moolji

Library of Congress Cataloging-in-Publication Data

Names: Khoja-Moolji, Shenila, author.
Title: Sovereign attachments : masculinity, Muslimness, and affective politics
   in Pakistan / Shenila Khoja-Moolji.
Description: Oakland, California : University of California Press, [2021] |
   Includes bibliographical references and index.
Identifiers: LCCN 2020053084 (print) | LCCN 2020053085 (ebook) |
   ISBN 9780520336797 (hardback) | ISBN 9780520336803 (paperback) |
   ISBN 9780520974395 (ebook)
Subjects: LCSH: Sovereignty—Religious aspects—Islam. | Masculinity—
   Political aspects. | Identity politics—Pakistan.| Pakistan—Politics and
   government.
Classification: LCC JC49 .K527 2021 (print) | LCC JC49 (ebook) |
   DDC 320.95491—dc23
LC record available at https://lccn.loc.gov/2020053084
LC ebook record available at https://lccn.loc.gov/2020053085

Manufactured in the United States of America

25 24 23 22 21
10 9 8 7 6 5 4 3 2 1

Dedicated to my beloved MHI

CONTENTS

ILLUSTRATIONS

ACKNOWLEDGMENTS

This book emerges from my commitment to study how gender frames the life of a nation. While I take Pakistan as a case in point, and expressions of sovereignty as an object of inquiry, the intersection of masculinity and militarism, as well as the reduction of Islam to a biopolitical discourse, is palpable in other contexts too. Indeed, militarism has permeated the intimate and the distant, the public and the private, calcifying gender, sexual, ethnic, national, and religious identities. Hence, while I tell a particular story of Pakistan in this book, I hope that my readers will draw broader lessons about gender, politics, and militarism. In all, the book is written from a stance of hope: hope for more capacious forms of living.

I am grateful for Lila Abu-Lughod, Ali Asani, Hussein Rashid, Leila Ahmed, Nancy Lesko, and Janet Cooper Nelson's sustained mentorship. They have been my intellectual and ethical guides for decades now. No words can ever express my gratitude for, and to, them. I started this project as a postdoc at the University of Pennsylvania, with the encouragement of Rogers Smith and Nancy Hirschmann.

Many colleagues and friends offered advice during the course of writing this book. My writing group with Oyman Basaran, Shruti Devgan, and Jay Sosa has been extremely generative; I am thankful for their close readings and friendship. The encouragement from my colleagues at Bowdoin College—in particular, Jen Scanlon, Marilyn Reizbaum, Elizabeth McCormack, Jill Smith, Doris Santoro, and Rachel Beane—was life-affirming. Elizabeth Pritchard offered much-appreciated advice on the intersection of religion and sovereignty.

Several colleagues read drafts at various stages of writing and provided invaluable feedback—Lila Abu-Lughod, Mary Ann Chacko, Karishma Desai, Mariam Durrani, Barbara Elias, Shehnaz Haqqani, Celene Ibrahim,

Ayesha Khurshid, Stephanie McCall, Natasha Merchant, Deepti Misri, Alyssa Niccolini, Laura Portwood-Stacer, Jyoti Puri, Maria Rashid, SherAli Tareen, Nicholas Tampio, and Asli Zengin—I am grateful to them for their insights and critical comments.

I benefited from several awards from Bowdoin College's Committee on Faculty Research. Research assistance from my students—Rahul Prabhu, Elise Hocking, and Ziyanah Ladak—was extremely helpful. Many thanks also to my editor, Reed Malcolm, and other staff at the University of California Press, who supported this book with great enthusiasm. I thank the University of Oslo for giving me permission to access their library, as well the staff at Bowdoin College Library for securing documents from the Danish Institute for International Studies. Abdul Sayed from Lunds University was most helpful in sharing the latest issues of some of the magazines.

Finally, my deep gratitude to my family and friends, including my *seva* families, for their patience and support. In the end, and in the beginning, *alhamdu li-llahi rabbil alamin.*

Introduction

THE PUBLIC LIVES OF SOVEREIGNTY

ON DECEMBER 16, 2014, SIX GUNMEN opened fire at the Army Public School (APS) in Peshawar. The gunmen were affiliated with the Tehrik-e-Taliban Pakistan (hereafter, TTP or Taliban), an umbrella organization that connects militant groups based primarily in the northwestern region of Pakistan. They killed 132 children, and nine teachers and staff. The attack is widely seen by the public as one of the deadliest in the country's recent history: "Pakistan's 9/11," as some have remarked.[1] Then Prime Minister Nawaz Sharif called it a "national tragedy," noting that "a line has been drawn . . . on one side are coward terrorists and on the other side stands the entire nation."[2] Making his way to Peshawar, he exclaimed, "I will supervise the [counterassault] operation myself. *These are my children and it is my loss.*"[3]

Sharif invoked the kinship attachment between a father and his children to harness permission for state action. He went on to remove a range of constitutional protections, including reviving the death penalty, advancing an amendment to establish military courts, and reforming laws in order to provide provincial intelligence agencies access to communication networks supposedly used by terrorists. His decisions had ample support from across the country's political spectrum. Most significantly, this moment allowed for an intensification of the army's assault operations against the Taliban in northwestern Pakistan.

The Taliban, for their part, insisted that they had attacked the school because the army was killing *their* kin. Muhammad Umar Khorasani, a Taliban spokesperson, explained, "We selected the army's school for the attack because the government is targeting *our families and females.* We want them to feel the pain."[4]

Both the state and the Taliban thus mobilized kinship feelings to legitimize their violence and cultivate consent for their actions. Since violence is often taken to be a paradigmatic performance of sovereignty, in staking a claim on legitimate violence, both entities advanced themselves as sovereigns.[5] Indeed, while sovereignty is often considered an absolute and indivisible quality of the state, Khorasani's statements highlight that nonstate actors too evince a will to sovereignty.[6] Emotions play a crucial role in this process. As Sara Ahmed reminds us, "subjects must become 'invested' in and attached to the forms of power in order to consent to that power."[7] Both Sharif and Khorasani's practices of violence were accompanied, preceded, and followed by attempts to solicit symbolic permission from their respective audiences. Sovereignty thus appears to not be a "given"; instead it is a relationship that has to be cultivated, as claimants hope to convince an audience of unknown others about their legitimacy to "take life or let live."[8]

These negotiations often unfold in public culture. Robert Hariman describes public culture as the domain where collective public opinion about governance and social welfare is formed through the means of cultural productions such as musicals, magazines, social media, art, advertisements, and memoirs.[9] The APS attack, in fact, led to a proliferation of mediatized productions from the state and the Taliban alike. From music videos released by the Pakistani army marking the Taliban as "the coward enemy" to the Taliban mimicking the same genre to mock the army for being "corrupt," both sought to influence public opinion. Often, militant media productions are viewed solely as instruments for propaganda or recruitment, while the state's productions are considered strategic rhetorical interventions in the service of national security.[10] In contrast, I view these cultural texts as objects whose circulation engenders and produces relations of sovereignty. They form the discursive and affective repertoire through which claimants to sovereignty interpellate multiple publics, binding them to their respective political projects. Studying them can give us a glimpse into statist and militant conceptualizations of the political, the imagined political community, and practices of exclusion/inclusion. It can advance an understanding of the affective dimension of sovereignty as a *felt relationship* between claimants and their publics. These texts thus are not solely functionalist instruments of recruitment or propaganda, but undertake ideological and affective work that requires interpretation.[11] I, therefore, make them the object of my analysis, and build on recent scholarship that reexamines classic assumptions of sovereignty by moving it out of the exclusive domain of geopolitics and legality, and into cultural and affect studies.

Focusing on the postcolonial nation of Pakistan, I engage in a close reading and interpretation of the print and online cultural productions of two key contenders for sovereignty: the Pakistani state and the Pakistani Taliban (which includes the Tehrik-e-Taliban Pakistan and its splinter groups). I ask: What discourses do the state and the Taliban mobilize to perform sovereignty? How do they conceptualize the political and the political community? Who is included and who is excluded? How does affect mediate political attachments and estrangements? What kinds of publics are formed? What are the implications of these analyses for our understanding of sovereignty in postcolonial contexts? I dwell in particular on the aftermath of crises—post-9/11 and post-APS—as such events prod claimants to sovereignty to come out in full force to reassert their status. This includes engaging in spectacular forms of counterinsurgency attacks as well as powerful cultural campaigns. These moments are often accompanied by the re-citation of old othering figures, and creation of new ones: fictionalized enemies, objects/subjects in danger, and agents ideally placed to undertake rescue.[12] Crucially, the post-9/11 Pakistani state has witnessed a shattering of the fantasy of absolute sovereignty and territorial wholeness due to the unilateral drone strikes by the United States and the occupation of territory by the Taliban. We therefore observe enhanced efforts by the state to perform sovereignty.

By juxtaposing the state and the Taliban I do not intend to dissolve their differences; nor do I want to give the impression that I endorse the Taliban's brutal violence, or, for that matter, state violence. The book's aim is not to draw an equivalence between the state and the Taliban. Instead, it seeks to describe and interrogate the discourses and affectivities of each performance of sovereignty to argue that our examination of sovereignty must account for its cultural and affective dimensions. It was Raymond Williams who pointed to the usefulness of juxtaposing "hitherto separately considered activities" for cultural analysis, as it may lead to the discovery of patterns and correspondences, as well as discontinuities.[13]

My examination shows the entanglements and shared repertoire of these seemingly antagonistic entities. It unveils the complicated imbrication of sovereignty by highlighting how scripts of gender and Muslimness become the very means through which sovereignty is performatively iterated in Pakistan. Both the state and the Taliban recruit strangers into relationships of trust, protection, and fraternity by drawing on and reinforcing gendered hierarchies, kinship feelings, and normative understandings of Islam. Such relationships become the structure of feelings that permits the classic and everyday acts of sovereignty that we immediately recognize: violence and governance. Feminist scholars have long argued that constructions and norms of gender and sexuality are crucial to the process of state formation and national belonging.[14] The gender and religious dimensions of political projects in Pakistan have therefore been well established.[15] What deserves scholarly attention is how these become the means through which the relationship of sovereignty is nurtured. Such an approach draws attention to affect and memory work, as well as the making of allied, counter- and ambivalent publics. It views political attachments as contingent and interacting with gender and religion, and also opens up the space for an exploration of political estrangements.

The Taliban and state texts are replete with gendered figurations, which I analyze to understand the constellations of ideas, affects, and histories through which relationships of sovereignty are established. These figurations include the paternal father, innocent child, mourning mother, brave soldier, resolute believer, perverse terrorist, and the dutiful or undutiful daughter. I have organized the book around them in order to study their political work. These figurations, of course, appear in multiple other contexts as well.[16] However, it is much more meaningful to untangle them in their local specificities of occurrence rather than to dwell on their aggregate versions.[17] Deconstructing these figurations exposes how the state and the Taliban foster attachment to their specific visions of the political by relying on and reworking prevailing attachments to particular scripts of gender and sexuality, normative Islam, the family, and imaginations of the past and future. The fantasy of absolute sovereignty is thus recreated through recourse to attachment to religion and family life. In a sense this study responds to Judith Butler's call to discern the role that attachment plays in binding subjects to disciplinary institutions, in this case the state and the Taliban.[18]

Whereas the Pakistani state identifies the territorialized nation as the primary site of belonging and control, the Taliban transform the Muslim community *(ummah)* into sovereign space, and control it by defining the correct practice of Islam.[19] Both target the body as the ultimate site for materializing their power, each drawing on discourses of gender, sexuality, and Islam to delineate who is permitted inside the political community and who threatens its integrity. Specifically, this book shows that relationships of sovereignty in the context of Pakistan are nurtured through performances of masculinity *and* Muslimness, a melding that I name as Islamo-masculinity, which gains affective intensity through kinship metaphors and memory work. The state, for instance, relies on discourses of heteronormative sexuality, Islamic warrior masculinity, and modernity to mark the "coward militants" for exclusion. It nurtures attachment to its project through the figure of the *jawan* (soldier) who invites trust, and even love. The Taliban, for their part, dispel the Pakistani state and army from the space of *ummah* by invoking memories of past national violence, particularly against other Muslims. This makes it possible for them to declare jihad on state institutions, a form of political violence that is traditionally not permissible against fellow Muslims.[20] To solidify their claim on the space of *ummah* and foster attachment to their project, the Taliban perform Muslimness through sartorial choices and adherence to religious rituals. Both the state and the Taliban mobilize women's figuration as kin to hail paternal and fraternal publics which acquiesce to state/Taliban violence in the service of protecting their fictive kin. The figure of the "violated Muslim sister" in the Taliban archives, for example, binds male readers as "brothers" who experience humiliation for allowing the violation of their sisters. To avenge past injury and forestall future ones, this fraternal public is called on to join the Taliban's political project. Women are also invoked to clarify the ideal styles of political attachment and gendered labor required for the reproduction of the state and Taliban. Accordingly, my examination of these figurations—the discourses that produce them, the affective publics that cohere through them, as well as their circulation and reiteration—allows for a theorization of sovereignty as an attachment that is nurtured through performances of Islamomasculinity and is intensified through recourse to kinship metaphors, affect, and memory.

However, we also encounter moments when attachments are formed in ways that are not in the service of power. Indeed, Lee Edelman and Lauren Berlant invite scholars to uncover the politics that proceeds from the breakdown of attachments.[21] The book, therefore, dwells on instances of political estrangement by examining figures (such as melancholic mothers) that express ambivalent attachments to the state. In some respect, the Taliban too exhibit ambivalent attachment, as Pakistan emerges as an object of both promise and betrayal in their texts. Such reworkings of attachment signal sovereignty to be a relationship across multiple entities that is tentatively and contingently forged. It is performative, as its work must be undertaken repeatedly for it to sustain force.

Although this study focuses on the TTP, they are not the only group that has challenged the sovereignty of the Pakistani state in recent years. Prominent among other such groups are the *ulama,* who ground their authority in long-standing religious and scholarly tradition; the Islamists, who seek to compel the state to institute their version of Islam; and imperial actors, such as the United States.[22] These groups are sometimes co-opted and at other times distanced by the state. However, the Taliban-state relationship warrants particular focus for a number of reasons. First, the ideological contestation put forth by the Taliban has, over time, gained widespread legitimacy. Pakistani cultural analyst Rafay Mahmood goes as far as to say that the Taliban's narratives "have supplanted those championed by Pakistan's traditional religious right-wing parties."[23] It is therefore important to analyze the Taliban's cultural productions, both to see them from a historical perspective—as an archive of a particular moment in the history of Pakistan—and to fathom how they condition present-day imaginations of nation, Islam, gender, and sovereignty. Second, groups such as the Taliban are often dismissed as "aberrations" or "irrational actors" due to their violent tactics. Cynthia Mahmood, however, notes that such terminology about perpetrators of violence perpetuates myths about them, rather than provides a grasp of the underlying conflict.[24] A close study of Taliban writings, however, shows that they draw on ideas that have been circulating in the South Asian context since at least the turn of the nineteenth century. They imbue new energy into them to advance their claims for political sovereignty. Their claims, then, are nostalgic *and* modern.

Finally, given that the Taliban aspire to control territory and have engaged in violence to that end, they are one of the most prominent nonstate performers of sovereignty in the context of Pakistan. Stathis Kalyvas argues that "insurgency can best be understood as a process of competitive state building rather than simply an instance of collective action or social contention."[25] Indeed, when the Taliban controlled the Swat and Malakand regions between 2007 and 2009, they engaged in state-like activities including collecting taxes, organizing policing, dispensing justice, conscripting fighters, and gathering intelligence. They mimicked the state in many other ways as well: they had their own flag, a *nasheed* (anthem), and judicial bodies. Crucially, the Taliban do not simply seek to terrorize; they also offer an alternate vision of everyday life and politics.[26] In this respect, I follow Faisal Devji and Talal Asad, who have called for resisting the pull to exceptionalize militants, and instead posit nonpathologizing rationales for militant violence.[27] In doing so, they read militant actions alongside other forms of political action. In particular, Asad observes that "The destruction of human beings and their ways of life . . . has been integral to the formation of modern society. Because every political founding and every commitment to political immortality is rooted in violence, it can be suggested that in an important sense modern terrorists belong to the same universe as democratic states waging wars."[28] Through this book, thus, I open up a hitherto understudied space that reveals correspondences in state and militant performances of sovereignty (their differences are patently discernable and well documented).

Such an approach to sovereignty focuses attention on public culture and the affective work of cultural texts. It calls for a consideration of practices in addition to violence through which sovereignty is performed and iterated. From a feminist perspective, sovereignty thus becomes a more useful analytic as it affords insights into how gender and sexuality constitute and are constituted through sovereign attachments. Yet its fluidity leaves room for the emergence of new assemblages in the future. Ultimately, *Sovereign Attachments* endeavors to excavate the imbrications of sovereignty with gender and religion. In this book, sovereignty acquires texture: it gains a history, is replete with figural nodes, emerges as performative, and has a cultural and affective dimension. The book thus offers directions for how we might study sovereignty by paying attention to gender, affect, and memory.

COMPETING SOVEREIGNTIES IN PAKISTAN

Studying Pakistan in the shadows of the War on Terror compels us to resist the default assumption that the state is the sole proprietor of sovereignty. Thomas Hansen and Finn Stepputat distinguish legal sovereignty from de facto sovereignty.[29] They note that while the former is grounded in formal ideologies of rule and legality, the latter materializes in the ability to kill, punish, and discipline with impunity, which can be performed by nonstate actors as well. The Pakistani state has had to contend with assertions of de facto sovereignty by militants and tribal groups, as well as the United States and China. The country not only has been at the forefront of the War on Terror as an American ally and proxy enforcer, but simultaneously has been termed a "terrorist safe haven" by the US Department of State.[30] Pakistan thus furnishes us with a distinctive site to study the enmeshment of multiple sovereignties in a postcolonial context.

While the book narrows in on the Pakistani state and the Taliban's knotted performances of sovereignty, the United States' imperial sovereign performances maintain an unstated presence.[31] To understand the entanglements of the United States with Pakistan, and the alliance of militants in the form of the Tehrik-e-Taliban Pakistan, we have to go back at least to the 1970s. It was during this time that the Soviet Union invaded Afghanistan, and American interest in the region grew as it sought to halt Soviet expansion. The Pakistani state was similarly geared toward curbing Soviet influence. US President Jimmy Carter signed a directive to covertly aid anti-Soviet operations in Afghanistan, staged via Pakistan. The US Central Intelligence Agency (CIA) trained instructors and members of the Pakistani Inter-Services Intelligence agency (ISI), who in turn trained Afghan and foreign fighters, known as the *mujahidin* (literally, those who engage in struggle) to fight the Soviets. By 1986, under the Reagan administration, the operation was considered the largest in American history since the Second World War.[32] America and Saudi Arabia funneled billions of dollars to the *mujahidin* in Afghanistan. Most of the funds and weapons, however, went to groups that espoused extremist interpretations of Islam.[33] Such rigid interpretations were, in fact, viewed as the ideal bulwark against the communist ideology. In particular, the ideology of jihad, described as holy war, was instrumentalized and used to recruit Muslims across the world. Osama bin Laden was involved in this effort too, funneling the *mujahidin* money, weapons, and fighters. More than three million Afghans were displaced and crossed the border into Pakistan. They found a hospitable home in the tribal border regions of the country, as they shared ethnic ties with the locals. New madrasas were opened to educate the young Afghan refugees.

After the withdrawal of the Soviet Union in 1989, civil war ensued among the Afghan factions. Afghanistan was divided into fiefdoms, with warlords fighting against each other and switching alliances.[34] Refugees kept crossing into Pakistan. In 1994, a movement of students from the eastern and southern parts of Afghanistan rose to challenge these warlords and end the conflict. They called themselves Taliban (literally, students). While the movement was composed of ethnic Afghan Pashtuns, they had strong ties with Pakistan. Many of the members, including the Afghan Taliban leader Mullah (Muhammad) Omar (d. 2013), had taken refuge in Pakistan during the Soviet occupation and had even studied in Pakistani Deobandi madrasas.[35] At the time, both Pakistan and the United States sided with the Afghan Taliban. Pakistan's support was also linked to a potential pipeline project through Afghanistan that was of interest to an American petroleum conglomerate, Unocal.[36] By 1996, under the leadership of Mullah Omar, the Taliban took the capital, Kabul, and over time gained control of three-quarters of the country. They called their state the Islamic Emirate of

Afghanistan and enforced a rigid interpretation of *sharia* (translated often as Islamic law).[37]

During this time, bin Laden also established his base in Afghanistan and started launching attacks on Western targets. In 2001, the United States held bin Laden and al-Qaeda responsible for the 9/11 attacks and began military operations in Afghanistan with NATO forces. As a result, the Taliban government was overthrown in 2001. In this effort, the United States again sought Pakistan's support and its president, Pervez Musharraf, agreed, in exchange for military aid, training, and compensation. After the invasion of Afghanistan, the United States placed its preferred leaders in government and has continued to fight the Taliban. At the time of this writing, in 2020, the United States had recently completed negotiating the terms of its withdrawal from the country.

The Making of the Pakistani Taliban

In the aftermath of the American and NATO invasion, several al-Qaeda and Afghan Taliban militants fled from Afghanistan to take refuge in Pakistan's tribal areas and launch counterattacks from there. They were initially welcomed by the locals, given that their shared ethnic code of *pashtunwali* called for hospitality and asylum. We learn from the biography of Baitullah Mehsud (d. 2009), one of the founding leaders of the TTP, that after the invasion he busied himself with transporting the *mujahidin* from Afghanistan to safe havens in Pakistan so that they could regroup and retaliate.[38] Mehsud's group at the time was called Tanzeem-e-Taliban.[39] Since the border regions of Pakistan were semiautonomous, in that the Pakistani government had let the local tribal chiefs manage the population with relative independence, the Pakistani army resisted engaging in military operations in the region at first. However, that changed with rising militancy and American pressure. In 2002, in an effort to eliminate al-Qaeda terrorists, the army deployed troops in Waziristan for the first time since Pakistan's creation.[40] In 2004, the United States also began its semicovert and legally questionable campaign of drone strikes.[41] In retaliation for military interventions in their own backyard and in support of their tribal affiliates across the border, in December 2007 several Pakistani militant groups formed an alliance, the Tehrik-e-Taliban Pakistan (TTP), under Mehsud's leadership. Anti-US and anti-state sentiments congealed in the form of the TTP. The Pakistani state banned the TTP in 2008 and has fought them ever since.

Although the Pakistani Taliban appear as a singular entity in Pakistani public culture, they are a heterogenous group, composed of different sub-groups, and shifting alliances. Leaders change often, members leave and rejoin, and groups dissipate due to ideological and strategic differences.[42] One of the earliest splits happened in June 2008 when two former TTP commanders, Maulana Hafiz Gul Bahadur and Mullah Nazir, separated from the TTP to form Muqami Tehrik-e-Taliban; they wanted to focus primarily on supporting the Afghan Taliban as opposed to attacking the Pakistani state. The group has periodically cooperated with the TTP, such as when it came together in 2009 to form the Shura Ittehad-ul Mujahidin, and has entered into deals with the Pakistani government to establish autonomy in its areas of operation.[43] In May 2014, the Mehsud faction decided to part ways from the TTP and declared Khalid Mehsud its leader, forming the TTP-South Waziristan.[44] Their spokesperson, Azam Tariq Mehsud, explained that the split was due to a disagreement regarding the TTP's practices, which they deemed contrary to Islam: "We consider the bombing of public places, extortion and kidnappings un-Islamic, and since the TTP leaders continued with these practices, we decided we should not share the responsibility."[45] The group, however, rejoined the TTP in 2017.[46] Another faction led by Omar Khorasani left in 2014, calling itself the Jamaat-ul-Ahrar; a few years later it splintered further into TTP-Hizbul-Ahrar.[47] It is rumored that as of August 2020 both have rejoined the TTP. Increasingly the TTP has become a magnet for other militant groups in Pakistan as well. Some groups outside the FATA (Federally Administered Tribal Areas, which were semi-autonomous until 2018) and Khyber Pakhtunkhwa regions, focused on sectarianism inside Pakistan and the Kashmir/India jihad, have expressed allegiance to TTP. Meanwhile, there are other niche, ad hoc groups, such as the Ghazi Force, that interlink with TTP but have their own targeted agendas.[48]

The Taliban factions also have varying levels of cooperation with other networks, such as al-Qaeda and now, Daesh.[49] In 2014, five commanders pledged allegiance to the Islamic State Khorasan (a Daesh affiliate in Afghanistan and Pakistan) and were dismissed by the TTP.[50] In July 2020, the TTP core group issued a statement in which it explicitly rejected the United Nation's claim that TTP might join the Islamic State Khorasan.[51] Some factions permit non-Pashtun and foreign fighters, others do not. While there is a sharing of knowledge and tactics between the TTP and their Afghan counterparts, there are also significant differences. The Afghan Taliban, for example, are opposed to targeting the Pakistani state. In contrast, most Taliban factions in Pakistan view the Pakistani state's support of coalition forces (United States and NATO) with suspicion and have taken it upon themselves to contest the state's authority through violence and cultural discourse. This remains a central point of contention and has led to fragmentation.

Given this fluidity, it is difficult to view the Taliban as a cohesive movement. However, it is possible to analyze the main constituent organizations' cultural products in order to understand their claims-making process. Indeed, the group continues to evince a will toward singular central authority even as it struggles with fragmentation. This is revealed by efforts such as the declaration of an amir to centralize command, establishment of consultative committees *(shura)*, publication of a code of conduct, and institution of punishment for detractors. In this book, then, "Taliban" operates both as a signifier for the TTP, as well as a set of anti-state and anti-US ideologies espoused by multiple groups that sometimes operate under the TTP banner and at other times splinter off from it.

The Taliban, as will become clear over the course of this book, contest the political authority of the Pakistani state, and argue that since God is sovereign, He alone exercises authority over the social and political lives of Muslims. Any state or entity that does not acknowledge this is considered apostate. They thus view the Pakistani state as illegitimate and believe that the Muslim community requires a different political formation, *khilafat,* to materialize God's will on earth. They posit themselves as agents who will inaugurate this sociopolitical order. The Pakistani state, for its part, does not reject God's sovereignty; the Objectives Resolution of Pakistan, passed in 1949, for instance, declares the sovereignty of God as its first principle. However, the state operates within the Westphalian state model, limiting the role of religion and religiously-derived authority.[52] The state and the Taliban therefore interpret divine sovereignty in different ways that have implications for how they envision the ideal political community and its institutions.

Things came to a head in 2007 when a group of Taliban-affiliated militants led by Mullah Fazlullah tried to institute *sharia* in the Swat Valley and the Malakand Division. They established training camps for fighters and took control of media apparatuses such as radio stations.[53] Crucially, they also controlled the means of violence, meting out punishments and policing the public and private lives of those who fell within their purview. They set up their own courts, prisons, and police, known as the Shaheen Commandos. They even erected a parallel civilian bureaucratic system to provide social services.[54] Said differently, the Taliban engaged in all the classic practices of sovereignty and, in doing so, emerged as a sovereign competitor on the national scene. To reassert control, the government launched military operations, followed by a peace agreement in February 2009. The terms of the agreement show how salient the control over means of violence was for the state, as it stipulated the following:

> The Taliban will recognize the writ of the government and they will cooperate with the local police; The Taliban will turn in heavy weapons like rocket launchers and mortars to the government; The Taliban will not display weapons in public; The Taliban will not operate any training camps; The Taliban will denounce suicide attacks; A ban would be placed on raising private militias.[55]

In exchange, the state agreed to institute *sharia* in certain areas and promised to gradually withdraw the army. The peace accords were soon compromised, and clashes resumed in a few months. However, the accords show that the state relinquished aspects of its sovereign right to rule in order to take back control over the right to violence. During that particular historical juncture, the Taliban were a formidable claimant of sovereignty in Pakistan.

Over the years, the Pakistani army, with American help, intensified its efforts to contain the Taliban and has had decent success. Some analysts today argue that the Taliban are no longer a threat; others, such as Ayesha Siddiqa, Amira Jadoon and Sara Mahmood, note that such groups often dissipate only to reunite or align with other networks later, and that a TTP comeback cannot be ruled out.[56] Recent TTP activity suggests the same. In September 2018, the new TTP amir, Noor Wali Mehsud (aka Abu Mansoor Asim), published a "code of conduct" document to promote cohesion and central control.[57] The document provides guidance on permissible and impermissible targets, and outlines punishments for detractors. During 2019, the TTP circulated leaflets in Wana warning the police to leave the South Waziristan region in three days.[58] They issued another one to caution residents of Miramshah to avoid playing loud music and getting polio vaccines.[59] It also demanded that women not leave their homes without being accompanied by a man, and included a threat of violence: "We remind you [residents] that similar statements issued by Taliban several times in the past had fallen on deaf ears, but this time we are going to take to task those who violate the Taliban order . . . There will be no use of DJs, neither inside the house nor in open fields and those ignoring the warning will be responsible for consequences."[60] The August 2020 reunification of several splintered TTP factions is viewed by some security analysts as an indication that their current leader's vision for a more cohesive TTP is coming to fruition.[61] Most recently, in November 2020, in an article published in *Mujalla Tehrik-e-Taliban*, he again urged readers to unite and avoid infighting.[62] The Taliban's strength and public contestations fluctuate, but they remain a subterranean force that can erupt under the right circumstances.

AFFECTIVE POLITICS, ATTACHMENTS, AND PUBLICS

In political theory, state sovereignty is often conceptualized from a juridical perspective, whereby a sovereign power establishes absolute authority over governance and violence in a given territory.[63] Joining a number of recent studies that reexamine such assumptions of sovereignty, feminist scholars such as Inderpal Grewal contest absolutist understandings of sovereignty, noting that other groups—from militias in the United States to Taliban in Pakistan—also evince a will to sovereignty.[64] Studies of para-statist organizations, tribal leaders, and militants point to how sovereignty can be yielded by nonstatist forces.[65] In the context of Pakistan, for instance, Anushay Malik writes about the authority exercised by a labor leader who enforced his own justice system, which was facilitated by armed groups of men; and Sanaa Alimia elaborates on how *maliks* in the former FATA operate as power brokers.[66] In addition, imperial practices of power also impinge upon our understanding of sovereignty as an exclusive domain of the state.[67] What we have then are cracks in the underlying assumption of sovereignty as unified in the state. These works compel us to consider sovereignty as nested, located across multiple nodes—local, national, and international—and distributed.

Ultimately, claimants of sovereignty seek control over bodies, over life and death. These claims, as Thomas Hansen and Finn Stepputat note, must be reiterated constantly in relation to other competing actors, who also hope to exercise more or less legitimate violence in a territory.[68] Sovereignty therefore can be viewed as an ongoing performance wherein competing sovereigns engage in practices that produce them as singular, natural sovereigns.[69] While violence is a prominent practice through which states and other claimants to sovereignty perform control over life and death, such exercises are often accompanied by negotiations in public culture in which claimants assign differential political value to bodies. Indeed, for Giorgio Agamben, the

capacity to decide on the outside, the exception, is an essential and defini-
tional feature of sovereign power.[70] Life caught in this exception is not freed
from sovereign power; instead it is included in the juridical order through its
exclusion and its *reduction* to biological fact, bare life. Feminist scholars from
Pakistan, such as Aneela Zeb Babar, Rubina Saigol, and Lala Rukh, furnish
us with examples of how popular and state-produced cultural texts—war
songs, art, and architecture—inform public opinion over who must die and
who deserves protection.[71] These cultural performances are not one-time
occurrences but have to be repeated in order to retain their force and intensify relations of sovereignty. Sovereignty, in that sense, is performatively
forged through discursive practices.[72]

Through their respective cultural texts, the state and the Taliban hope to
forge a public that aligns with their claims and responds accordingly. Michael
Warner describes publics as strangers who share a commonality by virtue of
being addressed and listening together; Lauren Berlant emphasizes the role
that shared feelings and sentiments play in the formation of publics.[73] The
cultural texts studied in this book mobilize affect and memory, binding
strangers into a public that consents to sovereign power. Indeed, Ann Stoler
argues that consent to domination is often made possible "by shaping appropriate and reasoned affect, by directing affective judgements, by severing
some affective bonds and establishing others."[74] Affect, in this formulation,
is understood as not residing *in* the subject but as producing the surfaces of
subjects and objects, giving shape to relationships.[75] For instance, when the
Taliban invoke the idea of *khilafat* in their magazines, they arouse a nostalgia
for past Muslim glory and stoke ambition for reproducing such a political
order in the present. They posit themselves as chosen by God to lead this
effort and, in doing so, nurture an attachment to their political project,
which simultaneously fosters ambivalence toward the state of Pakistan.
Likewise, when the army advances the figuration of the "mourning mother"
in its songs, it recruits mothers of slain soldiers and children to perform this
affective state. Mothers are permitted to grieve their loss but are called on to
reframe it as a sacrifice for the nation and to reattach to the state. In both
cases, allied publics are created that learn appropriate ways of attaching to the
Taliban or the state. These attachments are crucial to examine because they
illuminate the process of political formation and allegiance, at the level of the
individual as well as the collective. They also provide insights into how specific arrangements of power are held together.

Indeed, a number of feminist and queer theorists have productively taken up the concept of attachment to examine political formation.[76] In developmental psychology, the concepts of attachment and attachment systems introduced by John Bowlby are used to describe the processes and environments in which an infant seeks out a familiar caregiver during times of separation.[77] An alarmed infant is predisposed to seek protection from her primary caregiver even when the caregiver may be cruel. Therefore, Judith Butler argues that paying attention to processes of attachment can help explain how subjects may continue to tie themselves to punitive cultural forms and disciplinary institutions, even when they realize their exploitative effects.[78] Lauren Berlant, however, observes that attachment may also offer the possibility of remaking the world around us.[79] Her distinction from Butler creates space for the emergence of alternate possibilities and patterns within disciplinary regimes. This book endeavors to provide an account of how attachments to claimants of sovereignty unfold in a specific postcolonial context. Affect plays a vital role in this process, producing *feeling publics* that align with certain forms of power and disengage from others. By analyzing affectively laden cultural figurations, the book offers insights into the universe of attachments nurtured by the state and the Taliban. Indeed, Berlant notes that "one attaches to the world, or not, not in the mode of decision or emotion, but *thrown into architectures* of trust that are built from within in the process of being in life (including from desperation when there are no reliable anchors for trust)."[80] This thrownness of attachment appears in the book as I illustrate how attachments to political entities are intertwined with attachments to masculinity, heteronormative family life, honor, normative Islam, and past Muslim glory, as examples. That is precisely why certain gendered figurations appear repeatedly in both the state and the Taliban's claims-making processes, as they simultaneously represent and congeal these myriad forms of attachments.

Yet, in the book, we also encounter moments when the state and the Taliban fail to produce allied publics; that is, when subjects reject particular forms of attachment, express ambivalence, or even modify attachments toward different ends. On such occasions we may observe the formation of a counterpublic. Warner describes counterpublics as those that are at odds with the dominant public. The Taliban are an exemplary instantiation of a counterpublic in this book as they reorient political attachments away from the state and toward their own political project, even while maintaining an imitative posture toward the state (chapter 3). While the Taliban's cultural texts are a key part of the archive assembled for this research, I also study street protests and rallies, as they represent moments when attachments to the state appear to be ambiguous. Butler reads protests as "provisional versions of popular sovereignty," in which "the people" contest statist hegemony over meanings of life and death.[81] Protests by mothers of slain APS students are a case in point (chapter 6). Whereas the mourning mother performs emotional labor for the state by reframing the killing of her son into a sacrifice for the nation, the melancholic mother rejects state-ascribed meanings: instead of detaching from the lost object (her son), she holds on stubbornly and calls for state accountability. In doing so, she enters into an ambivalent attachment to the state, signified by her simultaneous attempt to seek redress from, and her scathing critique of, the state. Such performances of popular sovereignty signal the ambivalences that Berlant points to, creating possibilities for alternate arrangements with the state. Protests however are not always organized against the state. In some instances, protests bolster statist claims, becoming occasions for performatively reinscribing sovereign attachments. I examine such occasions organized in the aftermath of the APS tragedy, in which young boys dress up as soldiers during public demonstrations, literally becoming sovereign proxies (chapter 2).

Masculinity and Muslimness

In the context of Pakistan, masculinity and Muslimness emerge as salient performances through which the state and the Taliban foster attachments to their respective projects. In recent years, there has been a steady rise in studies that draw explicit connections between masculinity and state power.[82] Scholars have studied how male leaders and their sexual prowess are often read onto the state and how the liberal state functions as a purveyor of male domination.[83] That said, while masculinity is frequently coded in the male body, it is not a natural expression of the body. Theorized as a performance of power and domination, masculinity can be enacted by female-coded bodies as well, as Jack Halberstam instructs.[84] The de-linking of masculinity and maleness means that in addition to studying men and their histories as gendered beings, the study of masculinity can also account for, as Mrinalini Sinha argues, masculinity's "rhetorical and ideological efficacy in underwriting various arrangements of power."[85] Such arrangements exist not only in relation to gendered bodies, but also across institutions. Feminist international relations scholars therefore often invoke masculinity to analyze both the protectionist and punitive dimensions of the state.[86]

In the context of South Asia, a number of recent studies examine the co-articulation of masculinity and power, focusing in particular on the masculinization of Hinduism in contemporary India. This includes remasculinization of religious figures such as Ram and Lord Krishna by the Hindu right, as well as the categorization of women primarily as mothers or female warriors.[87] While gender and sexuality have been an enduring concern for scholars writing about Pakistan too, there is much less written explicitly on masculinity. Studies about male nationalist and political figures such as Mohammad Ali Jinnah and Allama Iqbal abound but often take a biographical approach.[88] That said, critical work on masculinity and its intersection with Islamism and piety movements is emerging.[89] My hope is to make a contribution to this nascent line of inquiry by paying attention to the construction and performance of masculinities as they lend weight to performances of sovereignty in Pakistan. I introduce the term "Islamo-masculinity" to identify the specific modality of masculinity that crisscrosses with normative Muslimness, which I observe in both the state and the Taliban's texts. Islamo-masculinity permits performers to mobilize both the privilege of normative masculinity and that of normative Islam, while demarcating aberrant masculinities. It relies on particular figurations of femininities in order to become relationally legible, and interlinks with discourses of heteronormativity and modernity. Islamo-masculinity *does* things; it mediates the relationships of sovereignty that exist between claimants and attentive publics, between the individual and the collective. This concept simultaneously draws on and departs from Bonnie Mann's helpful theorization of sovereign masculinity, grounded in the American context.[90] While emphasizing how sovereignty draws weight from, and gives weight to, masculinity, I note how the Pakistani context brings with it its own structural features, affective accruals, and histories.

Indeed, Muslimness emerges as a salient performance in sovereign contests in Pakistan. In the hands of the state and the Taliban, the *ummah* is transformed into a sovereign space from which certain bodies are excluded for failing to perform appropriate Muslimness. Muslimness, in these discussions, is expressed not only through pious acts, sartorial choices, and ritualistic practices, but also through conceptualizations of the political that advance the welfare of the *ummah*. The latter include conceptions of divine sovereignty and its relationship to state sovereignty. This debate has a long history in the context of Muslim South Asia. Following the death of the last

Mughal emperor in 1707, political sovereignty of India gradually shifted toward the British. It was consolidated first through the East India Company and then formally through the Government of India Act of 1858. Against this loss of political sovereignty, the Indian Muslim scholarly elite began to debate questions of divine sovereignty and its relationship to the intercessory authority of the Prophet as well as to the state.[91] These questions were ultimately concerned with examining authority structures that mediated the divine-human encounter. The present contestation over ideal polity for Muslims that I delineate in this book takes place against this historical background. As in the past, today too, both the state and the Taliban advance conceptualizations of the political that they believe represent a materialization of divine sovereignty on earth. They view themselves as forging a political community that permits Muslims to engage in pious acts and facilitates their welfare. Ultimately, these practices transform the *ummah* into a space of regulation and control, and Muslimness into a disciplinary discourse, as each decides on Islam's normative boundaries and exposes those outside them to death.

ARCHIVES OF SOVEREIGNTY

Economic liberalization, a boom in mobile technology, and growth of social media have increased the salience of mediatized cultural texts in shaping national political discourses across the globe. This holds true for Pakistan as well. Whereas before 2002, state-sponsored television and radio networks were the primary media outlets in the country, a large number of private media channels have been established since then. As of 2017, the Pakistan Electronic Media Regulatory Authority (PEMRA) had issued eighty-nine satellite TV licenses.[92] Today, television is one of the most dominant mediums for accessing news and entertainment. In addition, while internet connectivity remains a challenge, mobile technology has enjoyed greater penetration in recent years. According to the Pakistan Telecommunications Authority, by the end of 2018, teledensity (the number of telephone connections for every hundred individuals living within an area) had reached 74 percent, and the cellular mobile subscriber base stood at 150.2 million.[93] Broadband penetration grew to 28.3 percent in 2018 (up from 22.6 percent the previous year and from under 1 percent in 2012), with broadband subscribers totaling 58 million. Between 2017 and 2018, the country reduced the custom duty on smartphones, which resulted in increased rates of adoption. The number of newspapers and periodicals has declined—from 1,820 in 2007 to 539 in 2016—but there is a more pronounced trend of dual print and online publications.[94] These changes have shaped the ways in which Pakistanis access and consume media. Social networking sites, for instance, have become increasingly popular, with close to 32 million Facebook users in the country.[95] While state ownership of media platforms is limited, the state continues to exercise power through its regulatory body, PEMRA. In this changing mediascape, both the state and militants are increasingly utilizing mediatized and popular cultural productions to shape public opinion.

In order to study the state and the TTP, I engage in a close reading of their print and online cultural productions published in the shadow of 9/11, paying particular attention to how they describe their political projects and address the public. I focus specifically on certain recent events prominent in public culture, ones that prompted a national discussion and debate on sovereignty. These include the Taliban attack on APS, the military operations against the Taliban, the arrest and later release of nineteen-year-old Naureen Laghari for planning a terrorist attack, and the ongoing incarceration in the United States of a Pakistani woman, Aafia Siddiqui. I engage in a close reading of how these events are described by the state and the Taliban to observe the dynamic interplay of gender, affect, and memory through which sovereign attachments are forged. In the history of Pakistan these are only a few among many events that have generated intense public discussion; their selection therefore serves illustrative purposes, aiming to isolate how sovereignty is negotiated in public culture.

To study the state, I examine online and print texts circulated by the Pakistani army, as well as autobiographies of civilian political leaders. Following Timothy Mitchell, I see the state as a composite of institutions and practices.[96] Mitchell theorizes the state as not a singular actor, but as a decentered complex of power relations that systematically create the larger *effect* that we call the state. The cultural productions that I study are precisely the discursive practices that create the effect of the state as a coherent entity. National armies often perform sovereign functions and are therefore an important object of study. Scholars studying national armies note that while the army is a key institution of the state, it is also a force in its own right. Historically, for example, as Hansen and Stepputat observe, colonial domination in Asia and Africa was often handed off to naval forces, trading companies, and even private actors.[97] These entities acted in the name of their sovereign but also engaged in practices—including meting out excessive violence, reforming courts, and issuing legal verdicts—of their own accord.[98] As a result, much harsher forms of punishment and violence were experienced by those who lived in the colonies than those in the metropole. In Pakistan, the army has functioned as the *hukumat* (government) through multiple coups, and remains one of the most powerful institutions.[99] It has access to a large portion of the public budget and often operates as a welfare support system for its soldiers and their families.[100] With Pakistan imagined as a homeland founded for Muslims, the army also sees itself as a defender of Islam.[101] The army's cultural texts therefore become a salient means in and through which attachment to the state is cultivated.

Since the beginning of the War on Terror and in response to the changing mediascape, we observe a distinct uptick in the Pakistani army's media engagements. While the army's media arm, Inter Services Public Relations (ISPR), was established in 1949 as an interface among the armed forces, media, and the public, and has been publishing magazines, songs, and televisual dramas for decades, the frequency and quality of these productions has increased dramatically. Today, the ISPR engages in wide-ranging public relations, managing public opinion not only through press conferences, but also via adept use of televisual and social media, as well as literature. The ISPR hosts a YouTube channel and is active on Twitter and Facebook. Its official magazine, *Hilal,* originally published in Urdu, now is joined by a version in the English language, a version for women in English, and a version for children in both English and Urdu. Although the *Hilal* magazines circulate primarily within army circles and many of the authors are either army officers or their relatives, the ISPR is also active in producing media aimed directly at the everyday Pakistani citizen: music videos, short films, and documentaries. The agency also consults with private media organizations on films and dramas, and its website features electronic books that include first-person accounts by soldiers and their families.

Political commentator Haroon Rashid notes that the Pakistani military started revamping its media and communications strategy during the tenure of General Ashfaq Kayani, the chief of army staff between 2007 and 2013.[102] This included training its personnel as well as establishing an institutional system for creating a national narrative. Rashid further comments that it was the APS attack that occasioned a change in the army's understanding of the media's role in contemporary war.[103] The army's pivot toward media as a means to influence public opinion is visible through a cursory study of its press conferences. Asif Ghafoor, the former director general of ISPR, for instance, views media as playing a crucial part in the defense of Pakistan. He explains, "Media has a front-line role in fifth generation warfare ... You [journalists] are the opinion makers. Show all the good things in our country ... Create public awareness. Show them what has improved in Pakistan. This doesn't mean don't show the bad. The power which the media has, no other state institution at this time has that sort of power because there is fifth generation warfare and hybrid war."[104] On another occasion, Ghafoor noted that media is the first line of defense in "hybrid warfare."[105] Given this emphasis on media, the military's public relations materials—such as music videos, short films, press conferences, speeches, and English- and Urdu-language magazines, specifically *Hilal Urdu, Hilal English,* and *Hilal for Her*—become primary sources for this book's investigation.[106] I focus on issues published between September 2001 and July 2020, with an eye to how the army articulated itself during or in the aftermath of attacks—terrorist and otherwise. During the period under consideration, the APS attack features prominently. I therefore take that attack as a point of departure but then move backward in time to make sense of it. To give my analysis a genealogy, I also examined past issues of *Hilal Urdu,* particularly those published during the decades when Pakistan was at war—specifically, the 1965 and 1971 wars with India. *Hilal* has a long history. It was first launched as a biweekly in 1951, alongside the weekly ISPR magazine, *Mujahid* (first published in 1948). It took over from *Mujahid* as the weekly army magazine in November 1952 and transformed into a bimonthly and then a monthly magazine in 2007.[107] Examining past issues shows continuities as well as shifts in the army's discourse. Books featured on the ISPR website are also an object of study: *Dam-e-Lahoo* (2018, Cost of Blood, a novel, Urdu), *Junoon-e-Rukh-e-Wafa* (2018, Passion in the Face of Loyalty, a compilation of first-person accounts by army personnel and their family members, Urdu), and *Moonglade* (2018, a compilation of first-person accounts by army personnel and their family members, English).[108] An impressive number of scholars have studied the Pakistani army, providing descriptions of its capitalist dimension, political histories, and ethnographies centered on the lives of soldiers and their families.[109] This book contributes to this body of work by investigating how, through its aesthetic productions, the army hails publics that acquiesce to its authority.

To examine other performances of state sovereignty, I study the cultural texts produced by state leaders, in particular political autobiographies set against the backdrop of 9/11. These include those written by former Army General Pervez Musharraf, former Prime Minister Benazir Bhutto, and current Prime Minister Imran Khan. Through these texts, leaders inspire confidence in their abilities by drawing on prevailing codes of hegemonic masculinity and melding it with self-articulated normative Islam. In doing so, they perform Islamo-masculinity, through which they establish a relationship of trust with their reading publics.

To study the Taliban's performances of sovereignty, I examine their communication materials, in particular print and online magazines, which have proliferated with the rise in digital technology and the ease of creating user-generated content. Specifically, I engage in a close reading of a number of magazines published between 2011 and 2020: *Ihya-e-Khilafat* (Urdu, issues 1 to 14, 2011 to 2017), *Azan* (English, issues 1 to 6, 2013 to 2014), *Mujalla Tehrik-e-Taliban* (Urdu, issues 1 to 8, 2016 to 2020), *Ihya-e-Khilafat* (English, issues 1 and 2, 2014), and the women's magazine *Sunnat-e-Khola* (English, issues 1 and 2, 2017).[110] Throughout the book, when citing from the Taliban magazines, I have retained the punctuation, spellings, and syntax in order to give readers a glimpse into the original texts. I also examine Taliban videos, recorded speeches of leaders available online, autobiographies of militant leaders such as Baitullah Meshud, the most recent TTP code of conduct document (2018), and leaflets and pamphlets used for local communication.[111] Most of these materials are in the Urdu language, indicating the TTP's desire to transform itself from an ethnic to a national movement.[112] Indeed, as the editors of *Sunnat-e-Khola* note, "Tehrik e Taliban Pakistan is not only a pukhtoon tehrik [movement] but it has members from all over Pakistan. Hundreds of people from Punjab, Sindh, Balochistan and tribal belts have joined Tehrik e Taliban."[113] The Taliban's recent ventures into publishing in English signal their aim to also speak to more urban, middle-class Pakistani and diasporic audiences. These audiences include insiders who are already aligned with the mission, potential recruits who could be convinced, as well as oppositional audiences such as the state.[114] Since the magazines often rely on the labor of a few committed members who edit and write, they are published with breaks or conclude abruptly, only to be replaced by new ones when conditions stabilize.

While the Taliban's cultural texts cover a broad range of topics, for the purpose of this book, I focus in particular on their conceptualization of the political vis-à-vis the Pakistani state, and the recurring gendered idioms through which a relationship of sovereignty is established with the reading publics. The magazines include extended features explaining the theological necessity of instituting *khilafat* and critiques of the Pakistani government and army. Articles regularly contain citations from the Quran, the hadith, and the stories of companions of the Prophet *(sallallahu 'alayhi wa alayhi wa sallam)*, which function as evidence of the truth-claims of the authors.[115] In addition, we find interviews with *mujahidin* and statements by leaders. Issues often also contain sections on history in which excerpts from the writings of prominent historical figures are shared.[116] Some magazines include a list of recent Taliban activities as well. The Urdu edition of *Ihya-e-Khilafat,* for example, contains a record of bombings, kidnappings, and arrests, as well as the number of injuries and deaths. Many of the magazines include visuals, featuring images of slain soldiers or civilians, Taliban fighters, and the enemy (construed broadly). The cover pages of the magazines often show men in military gear, typically with rifles or Kalashnikovs. The writers of *Azan, Mujalla Tehrik-e-Taliban,* and *Ihya-e-Khilafat* (Urdu and English) are predominantly men, except in a couple of instances where writings of female scholars such as Zaynab al-Ghazali are reproduced or where rare female authors make their appearance.[117] In contrast, articles in *Sunnat-e-Khola* are written predominantly by women but also feature several male voices.[118]

While the Taliban's texts provide one glimpse into how statist performances of sovereignty reverberate, I inspect other entanglements through a study of popular media that engage with statist claims. Specifically, I examine news reports, television talk shows, citizen-generated popular songs, and posters at political rallies related to the events foregrounded in the book (the APS attack, Naureen Laghari's release, and Aafia Siddiqui's incarceration, in particular) to glean how "the people" echo or alter statist performances. I consulted Pakistan's three largest Urdu-language newspapers—*Jang Daily, Express Urdu,* and *Nawa-i-Waqt*—and two major English-language newspapers—*Dawn* and the *Express Tribune*—as well as talk shows featured on both the state-sponsored Pakistan Television Network and private channels such as ARY News, Dunya, and Samaa. I also follow the discussion of these events on social media through hashtags such as #NaureenLaghari and #APSattack as well as user-generated content on YouTube.

Figurations as Method

An analysis of state and Taliban cultural texts reveals recurring gendered figurations, that are simultaneously specific to the historical moment under study and carry the residue of the past. Donna Haraway describes figurations as distillations of shared meanings through which we make sense of the world around us.[119] Likewise Imogen Tyler identifies "figurative methodology" as a useful approach "to describe the ways in which at different historical and cultural moments specific 'social types' become overdetermined and are publicly imagined (are figured) in excessive, distorted, and caricatured ways."[120] By unpacking figurations and following their social and political work, we can discover the terms, registers, and affects through which sovereign attachments unfold in Pakistani public culture. Figurations, however, carry within them seeds of contradictions. They can be taken up and molded in ways that were not originally intended. That is precisely what happens to certain state-produced figurations—on one hand, the Taliban mold them for the purposes of advancing their own, alternate claims of sovereignty, and on the other, diverse publics take them up in ways that at times contest the state's objectives. It is during such moments that the constructedness of figurations—and the fragility of sovereign attachments—becomes most apparent.

Each chapter takes a particular figuration as its point of departure. The first three chapters (Part I) consider different personifications of sovereign power: the head of the state, the soldier, and the *mujahid*. Through these figurations the state and the Taliban articulate themselves as ideal sovereigns and foster attachment by performing Islamo-masculinity that invites trust and confidence in their respective political projects. The next three chapters (Part II) illustrate how relationships of sovereignty are intensified through recourse to kinship, affect, and memory. Paying attention to how women are figured in performances of sovereignty, these chapters examine women's contribution to the Islamo-masculinist claims of the state and the Taliban through gendered labor (the *mujahida* and the army woman), and embodied and affective comportments (*betis*, *behans*, and mourning mothers). The attack on APS functions as an anchor for some of the chapters of the book. The episode was elevated to the level of a crisis and has become an enduring part of national collective memory.

The first chapter engages in a close reading of the political autobiographies of three state leaders, elaborating on the distinct performances of Islamo-masculinity through which they bid for the confidence of their reading public. The next chapter scrutinizes the figuration of the soldier *(jawan)* in the ISPR's media productions as another performance of Islamo-masculinity through which a relationship of trust is established between the army and its audience. The soldier, however, relies on its foil—the militant, an object of hate—to become an object of love. The chapter traces this dyadic construction, paying attention to how discourses of masculinity, sexuality, modernity, and Islam are mobilized in the process. In the third chapter, I place these readings alongside the figure of the *mujahid* that appears in the Taliban magazines. A close reading of the magazines illuminates the Taliban's ambivalent attachment to Pakistan and their simultaneous creation and regulation of the sovereign space of *ummah*. The Taliban stake a claim on this space by performing their own version of Islamo-masculinity, which both corresponds to and departs from the state's versions. These three chapters together provide a glimpse into competing performances of sovereignty that rely on masculinity and Muslimness to produce allied publics.

In the second half of the book I focus on figurations of women in the drama of sovereignty. The fourth chapter explores the figures of the *muhajira/mujahida* and the army woman as ideal women-subjects for the *khilafat-* and nation-building projects, respectively. These women reiterate state and Taliban assertions of sovereignty by buttressing their claims to Muslimness as well as by performing subordinate femininities. The fifth chapter examines women's figuration as *beti*s (daughters) and *behan*s (sisters) across state and Taliban archives to reveal how sovereignty is performed through recourse to kinship feelings. The resulting paternal and fraternal publics clear the way for the sovereign functions of rescue, protection, violence, and rebuke. The chapter however also provides a glimpse into how publics may rework these feelings to enter into oppositional relationships with sovereign power. The sixth chapter expands this theme to showcase women's emotional labor in forging sovereign attachments through the figure of the mourning mother as well as women's refusals to do so through the figure of the melancholic mother. Together, the three chapters in Part II outline how sovereign attachments gain intensity through affect, kinship, and memory. The conclusion reflects on the complicated imbrication of sovereignties considered in the book.

There is both a specificity and a generality to this study. Even though Pakistan is foregrounded, the dynamics outlined in the book—the contingency of sovereign attachments, the mobilization of kinship feelings, the appeal to religion, and the construction of hierarchies of masculinities—emerge in other contexts as well.[121] Their effect in relation to the ideological subordination of women and ethnic minorities also resonates elsewhere.[122] Yet expressions of sovereignty take on a *specific* form in postcolonial contexts.[123] In the case of Pakistan, for instance, concerns around sovereignty are intricately linked with recent as well as past ruptures in assumptions of absolute sovereignty, including unilateral US drone strikes and the secession of regions not fully articulated within majoritarian nationalism, as occurred in East Pakistan in 1971. The interplay of divine sovereignty with state sovereignty and tensions around what it means to be Muslim also factor in. Thus, this book's examination of performances of sovereignty in Pakistan, with attention to its discursive and affective dimensions, offers both specific insights into the Pakistani case and possible directions for the cultural study of sovereignty in other contexts.

Death and Detritus

The 2014 APS attack by the Taliban elicited a strong response from the state. The government initially sought the death penalty only for terrorist-related offences but later expanded it to apply to all capital crimes, including murder and blasphemy.[124] According to Amnesty International, within the first year of this expansion, 326 people had been put to death in Pakistan.[125] Terrorist attacks are horrific, but the responses to them and their ongoing effects are atrocious too, as they breed both security *and* insecurity. For instance, after ousting the Taliban from Swat during a bitter battle between 2007 and 2009, the military stayed in the region to undertake infrastructure and development projects. They rebuilt hospitals, schools, and museums. They also instituted checkpoints to ensure that the Taliban would not return. While the military had been welcomed earlier, it was soon viewed as a nuisance—a body that incited fear. Reheela, a woman living in Waziristan, explained this condition of fear, the dread of being caught between the Taliban and the army: "We are afraid of the Taliban and also of the army" *(Taliban say bhi dar lagta hai, Fauj say bhi dar lagta hai).*[126] During these state-Taliban encounters, millions of people were displaced and they are only slowly returning to rebuild their lives. A formerly displaced woman, Aaliya, recalled that in 2009, she had to move out into the mountains as a result of the Taliban takeover: "My children and I would sometimes live on one mountain, and at other times on another."[127] When Aaliya returned, her house had been demolished.

Butler writes that even when life is not destroyed by war, something of life is destroyed when other lives and living processes are destroyed.[128] In addition to the loss of lives, the sovereign contests between the Taliban and the state have damaged the region such that it is now unable to sustain and organize life in ways that are livable. Ordinary people thus find themselves at the crossroads of competing sovereignties. Malala Yousafzai reflects on this general condition of precarity when she writes: "How can a mother buy food for her family when the market is a warzone? How can children gather for a game of cricket if a bomb could go off under their feet?"[129] What we have then is the enervation of life in many forms—from the decimation of bodies and the destruction of built environments, to the symbolic violence of masculine hierarchies, female subordination, and hardening of religious identities. While it is the latter that this book tracks, it is the former that prompted the research investigation.

PART ONE

Sovereign Islamo-Masculinities

ONE

Narrating the Sovereign

THE HEAD OF THE STATE

RECALLING THE MOMENTS FOLLOWING THE 9/11 ATTACK, Pervez Musharraf, then president of Pakistan and its former military head, writes in his memoir, *In the Line of Fire* (2006):

> [Colin] Powell was quite candid: "You are either with us or against us" . . . [US Deputy Secretary of State] Armitage. . . told the director [of Pakistan's Inter-Service Intelligence] not only that we had to decide whether we were with America or with the terrorists, but that if we chose the terrorists, then we should be prepared to be bombed back to the Stone Age. This was a shockingly barefaced threat . . . . I made a dispassionate, military-style analysis of our options, weighing the pros and cons . . . . Underlying any leader's analysis has to be a keen awareness that on his decision hangs the fate of millions of people and the future of his country . . . . I war-gamed the United States as an adversary.[1]

Musharraf had come to power in 1999 after removing Nawaz Sharif through a military coup. In 2001, he found himself in the midst of the Global War on Terror. He ultimately sided with the Americans, allowing them access to Pakistani airbases and personnel with which to fight the war in Afghanistan. What is of interest to me is that, in this autobiographical text, written five years later while he was still in power, Musharraf produces himself as an analytical leader who skillfully engaged with American bullying. The text not only narrates a past but also fashions Musharraf as an ideal leader for *the present* by inviting conviction in his capabilities. His autobiography can thus be viewed as an object that mediates a relationship of confidence and trust between him and the reading public. This attachment ultimately fosters the public's consent for his sovereign exercises of power. In this chapter, I examine political autobiographies of heads of the Pakistani state written in the shadow of the Global War on Terror. I posit these texts as performative acts that bind subjects to the sovereign. Their study reveals how state leaders locate threat and injurability in other bodies, and assign themselves, and through them the state, the right to govern and engage in violence.

While expressions of national sovereignty are diffused across multiple institutions and leaders, the head of the state often appears as the nation's symbolic apex. Gendered usually as male, he is imagined as the patriarch, the guardian of the masses, and a savior. Milinda Banerjee notes that such imaginations of the head of the state result from the desire for embodied, concrete, and visible forms of sovereignty.[2] In a similar vein, Najeeb Jan argues that while modern liberalism assumes that rule of law has replaced the sovereign (that is, monarchical sovereignty), it is still the sovereign who gives force to law.[3] He therefore calls for studying the personifications of sovereign power in order to understand how this power circulates symbolically. Studying the autobiographies of state leaders can furnish us with insights into a dominant personification of sovereignty as well as into the discourses and affective exchanges that leaders mobilize to hail an allied public.

Autobiographies are memory acts through which writers present their lifeworlds for the consumption of the reading public. These presentations are not disinterested; writers carefully decide which events to highlight and which ones to leave out. They also provide readers with an interpretive frame for understanding their actions and decisions. Autobiographies of state leaders memorialize not only the life of the leader but also that of the nation. In her analysis of autobiographies written by postcolonial state leaders, Elleke Boehmer observes that the leaders' lives often follow the arc of national development and in so doing supply the nation with a self-determining history and a myth of progress.[4] In this chapter, I examine autobiographies written by Pervez Musharraf (chief of army staff, 1998–2007; chief executive of Pakistan, 1999–2002; president, 2001–2008), Benazir Bhutto (prime minister, 1988–1990 and 1993–1996), and Imran Khan (prime minister, 2018–present). All three were active in the political landscape during 9/11 and the ensuing War on Terror. Their autobiographies expressly take up the topic of terrorism and set out to either validate statist policies (as is the case with Musharraf) or provide an alternate vision for Pakistan (Bhutto and Khan). By examining these texts, we can understand how state leaders set in motion what the public identifies to be the domain and body of the sovereign, and how the discourses they mobilize fashion attachment to themselves and to Pakistan.

Written in English and often published simultaneously in Pakistan and Western countries, the autobiographies considered in this chapter are aimed at a particular public—urban, upper-/middle-class Pakistanis, as well as foreigners.[5] In the texts, leaders tell tales of the past replete with characters that threaten the integrity of the nation as well as heroes whose supernatural courage is needed to rescue us. To articulate themselves as singular, inviolable sovereigns, each leader mobilizes different discourses. Yet, masculinity emerges as a salient idiom across all three; it appears not only as a set of values historically associated with male-coded bodies, such as strength, athleticism, and physicality, but also as a practice of power through which domination is enforced. The latter performance of masculinity is visible when all three leaders caricature the masculinities of their competitors. The discourse of masculinity, however, is crisscrossed with, and draws its weight from, other discourses, in particular that of Islam. Each leader advances a specific version of an Islamic subjectivity required for national welfare. In doing so, they also demarcate improper interpretations of Islam, often those harbored by militants. We thus encounter in the chapter three unique and overlapping performances of Islamo-masculinity, which simultaneously nurture confidence in the sovereign and skepticism about competitors. Autobiographies, of course, are one element of a broader corpus of cultural productions related to the leaders under consideration; my reading, therefore, is not meant to provide a comprehensive assessment of their (often fluid) performances of Islamo-masculinity during the course of their careers. Instead, I engage specific texts, written under specific sociopolitical conditions, to glean the salient discourses and affects through which relationships of sovereignty unfolded at particular historical junctures.

MILITARY MASCULINITY

Pervez Musharraf was made chief of army staff in 1998 by the then-Prime Minister Nawaz Sharif, who a year later attempted to remove him from the position. Musharraf was on his way back to Pakistan from a trip to Sri Lanka when Sharif ordered that his plane not be allowed to land. A number of senior army officials launched a coup; Sharif was relieved of his command, and Musharraf installed himself as the chief executive of Pakistan. While Musharraf did not institute martial law, he did amend the constitution to allow himself to be the head of both the civilian and military branches of the state. Musharraf promised swift elections, which did not happen until three years later. In the meantime, through a referendum that Musharraf himself admits had irregularities, he installed himself as the president of Pakistan in 2001.[6]

The 9/11 attacks created the conditions that extended Musharraf's rule, as the United States looked to him for collaboration in the War on Terror. In return, Musharraf received economic aid, which artificially propped up the economy, giving a semblance of progress. He did, however, endorse the creation of private media channels, leading to a boom in the Pakistani mediascape that continues to the present. Over time, as the United States began unilateral drone strikes in Pakistan, Musharraf's popularity began to wane. However, he continued to enjoy support from segments of the Pakistani elite, who viewed his agenda of "enlightened moderation" as a way to curb the influence of extremists, particularly the Taliban.[7]

Written at a time when Musharraf's popularity was declining, *In the Line of Fire* attempts to regain the population's confidence. The text fashions military masculinity as the ideal sovereign masculinity, and constructs Musharraf, the military man, as a paradigm of patriotism and physical strength predestined for national leadership.[8] Musharraf emerges as such against the figure of the corrupt, nonmilitary politician, and his moderate religious stance provides the ideal foil against the zealous militants. The autobiography naturalizes the connections across military, maleness, patriotism, moderate Islam, and sovereign power, working through and with already prevailing positive sentiments associated with the army in Pakistan. Yet in its striving, it also reveals the constructed nature of its own project by providing evidence of moments when soldiers act in ways that can be deemed as less than patriotic.

The Military Man as the Ideal Sovereign

The male body is highly *visible* throughout *In the Line of Fire*. Musharraf recounts moments in his childhood and adulthood when his superior physical prowess and strongheadedness were his saving graces. We learn about the occasions when Musharraf stood up to bullies, including punching and thrashing a boy who harassed his older brother, which earned him the title of "*dada geer* ... a tough guy whom you don't mess with."[9] When his family moved to a rough neighborhood, the only way to survive was to be street-smart: "needless to say ... I was one of the tough boys."[10] In college, he competed in "gymnastics, cross-country running, bodybuilding, and athletics," and was praised for his "muscular physique."[11] Through these narratives, Musharraf produces tough masculinity as a natural characteristic of some male-coded bodies, and the text tacitly suggests that one is born, not made, a soldier. This logic is informed by, and has implications for, the types of men who are considered to be a good fit for the military and those who should be excluded. While I dwell on this more in the next chapter, military recruitment policies betray a preference for men from the Punjab and Khyber Pakhtunkhwa provinces, who are imagined as being naturally tough. In turn, this tough masculinity, as a property of some ethnicized bodies, inclines these men toward the military and ensures their success in it. However, being neither Punjabi nor Pashtun, Musharraf delinks male prowess from ethnicity, connecting it instead to an athletic made body. For example, he notes that it was his tough nature that enabled him to travel to some of the harshest terrains deep in the Himalayas where few dared to go. Describing juvenile play, he uses terminology often employed during war: "We threw stones at each other and made shields with which to protect ourselves. Each gang had its own flag. Even at that age I was very good at making strategies and planning tactics to ambush and trap other gangs. We would lure them into an area, ambush them, and run off with their flag to the top of a hill. It was defeat for them and victory for us!"[12] His toughness also aided him during close brushes with death, including two assassination attempts.[13]

Though tough masculinity seems to be an inherent property of some male-coded bodies, for Musharraf, the military's institutional trainings also have a central place in its production as they harness this raw quality and channel it appropriately. These trainings engender in the future-soldier appropriate dispositions toward both the nation and fellow army members. Musharraf therefore painstakingly describes the rigorous training that elite soldiers undergo and the fraternity, loyalty, and obedience that such trainings impart.[14] Through careful techniques, men are transformed into a distinct class of people: "a breed that willingly dies for its country without question."[15] To produce this breed, according to Musharraf, a man is first "taken apart and put back together differently" and instilled with "discipline and respect for authority."[16] The breaking-down of the future-soldier is necessary for his later inclusion in the fraternal collective of the military—so that he learns "how to be a man" and cannot be broken again.[17] Soldiers are not only toughened up physically but are also "taught how to command men and get the best out of them."[18] In order to motivate his subordinates, Musharraf explains that he used to lead from the front and aimed to be better than them: "I would compete with my men in everything and would treat them to a cold drink if [I] lost . . . All this endeared me to my men, who started looking up to me. They loved me because I was just and compassionate."[19] He recounts a number of military operations where he succeeded due to his men's personal attachment to him. Through these narratives we learn that an ideal military man is not only tough but also a leader who can command moral authority and respect.

For this military man, Pakistan emerges as an object of intense love, and his fellow soldiers and citizens feature as kin. However, Musharraf argues that even though the military man cares for his fellow citizens, he is logical and able to exercise control over himself. He is thus simultaneously a figure who commands intense passion (for the nation and fellow citizens) and dispassion (when it comes to the task at hand). In contrast to the politician, who thrives on public emotions, the military man can separate facts from feelings in order to secure the interests of the nation. In the passage where he discusses Colin Powell's ultimatum, Musharraf articulates himself precisely through these frames: even though he was incensed by the demands of the US Secretary of State, like a good, dispassionate soldier, he put his emotions aside and made a "tactical" and "rational" call that was in the national interest.

Musharraf's autobiography can be theorized as what Salih Aciksoz calls a "consecratory act," which elevates not only Musharraf but also the figure of the military man to the domain of the national and masculine sacred.[20] The text is simultaneously about Musharraf and about the institution of the military. Musharraf's construction of military masculinity, however, includes a paradox. As Elizabeth Spellman and others have noted, in Cartesian dualism, emotionality and the body are often coded as female, while rationality is linked with masculinity.[21] Military masculinity comprises associations not only with rational thought but also with passion: these associations place the military man in an ambiguous relationship with normative gender codes. He is simultaneously hypermasculine *and* connected to his feminine, emotional side. This apparent contradiction is constitutive of sovereign military masculinity (as the next chapter will show further): the delicate balance between toughness and emotion secures the sovereign as both ruthless (during wars) and compassionate (toward his subjects).

The "Corrupt" Politician and the "Uninformed" Terrorist

The status of the military man in *In the Line of Fire* is established through differentiation from other masculinities. Specifically, both the politician and the terrorist are posited as classic forms of lesser masculinities, unauthentic Muslims with dubious loyalty to Pakistan. Whereas the politician is corrupt, self-interested, and in thrall to foreign cultural mores, the terrorist is detached from reality and is uninformed about Islam. These divergent characteristics cast their respective political claims as suspect.

Throughout the text, Musharraf is keen to distinguish himself from politicians. He resists even labeling himself with the term—this in spite of the many instances where he acted as a politician, such as when he facilitated the creation of the Pakistan Muslim League (Q), the party he backed in the 2002 elections.[22] Instead, in the autobiography, Musharraf portrays himself as a soldier who only reluctantly entered the arena of politics. During his college days, when he was persuaded to run in elections, he "didn't enjoy it a bit."[23] Emphasizing his disinterest, he frames politics as a substandard realm of activity for a soldier. To cast doubts about the loyalty of politicians to the nation, he points out that they often attend foreign universities and are disconnected from Pakistan's culture and history.[24] He also alludes to past failures of political leadership due to leaders' lack of local knowledge.[25] In contrast, Musharraf endeavors to present himself as thoroughly belonging to the soil. Whereas politicians—such as his rivals Bhutto and Sharif—come from wealthy backgrounds, he hailed from a middle-class family and had to work hard, against all odds, to climb to the top.[26] His background permits him—and through him, the figure of the soldier—to stake a more authentic claim on sovereign power. It also allows him, in contradistinction to the elite, foreign-educated politician, to forge intimacy and closeness with the average Pakistani.

In terms of specific politicians, we learn about the gross power plays of Sharif—a businessman elected prime minister of Pakistan three times. Not only was he involved in financial corruption, but he also maintained "goons" who assaulted his opponents, including launching an attack on the Supreme Court.[27] Musharraf lists Sharif's many "undemocratic actions," including his unreasonable requests to remove army officers.[28] Sharif also sought to centralize authority by passing an amendment to the constitution that would make him *amir-ul mominin* (commander of the faithful), a move Musharraf views as an overreach. Likewise, the Bhutto dynasty appears in the autobiography as power hungry, with Zulfiqar Bhutto functioning as an "autocrat" and Benazir Zulfiqar treating "the party and the office like a family property."[29] This information about the corruption of politicians works to clear the way for the military man to emerge as a noncorruptible moral force.

Represented by Musharraf, the military man and the institution of the military are held up as the ultimate saviors of Pakistan. Supporting this framing, Musharraf says, "in crises, everyone sees Pakistan's army as the country's savior," and "the Pakistan Army has always been held in high esteem as the only powerful stabilizing factor in the nation."[30]

As the politician consolidates the military man's power, so too does another figuration: the terrorist. In the text, the terrorist appears as a foil for the brave soldier and legitimizes Musharraf's extended military alliance with the United States. Whereas the al-Qaeda terrorist is foreign and hence written out of the nation from the beginning, the Taliban militants are not. They were the *mujahidin* who were prepared by the United States, Saudi Arabia, and Pakistan to resist the Soviet occupation of Afghanistan in the 1980s. Therefore, as Musharraf explains, Pakistan looked to them as a force of peace in war-ravaged Afghanistan after the Soviet exit: "We had hopes that Taliban, driven by religious zeal based on the true principles of Islam, would bring unity and peace to a devasted country."[31] These hopes were dashed when they instituted their own version of governance, which Musharraf terms a "primitive regime."[32] Eventually, for Musharraf, the Taliban slip into the category of terrorists. In the text, terrorists are pathologized as "radical," "criminals," belonging to a "cult," "caught in a time warp," "perverting our faith [of Islam]," and "detached from reality."[33] They seem to have "personality disorders," are of "an uninformed religious bent," and come "from dysfunctional families."[34] Musharraf alleges that they "become terrorists just for the money," and hence also refers to them as "mercenary" and "rats."[35] The former Taliban *mujahidin,* thus, become menacing children of the state because they are duped by zealous clerics.[36]

At the same time, Musharraf is careful to ensure that the figure of the terrorist does not subsume those fighting in Kashmir for their self-determination, a project that aligns with Pakistan's interests in the region. To that end, he mobilizes the figure of the freedom fighter: "sometimes a man can be a legitimate freedom fighter in one context and a terrorist when he does something else."[37] He critiques Western counterterrorism policies that fail to distinguish between these different kinds of struggles: "The West rejects militant struggles for freedom too broadly. The US and Europe too often equate all militancy with terrorism; in particular, they equate the struggle for freedom in Indian-held Kashmir with terrorism."[38] Alluding to the violence of the Indian state in Kashmir, Musharraf argues that such state actions also constitute terrorism:

Pakistan has always rejected this broad-brush treatment. We demand that terrorism be seen "in all its forms and manifestations." This is a serious statement, because when states kill innocent civilians in an effort to crush struggles for freedom, we call it "state terrorism." I feel that the killing of innocent civilians, whether by a state or by any groups, is terrorism. A state causing atrocities and killing civilians in violation of resolutions passed by the UN Security Council is certainly carrying out state terrorism. I differentiate between killing civilians as collateral damage in an attack on a military target on the one hand and targeting civilians intentionally on the other.[39]

Musharraf not only distinguishes between terrorists and freedom fighters, but also expands the definition of terrorism to include states that occupy, maim, and kill civilians. State violence to defend sovereignty, however, remains legitimate and civilian deaths during such encounters are classified as collateral damage. The military man's sovereign power remains intact.

The Unraveling of the Military Man

Even as the military man is valorized as the ideal sovereign, there are moments in Musharraf's autobiography that unravel this very claim. These occur when soldiers violate rules, plan attacks on their superiors, or play politics. In doing so, they perform acts that can be deemed less than patriotic. Musharraf's text is littered with such evidence, which punctures the imagined sacredness and inviolability of the military man.

Consider the 1971 India-Pakistan war, which led to the loss of East Pakistan. In the imaginary of the Pakistani army, 1971 is lodged as a moment when its own officers, those belonging to the East Bengal Regiment, revolted. The scene of brothers killing brothers evokes a deep sense of betrayal and loss.[40] Recalling the day when he and his troops were informed about the cease-fire and the surrender of Pakistani soldiers, Musharraf notes: "I broke down and cried. All my brave soldiers cried with me. It remains the saddest and most painful day of my life. My anger at the generals who had taken charge of government, and at some of the politicians of the time, still makes me see red."[41] Defeat on the battlefield is perhaps the most visceral undoing of the soldier; what is more hurtful is that this loss was engineered by fellow soldiers. In Musharraf's autobiography, the defeat of 1971 figures as a ghost that continues to haunt the present. It seems to inform his desire to both avenge this past defeat and forestall any future threats to Pakistan's sovereignty. The haunting is thereby transformed into an impetus for renewed efforts to ensure that the present-day unruly brothers (the Taliban) are kept in line, so that a cohesive Pakistan can be secured.

Musharraf also relates the story of the noncommissioned officers of the elite Special Services Group who had helped facilitate an assassination attempt on him. He, however, resignifies these officers as having fallen prey to the extremists' propaganda: "it is almost impossible to guard against extremists' indoctrinating the lower ranks in any armed forces."[42] Musharraf thus constructs a hierarchy of soldiers, with the low-ranked soldiers the least connected to the core and hence at risk of being duped by terrorists. With the blame fully shifted onto the terrorist who takes advantage of the low-ranked soldier's inexperience, the officer class—the military man—is protected from defacement. Yet, these narratives continue to hint at the fragility of the military man's claim to sovereign power, for the Special Services Group is composed of elite commandoes.

In the autobiography we also encounter senior generals whose behavior is less than ideal. Musharraf writes about General Ayub Khan, under whose leadership the country saw significant economic expansion during the 1960s. However, Musharraf points out that the benefits of this growth were concentrated in the hands of a few industrialist families.[43] Khan's successor, Yahya Khan, receives criticism for his "callous" response to the 1970 cyclone in East Pakistan.[44] Musharraf also censures him for his "small coterie of military" men who, along with Zulfiqar Ali Bhutto, precipitated the breakup of Pakistan.[45] The autobiography recounts the excesses of General Zia ul-Huq's regime, including inhumane punishments, such as lashings, that Musharraf himself witnessed and tried to stop.[46] In Musharraf's observation, Zia started to overemphasize religious rituals in order to bolster his political base and appease the religious lobby.[47] Naturally, Musharraf includes in his book the betrayal of Lieutenant General Ziauddin, who sided with Sharif to help depose him.[48] Ziauddin is presented as a less-accomplished officer and thus not really a soldier; he was "only the head of our premier security service, ISI ... but Ziauddin did not command any soldiers."[49] Sharif's attempted dismissal of Musharraf also exposed a number of other soldiers who broke the chain of command, such as Tariq Fateh, who did not get to the Karachi airport in time to help Musharraf.[50]

While in the autobiography, the military man emerges as the ideal sovereign when measured against the politician and the terrorist, the text provides evidence for the desecration of this very sovereign masculinity through stories of soldiers who fail to perform normative military masculinity. These soldiers' unsoldierly acts throw a wrench in the didactic and affective work that the text is supposed to do for its readers. They show not only that the military man is socially and culturally constructed but also that his connection to sovereign power is socially produced too—through discursive acts like the autobiography itself. The text thus both nurtures attachment to the military male and holds the potential for fraying that very attachment.

SOVEREIGN FEMALE MASCULINITY

Benazir Bhutto, the twice-elected prime minister of Pakistan, boasts the honor of being the first woman to lead a Muslim nation.[51] Born in 1953, she was assassinated in 2007 after returning to Pakistan from a self-imposed exile. Her initial popularity came from being the daughter of Zulfiqar Ali Bhutto, the Pakistani leader who founded the Pakistan Peoples Party (PPP) in the 1960s and was the country's president and then prime minister between 1971 and 1977. He was ousted by General Zia ul-Huq, and was later hanged in 1979 for complicity in an opponent's murder. His years in prison and then execution, combined with Zia's repressive policies, catapulted his reputation and his daughter to national glory. When Zia died in 1988, Benazir Bhutto was voted into office.

Over time, Bhutto and her husband, Asif Ali Zardari, were indicted for largescale corruption, charges that they contested. Zardari is popularly known in Pakistan as "Mr. Ten Percent"—to get a contract for any government project in Pakistan during Bhutto's tenure, one supposedly had to give Zardari kickbacks from the proceeds.[52] After Bhutto's second term, Zardari's bank accounts in Switzerland were frozen, and Swiss authorities charged him with money laundering. He was arrested by Pakistani authorities in 1996, and in 1999 both Bhutto and Zardari were convicted; however, Bhutto evaded arrest through a self-imposed exile. She spent the following several years in London and Dubai during which she reinvented herself as an advocate for democracy, traveling to Western countries to deliver lectures on democracy and Islam. By 2007, pressure was mounting against President Musharraf, and the Americans were ready to move on from him. They found in Bhutto a candidate to back and brokered a power-sharing arrangement between the two. Musharraf saw it as an opportunity to hold onto power, even if shared. Bhutto, in turn, asked that the corruption charges against herself and her husband be dropped; Musharraf obliged.[53] Bhutto, however, was assassinated shortly after reentering the country. In a classic dynastic politics move, she bequeathed the political party to her son Bilawal, then a minor.

Bhutto's autobiographical texts coincidently map onto the beginning and the end of her political career. Her first book, *Daughter of the East: An Autobiography* (1988; published as *Daughter of Destiny* in 1989 in the United States) comes closest to the genre of national autobiography, in which the personal and the political are intertwined. In it, she describes the arrest and execution of her father by the military regime and details her own detention in various forms, culminating with her election in 1988. Her second book, *Reconciliation: Islam, Democracy, and the West* (2009), was written to coincide with her return to Pakistan. It is presented as a philosophical treatise aimed at explicating the overlapping elements between Islam and modernity. The text draws on academic research, and while Bhutto's personal views—such as her criticism of Musharraf—seep through, it presents itself as a disinterested account. The two texts are connected—both are invested in producing Bhutto as the ultimate, even final, hope for a democratic Pakistan.

Through these texts, Bhutto establishes herself as the ideal sovereign by performing a distinct form of masculinity: a female masculinity that hinges on balancing traditional practices and codes associated with both femininity *and* masculinity. Furthermore, she posits democracy as a form of governance that can tackle both military authoritarianism and religious fundamentalism. In doing so, she furnishes an interpretation of Islam that aligns with democracy and can withstand both militants and the military.

Bhutto's Gender Play

Bhutto belonged to a politically prominent, wealthy family in Sindh, and as feudal lords she and her family lived on rents collected from tenants and indentured laborers. Her entrance into the masculine domain of Pakistani politics was thus predicated on the traditional sources that have permitted such entry—wealth and political connections. However, it is one thing to access a masculine domain and quite another to persist in it. To maintain leadership of her party and nation, Bhutto forged a distinct sartorial style that permitted her to straddle femininity and masculinity. She also mobilized kinship metaphors and masculine codes of honor to appeal to the Pakistani national public. In doing so, she performed a unique form of sovereign masculinity: a sovereign female masculinity. Indeed, if masculinity is a social and cultural construction of power and domination, and not a natural expression of the body, then females too can partake in it and reap its rewards. Todd Reeser, however, notes that the masculinity performed by women is not simply male masculinity transposed onto the female body; it is instead, "another type of masculinity that may nonetheless have connections to male masculinity."[54] Female masculinities are often studied by examining women who are perceived as masculine, such as tomboys or female body-builders.[55] In reading Bhutto, however, I am more concerned with how female-coded bodies take up and play with already-circulating codes and practices of masculine power. While in *Daughter of Destiny*, Bhutto proudly claims that she had "transcended gender," a close reading of her autobiographies reveals that she instead forged a gender performance that relied on traditional codes of both masculinity and femininity.[56]

Bhutto was acutely aware of how her female-coded body was read within the Pakistani political sphere. In *Reconciliation*, she notes, "Like most women in politics, I am especially sensitive to maintaining my composure, to never showing my feelings. A display of emotion by a woman in politics or government can be misconstrued as a manifestation of weakness, reinforcing stereotypes and caricatures."[57] From her father, Bhutto learned that stylizations of the body were crucial in desexualizing her for a Pakistani public. On one occasion, her father gave her his Mao cap, instructing her to wear it when she spoke with people in the tribal areas.[58] He also guided her to be careful about the placement of her scarf: "Sometimes your dupatta [scarf] falls off your head while you're speaking. Remember to put it back up."[59] When in power, Bhutto fashioned a clothing style that would mimic men's and hide her curves. Consider the following photograph (figure 1). Here, Bhutto is seen alongside a French leader, Jacques Chirac, wearing a modification that she introduced to Pakistani women's clothing style—one that included a coat over the *shalwar kameez*. Bhutto's fashion choice both adopted and offset masculinity—her red lipstick, Chanel bag, and heels emphasized her femininity, while her reinvented *shalwar kameez* incorporated the men's power suit into women's clothing repertoire.

Bhutto drew on prevailing sensibilities around women's status in Islam as well as the language of kinship to desexualize herself and garner support. *Daughter of Destiny* covers a visit to the northwestern frontier province where, as she explains, "it was also necessary to convince the male-dominated Pathan society that a woman could lead them."[60] In the speech she reports giving to them, therefore, she situates herself as an inheritor of qualities associated with

FIGURE I. Benazir Bhutto with Jacques Chirac in Paris. October 25, 1995. Credit: Gilles Bassignac / Gamma-Rapho via Getty Images.

women from the Prophet's family: "People think I am weak because I am a woman . . . do they not know that I am a Muslim woman, and that Muslim women have a heritage to be proud of? I have the patience of Bibi Khadija, the wife of the Prophet, Peace be Upon Him. I have the perseverance of Bibi Zeinab, the sister of Imam Hussein. And I have the courage of Bibi Aisha, the Prophet's favorite wife, who rode her own camel into battle at the head of the Muslims."[61] Bhutto often called herself the "people's sister" in order to create a familial connection with her audience: "I am the daughter of martyr Zulfiqar Ali Bhutto, the sister of martyr Shah Nawaz Khan Bhutto, and *I am your sister as well.*"[62] When she decided to get married, she assured people that her "marriage would have no bearing on [her] political career."[63] When she returned from London to run for elections, crowds welcomed her with slogans of "my sister, your sister, Benazir."[64] Through these kinship metaphors, she invited audiences to trust her as they would their own female relations.

Bhutto's practice of masculinity also included a reiteration of prevailing hierarchies of masculinity. In *Daughter of Destiny,* for instance, she mobilizes masculinity's connections to physicality and honor to ridicule her opponents. To stake a claim on her father's political party, she discredits other members of the party who opposed her leadership, using terms such as "old uncles" to signal their outdatedness.[65] On other occasions, she calls her opponents "old-style politicians."[66] Men who opposed her father appear as "small," "provincial," and "myopic."[67] She uses terms such as "cowards," *besharam* (without shame), and "shameless cowards" when speaking to or about the soldiers who came to take her to detention.[68] Elsewhere, she co-opts gendered vernacular to register her disdain for the army chief, Zia: "Unlike the childhood image I carried of a soldier as tall and rugged with James Bond nerves of steel, the general standing in front of me was a short, nervous, ineffectual-looking man whose pomaded hair was parted in the middle and lacquered to his head. He looked more like an English cartoon villain than an inspiring model for the leader of the Pakistani army. And he seemed so obsequious, telling me over and over how honored he was to meet the daughter of such a great man as Zulfiqar Ali Bhutto."[69] Noting that it was her father who had appointed Zia as general, bypassing other senior officers, Bhutto questions Zia's manhood and honor: "in our culture, one does not betray one's benefactor."[70] These discursive strategies invoke and reproduce masculinity's link with physicality and honor to construe Zia and other soldiers as dishonorable and unmanly.

Bhutto thus furnishes us with an example of how a woman can participate in sovereign masculinity in the context of Pakistan. She performed a unique blend of masculinity and femininity—female masculinity—to foster an allied public that found solace in traditional gender codes. Through careful aestheticization of her female-coded body, she relieved the anxieties of those who feared women in leadership positions. Through the use of kinship metaphors, she transformed herself into the people's sister, mobilizing familial notions of trust and protection. And, while forging this new gender performance, she summoned traditional gender associations—masculinity's link to the male body and honor—to banish her opponents.

The Symbol of Democracy

In contrast to Musharraf, who drew his power from positing the military as Pakistan's savior, Bhutto tied her claims to sovereignty to democracy and moderate Islam. *Reconciliation* encourages readers to differentiate between military and civilian rule, as well as to distinguish moderate Islam from extremism. A recurring phrase in *Reconciliation* is "Democracy versus Dictatorship, Moderation versus Extremism."[71] Whereas Islam is committed to moderation and democratic principles, dictatorship, Bhutto argues, is more aligned with extremism. She notes, "The battle for hearts and soul of Islam of today is taking place between moderates and fanatics, between democrats and dictators, between those who live in the past and those who adapt to the present and plan for a better future."[72] Against this background, Bhutto presents herself as a leader who can carry forth the best of Islam and democracy. In this way, Bhutto aligns herself with the US imperial project that had for decades posited democracy as an alternate ideology to Islam and then resolved this tension through the creation of "moderate Islam." Bhutto reaffirmed this narrative.

Bhutto's advocacy for democracy took shape in the context of resistance to military rulers—first Zia and then Musharraf—as well as her later alignment with the United States during the War on Terror. In *Daughter of Destiny,* she portrays the army as the paramount threat to democracy, and understandably so: General Zia had overthrown her father and then established eleven years of repressive rule. In *Reconciliation,* she draws a direct connection between dictatorship and extremism, asserting Zia and Musharraf as ineffective in the face of increasing radicalization. She blames them for working with the religious right to legitimize their rule and for causing widescale deprivation that pushed people toward extremism. Throughout the book, Bhutto applies labels such as "king," "dictator," and "authoritarian" to Musharraf.[73]

While in self-imposed exile, Bhutto wrote extensively for Western media outlets, criticizing the Musharraf government and drawing on the language of democracy to foster support for herself. In an article she wrote for the *New York Times,* she criticizes Musharraf for relinquishing sovereignty: "The current government of Pakistan has ceded large areas of our nation to the pro-Taliban and al-Qaida forces claiming that these areas are ungovernable."[74] Writing for the *Huffington Post,* she stokes fears of a takeover of Pakistan by the religious right: "they will attempt to run our country like they run the political madrassas."[75] Similarly, in the *Washington Post,* she observes that "within our intelligence and military are elements who sympathize with religious extremists."[76] She cautions readers of the *Wall Street Journal* that "for the first time in Pakistan's history, the number of religious-based parties is rising, and suicide bombings are becoming a common occurrence of daily life."[77] By pointing to the military's support of the religious right, Bhutto attempts to steer attachments away from both.

With the military and the religious extremists cast as improper sovereigns, she presents herself as the harbinger of democracy and moderate Islam in Pakistan. Reflecting on the moment she became the head of her father's party after his death, she notes, "Whether I had ever wished it or not, I was the leader of not only the Pakistan Peoples Party but the entire democratic opposition in Pakistan. I was the symbol of democracy."[78] Writing about the day she was sworn in as prime minister in 1988, she exclaims, "This was the moment of democracy . . . I returned democratic governance to the people of Pakistan."[79] And again, she imagines her return from self-imposed exile in 2007 as being "the beginning of a long journey for Pakistan back to democracy."[80] Democracy appears in both of her texts as a competing form of governance under which moderate Islam can thrive, one that can keep military, militants, and militarism at bay. A vote for Bhutto thus meant a vote for democracy and moderate Islam.

REDEMPTIVE MASCULINITY

Born in 1952, Oxford-educated Imran Khan represented Pakistan in international cricket and led the country to its first World Cup win in 1992. He subsequently focused his efforts on philanthropy and went onto establish Pakistan's first cancer hospital in 1994. In 1996, Khan launched his political party, Pakistan Tehrik-e-Insaf (PTI), literally, Pakistan Movement for Justice. The party was fairly unsuccessful in the early years, winning only a single seat in the 2002 elections. However, he persevered and after twenty-two years Khan was elected prime minister in 2018. In his person, we find someone who has consistently made the impossible possible: the '92 World Cup victory; the promise of a cancer hospital with free treatment for the needy; PTI's successful incursion into an enduring two-party political system. These miracles are central to the promise of Khan. To some, he is a messiah who will save Pakistan; to others, he is a self-important former cricketer riding the global wave of nationalism that has elected the likes of Donald Trump and Jair Bolsonaro. In this respect, there are those who believe that Khan's rise to power was carefully fashioned by the Pakistani army in order to displace his predecessor, Nawaz Sharif, whose corruption and affinity with India were becoming increasingly problematic.[81]

I am interested less in adjudicating how Khan came to power and more with how he articulates himself as an ideal sovereign in his autobiography, *Pakistan: A Personal History* (2011). Khan's text draws on his life and success on the cricket field to inspire confidence in his abilities to master the field of politics. He secures attachment to himself through recourse to normative masculinity and the redemptive powers of Sufi Islam. A key purpose of the autobiography seems to be to garner electoral support by providing an explanation of his political philosophy. Just as he was able to win the World Cup for Pakistan, he promises to lead the nation to prosperity.

The Promise of Cricket and Sufi Islam

When Khan returned to Pakistan after winning the World Cup in Sydney, he was hailed as a hero. He had come out of retirement at the age of thirty-nine to lead the floundering cricket team to victory, all while battling ruptured cartilage in his shoulder. He had redeemed Pakistan. He was the epitome of what sheer determination and ambition could achieve. In *Pakistan: A Personal History,* Khan suggests that his athleticism and sportsmanship have prepared him uniquely for the field of politics. He highlights his hard work and fortitude by providing examples from his life as an athlete: his intense focus on preparing his body for each game, the tactics he used to unite the team, the tough decisions he had to make as captain, and his courage in living with the consequences. Even now, in his sixties, his daily workout routine is a topic of popular interest in Pakistan. His party, PTI, harnesses this interest by sharing videos of him training. These videos highlight him as a tough, virile leader who bestows this virility onto his party. At the same time, they function as a taunt against his opponents. Consider a tweet from the PTI official account that shows Khan doing push-ups alongside members of his team: "@ImranKhanPTI training his tigers! . . . Be very scared Nawaz sharif [*sic*] . . .," it warns.[82] Khan's athleticism, and the consequent redemption of the Pakistani cricket team, is offered as a promise to the nation: just as he was able to save the team, he can save the nation too.

Khan's turn to Sufi Islam further bolsters his redemptive appeal. In his autobiography, he tells the story of his religious transformation, which entailed examining his "hedonistic lifestyle" and becoming critical of the rampant materialism and individualism to which he had subscribed.[83] He started contemplating the contingencies of life, including those in sports, and gradually turned to Sufi teachings to learn more about the existence of God. Khan narrates his personal story of religious awakening to invite readers to also return to the fundamental tenets of Islam. He pines for the revival of an unadulterated Islam so that Pakistanis can fulfill the purpose for which their state was created. This "return to Islam" discourse shares eerie similarities with Islamist discourses that imagine such a return as a way to rid the present of its contaminations.[84] However, Khan pursues an esoteric interpretation of Islam and has combined it with the study of nationalist philosophers such as Allama Iqbal; therefore, his Islam is unlike that of the Taliban, which emphasizes a dogmatic approach. Indeed, in *Pakistan: A Personal History*, when explaining his decision to enter politics, Khan notes, "I had a life that many young people, in Pakistan and elsewhere, dreamt about—I was a rich and glamorous cricket star, jet-setting all over the world. Politics was considered a dirty business for those who could not do anything else."[85] Yet it was his sense of duty as a spiritual person that guided him to politics: "a spiritual person takes on responsibility for society, whereas a materialist only takes responsibility for himself."[86] In taking responsibility for society, Khan seems akin to a Sufi saint through whom the masses can acquire deliverance. While in Islam redemption is often linked to personal piety, a variety of religious figures can perform the intercessory role alluded to in the Quranic verse in which God asks, "Who is there who may intercede with Him save by His leave?"[87] While Prophet Muhammad plays the most important intercessory role, in Sufi Islam, *pirs* (guides), imams, and saints are also understood to be bestowed with this divine gift. Their piety can invite God's favor not only for their own souls but also for those associated with them. Khan's turn to Sufi Islam and his sense of responsibility for society qualify him as a figure who could invite God's favor and offer redemption to the nation through his own religious strength. Indeed, in the popular press Khan is often referred to as a "messiah" and "seer."[88]

In Khan's text then we find an alluring imbrication of sports masculinity and saintly authority—like an exceptional sportsman, he inspires trust because he is willing to go the extra mile; like a Sufi saint, he invites divine favor and offers salvation.[89] While Khan appears to be an aspirational leader, his masculinity is difficult to emulate. He is thoroughly bourgeoise, educated at elite Pakistani and English institutions. He also signifies a religious transformation that is not easily accessible, as spiritual knowledge cannot be willed but is bestowed by God. Thus, not only do his social class and cricket career elevate him but his successful turn to religion later in life adds to his messianic quality. Perhaps that is precisely why he has intense appeal in Pakistan.

The Outsider, Now on the Inside

Khan's autobiography positions him as a redeemer figure by establishing his outsider status. His turn to Sufi Islam from a hedonistic lifestyle, as described above, is one way in which he becomes an insider to Pakistan and Islam later in life. His perspective as a former outsider gives him an opportunity to study Islam from a disinterested position through which he apparently arrives at Islam's true meanings, inaccessible to insiders, who are too close to see it properly. The other dimension of his outsider status is his lack of familial affiliation with politics. According to his autobiography, this gives him a distinct advantage over his fellow politicians, as he is not invested in the same power dynamics as them. He thus emerges as interested solely in redeeming Pakistan's and Islam's sovereignty.

In *Pakistan: A Personal History,* Khan distinguishes himself from his rivals by noting the incompetence that inevitably emerges when a model of family dynastic politics is followed—something common to his rivals Bhutto and Sharif. He points specifically to the corruption charges that engulfed both the Bhutto and the Sharif families.[90] He also offers a scathing critique of Musharraf, a military-turned-civilian leader, and his successor, Zardari, Bhutto's husband, who engaged in military operations in Waziristan. In Khan's view, both Musharraf and Zardari disgraced the nation by aligning with the United States: "I found Musharraf and Zardari's total subjugation of Pakistan's sovereignty to the US as the ultimate humiliation."[91] He goes on to critique Musharraf's engagement in the War on Terror, noting that he "took us into the 'war on terror' when no Pakistani had been involved in the 9/11 attacks and al-Qaeda was a CIA-trained militant group based in Afghanistan, and there were no militant Taliban in Pakistan. He also gave US intelligence agencies a free hand to pick up any Pakistani citizen or foreigner suspected of terrorism."[92] Continuing, Khan observes that "today in Pakistan, with drone attacks and raids in our cities, our sovereignty is compromised by those who are puppets of the US."[93] He is bothered by how frequently Pakistani citizens are incarcerated by the American government without trial. He assigns the blame for these outcomes to the existing Pakistani political elite, "who shamefully accepted dollars in exchange for turning on [their] own people."[94] Khan thus critiques both past and contemporary forms of imperialism. Himself a Pashtun, he never tires of pointing to the fact that Afghanistan, where Pashtuns reside, was never colonized. He also expresses his desire to emancipate Pakistanis from their economic and political servitude to the West and to raise the "nation's self-esteem": "How can Pakistanis ever be encouraged to achieve their potential while we remain a cowed nation that cannot operate without international aid?"[95] Khan thus promises to restore Pakistan's sovereignty by ridding it of both internal and external threats. He offers himself as the outsider who will take on both politicians and army generals: "I am the head of the party that is battling to take on a political elite that has for more than six decades stymied this great country, depriving it of its God-given potential. Ruled alternately by military dictators like President Musharraf, or as a fiefdom by families like the Bhuttos and Sharifs, Pakistan has drifted far from the ideals of its founders."[96]

While Khan criticizes specific political leaders for their incompetence, he is careful to spare the army from this critique. For instance, even as he censures Musharraf, he holds the army in a positive light, empathizing with soldiers who must have felt humiliated when the United States unilaterally entered the Pakistani airspace to capture Osama bin Laden: "There is a feeling of humiliation within the army, similar to that felt after the surrender of 90,000 soldiers in East Pakistan in 1971."[97] And even though he rebukes the army's policies and its Westernized outlook, in a true nationalist manner, he does not tolerate the army's emasculation by imperial sovereigns.[98] Khan's movement between the registers of pride and critique makes him an appealing figure for Pakistanis who also experience this ambivalence, feeling the same sense of humiliation regarding the army's alliance with the Americans but remaining invested in the same sovereign body for security and protection.

PERFORMING ISLAMO-MASCULINITY

The autobiographical texts considered in this chapter are one element of a broad corpus through which relationships of sovereignty are fashioned between the heads of the state and multiple reading publics. Their close study reveals masculinity—as a discourse of power and an aesthetics of the body—not only as a salient idiom in the constitution of sovereign power but also as a means through which this relationship is nurtured. The authors rely on and mobilize sovereignty's longstanding historical association with masculinity to nurture allied publics.[99] They do so by invoking various characteristics of normative masculinity: physicality, toughness, hierarchies, honor, and virility. Masculinity, however, appears in various aesthetic forms: the military (Musharraf), the female (Bhutto), and the athletic (Khan). While in each case certain enduring elements of masculinity, such as its connection with strength, are invoked, new connections emerge as well, as it is co-articulated with other discourses such as femininity, in Bhutto's case, or Sufi Islam, in the case of Khan.

Crucially, in each of the instantiations that appears in this chapter, sovereign masculinity gains force through recourse to normative Islam. Each leader constructs a version of Islam that he or she then advances as being crucial for the welfare of the nation. This version of Islam often becomes legible by contrast with improper practitioners. In Musharraf's case, for example, the terrorist is identified as "perverting our faith [of Islam]" and being of "an uninformed religious bent." By defining this improper Muslim, Musharraf seeks control of the space of *ummah* through his own "enlightened" version of Islam. In Bhutto's case as well, it is the fundamentalist interpretation of Islam that is deemed to be incompatible with democracy. She thus constructs "moderate Islam," as the variant of Islam that can coexist with democracy. Finally, in Khan's case, the redemptive powers of Sufi Islam meld with his athletic masculinity, transforming him into a messianic sovereign. It is, therefore not just masculinity that mediates the relationship of sovereignty, but masculinity that is tied to a version of normative Islam: Islamo-masculinity. All three state leaders perform Islamo-masculinity to lay claim to sovereign power and recruit allied publics. Islamo-masculinity thus works as an affective glue, adhering the reading publics to the claimants of sovereignty. Here, adhesion involves giving one's support and allegiance.[100]

In the next chapter, I dwell on the figure of the soldier (*jawan*) as a proxy for the sovereign who engages in violence and sacrifices on behalf of the nation. Like the head of the state, he too performs sovereign Islamo-masculinity, producing a public that feels confidence in him and, through him, in the army. The sovereign thus is not a coherent, singular whole but is composed of multiple nodes that vie for a semblance of wholeness and singularity. In the autobiographies considered in this chapter, for instance, the civilian leader performs sovereignty in relation to the military, imperial sovereigns, and internal competitors, such as the Taliban. This self-narration of sovereignty at times sits alongside and at other times overlaps with the military's articulations of sovereignty. Sovereignty thus remains an open and ongoing project, even as we detect symbolic singularities in the figures of the head of state and the soldier.

TWO

Identity, Alterity

THE SOLDIER-MILITANT DYAD

THE SOLDIER, OR *JAWAN*, IS A PROMINENT figuration through which the Pakistani national public understands the functions of the sovereign. Usually used to refer to soldiers who are not officers in the Pakistani army, the Urdu term *jawan* literally translates to young man, an articulation that draws on sedimented ideas about youth as a time marked by strength, muscularity, and agility.[1] Like young people in general, the *jawan* is imagined as being idealistic and passionate, willing to go to extreme lengths to protect his nation. He is a synecdoche for the nation: his strength and resolve represent that of the nation, and his weaknesses and defeat stir up intense anxiety since they foretell the demise of the nation. He also connects the national present to the Muslim past by embodying the strength and bravery of prior Muslim warriors. The *jawan* thus furnishes us with yet another performance of Islamo-masculinity.

The Inter Services Public Relations (ISPR) archives hold insights into how attachment to the *jawan,* and through him to the state, is forged as readers are invited to both place their trust in his ability to protect them *and* to pray for his protection against enemies. Indeed, the soldier must be presented as not only strong but also vulnerable, for his vulnerability delivers a pretext for preemptive state action. He thus lives in what David Palumbo-Liu calls "the gray zone," shuttling between strength and weakness, invincibility and vulnerability.[2] A poem in the ISPR's *Hilal Urdu* magazine elucidates these simultaneous logics:

Our army's *jawan*, Keepers of our trust,
Our heart, our life, May they be protected by God.[3]

The *jawan* thus evokes intense admiration and stirs the paternalistic sentiments of the nation. In this chapter, I examine this figure in the cultural texts produced by the ISPR to observe how the everyday citizen's attachment to the state, and in particular to the army, is nourished through him. The affective economies of love for the *jawan* bind individuals to him as well as to the collective, the nation. Attachment to him, however, relies on the construction and expulsion of difference, in the form of the militant. The specific avatar of the militant that this chapter tackles is the *talib,* the plural of which gives the Taliban its name. While other portrayals of militants also circulate in the Pakistani public culture, including the non-Muslim terrorist often associated with India, the cultural texts presented here relate to the counter-insurgency military operations in the aftermath of 9/11 and the attack on the Army Public School, which center on the Taliban.

Distance and difference are created between the *jawan* and the *talib* through recourse to discourses of heteronormative sexuality, Islamic warrior masculinity, and modernity. These discourses produce the *talib* as an object of disgust. However, even as the state constructs the *talib* as the Other, he remains indispensable for the constitution of the *jawan.* Upon close reading, we sense an unintended intimacy between the two, for the *jawan*'s hypermasculine strength becomes legible only in relation to the cowardice of the *talib;* he emerges as properly heterosexual in comparison to the *talib's* sexual perversion; he appears as a national subject next to the provincialized outlook of the *talib;* and his claims to correct interpretation of Islam are weighed against the *talib's* lack of religious understanding. The *talib,* hence, is constitutive of the *jawan.* The dyad of the soldier-militant then emblematizes the simultaneity of identity and alterity in the cultural texts of the Pakistani army. It delineates how the emotions of disgust (for the *talib*) and love (for the *jawan*) mediate the relationship of sovereignty.

STAGING LOVE AND DISGUST

The ISPR's popular cultural productions include music videos, short films, and melodramas that combine fact with fiction. As scripted, carefully edited and choreographed texts, these productions are performative acts that stage the power of the state.[4] They cast the state's counterinsurgency operations, which at times include an extended scope for violence, as legitimate and necessary. These staged performances are useful not only for their content and visualities but also for what they *do* in the world as they circulate. I examine a number of ISPR's moving texts, particularly music videos and short films released in the aftermath of the APS attack as well as those that engage with the broader context of the War on Terror, to glimpse these dynamics. While in this chapter I am primarily focused on analyzing these videos, I also bring to bear evidence from the ISPR magazines, *Hilal* (Urdu and English versions), to trace the genealogy of some of the ideas. To examine how these texts forge an allied public, I explore pro-state rallies as well as media productions by private citizens in which we encounter the *jawan-talib* dyad.

In recent years, the reach of ISPR's music videos has grown exponentially. This is partly due to the accessibility of these videos via YouTube, as well as to their thematic alignment with an already popular genre of patriotic songs, *milli nagmay*.[5] Such songs are an established element of the Pakistani public culture and state-making process. They not only reflect the state's imagination of itself and others, but also produce it. The genre thrived during the 1965 war with India and then again in the 1971 effort to prevent the secession of East Pakistan. The *milli nagmay* of those days are etched in public memory through their repetitive circulation on the anniversaries of these wars. Having grown up in Pakistan during the 1980s, I remember listening to patriotic songs by Madam Noor Jehan (1926–2000) that were first released in the 1960s. The tunes received primetime coverage on national television. Many of them were dedicated to soldiers—"Aye watan kay sajeelay jawano" (O nation's beloved *jawan*) and "Aye puttar hattan te nahi wikde" (Such sons cannot be purchased)—producing the soldier as an object of intense love and establishing a relationship of kinship between soldiers and those enjoying the songs. The broadcasts were often accompanied by images of soldiers who died during the wars—the *shahid jawan* (martyred soldiers); their names are etched in my memory: Rashid Minhas ... Rana Shabbir Sharif ... Muhammad Hussain Janjua ... Muhammad Akram ... Raja Muhammad Sarwar ... Raja Aziz Bhatti ... Muhammad Mahfuz .... I still get goosebumps when I recall the songs, such is their affective resonance.

While the ISPR's contemporary productions are not often termed as *milli nagmay,* they are the most recent iteration of this genre. Like Madam Noor Jehan's songs, these music videos and short films bind viewers and listeners into an imagined collective called the nation, and produce the soldier as an object of the nation's love. Moreover, the army is not the only entity that participates in the affective economy of love for the soldier; this political project relies on other actors too. In the aftermath of the APS attack, for instance, a number of celebrities released commemorative videos invoking similar themes of identity and alterity through the soldier-militant binary.

These productions were an echo of those produced by the ISPR. The more the *jawan-talib* dyad circulates, the more affective it becomes, and the more it sediments the difference between the *talib* and *jawan,* for as Sara Ahmed reminds us, it is the accumulation of affective value that shapes the surfaces of bodies and worlds.[6] I thus view such productions as instances when statist claims to sovereignty—through the production of Self and Other—are performatively reiterated, as publics consent to sovereign exception.

The Talib *as a Coward*

The ISPR's music video "Bara dushman bana phirta hai" (hereafter, "Bara dushman") was released in January 2015 to coincide with the reopening of the APS in Peshawar. As of January 2021, "Bara dushman" boasts over twenty-eight million views on the official ISPR YouTube channel, where it was uploaded for the first time in February 2018.[7] This channel, notably, is only one of several places where the video can be accessed. In all likelihood, therefore, the video has had much wider circulation than this number indicates. It has even been called "the song of the decade."[8] The singer, Azaan Ali, is a boy of no more than ten years. In the video, Ali sings in the voice of a (male) child victim of the APS attack, narrating the events of the day when he and his fellow classmates were attacked. Instead of the gory details, the video highlights the feelings and thoughts of the child as he tries to interpret the event and, posthumously, console his parents. He also alerts the terrorist of his impending ruin. In addition to the child singer, many other schoolchildren participate in the chorus, imparting a sense of collective strength.

The chorus stanza, *"Bara dushman bana phirta hai, jo bachon se larta hai"* (And you're the mighty coward for the children you fight; all translations from ISPR), conveys a form of sarcasm that comes out of hero-speak.[9] Its syntactic arrangement is notable: put together, the two verbs, *bana* (acts) and *phirta* (goes around), are an unusual predicate construction that, in juxtaposition to *bara* (big), takes the "bigness" of the enemy down a notch. It is thus a taunt of sorts, mocking the militant for pretending to be a mighty "enemy" (*dushman*) while attacking defenseless, unarmed children. The taunt, as a linguistic device, undermines the militant. That it is a child (the singer) who is doing the taunting signals the adult militant's inability to come close to even the strength of a child, adding another layer of insult. The ISPR's translation of *dushman* as "coward," when a more precise translation would have been "enemy," exposes the tight connections that the institution seeks to draw between cowardice and the figure of the militant. In contemporary cultural discourses, a coward is a subject position taken up by inferior masculinities, invoking fears of effeminacy.[10] ISPR's framing of contenders to sovereignty as "cowards" has precedent in its earlier cultural texts as well, although at that time it was in relation to a different enemy—Indian soldiers. In an article entitled "Sherni" (Lioness) published in *Hilal* during the 1971 India-Pakistan war, author Captain Aijaz Mehmood refers to Pakistanis as lionesses and their Indian counterparts as "coward jackals."[11] He explains that during the 1965 India-Pakistan war, the cowardly enemy moved toward the borders without announcing its intentions. However, he reminds his readers that the enemy was still defeated and will be once again.

In "Bara dushman," the construction of the *talib* as a coward also relies on the innocence embodied by his victim: the child. As proverbial subjects-in-process, children are conceptualized as being outside politics and societal corruption. As such, they embody aspirations for a positive and prosperous future, and any threat to them is read as a threat to that promised future. Children, therefore, trigger the intense protective impulses of the nation. "Bara dushman" works through the visualities, sounds, and histories of these associations to create a sensation of deep mourning for the loss of the children killed in the APS attack and the futures associated with them. The video blames the *talib* for this loss and in doing so, primes the audience to hold him responsible:

Main aaney wala kal hoon woh mujhe kyun aaj marey gaa

You want to destroy me today for I am the tomorrow

While the video certainly plays with sedimented assumptions about children, it also rescues the children lost in the APS attack from being cast as victims. The return of the dead male child (the song's narrator) is simultaneously haunting and daring. He is no longer a silent victim but is able to tell his story; a story that features his strength in the face of the attack:

Tumhara khoon hoon na isliye acha lara hoon mein
Bata aya hoon dushman ko kay us se to bara hoon mein

With my parents' blood in my veins, I valiantly fought
So you learn the lesson I'm stronger than you thought

The "you" in the second verse refers to the coward militant and pits him once more against the child, who emerges as "stronger" and "bigger."

The child's bravery is further established through various visual techniques. The lead singer and the other children who participate in the chorus almost always look directly at the camera, with determined gazes. In many instances, they raise their fists in the air, bang on their desks, and hold up their index fingers as if gesturing warnings from the beyond. One scene in particular is quite powerful. Here, we find a young schoolgirl, perhaps eight or nine years old, sitting in the schoolyard after the attack. The yard is littered with broken chairs, bent desks, and torn books. In the background, we see bookshelves that have fallen down and wall posters that are now slanted. Dust is everywhere. Unlike the other children in the video, who appear extremely tidy, this girl looks a bit disheveled. Her shoes are covered with a thick layer of dust, perhaps as a consequence of running away from the militants. Her ponytail has come loose. She sits on the ground, with her back against a pillar, as if to catch her breath. Even in this state, she is unafraid and looks directly into the camera and sings, though we continue to hear the male child's voice:

Main aisi quam se hoon jiske woh bachon se darta hai

For I belong to the brave nation whose children you fear

The nation is thus discursively produced as a united, brave collectivity that stands in opposition to the militant. The video frame then moves to a boy who has climbed up a tree and is now looking downward, a stance that adds to his dominance. He joins the girl in completing the verse. The children's fortitude, unwavering stance, and direct, dogged glances into the camera simultaneously project the strength of the nation and declare the cowardice of the militants. Crucially, the children gain a new political life in national cosmology.

Towards the end of "Bara dushman," the narrator warns the *talib* never to return, as his brother and father remain behind, together with the rest of the nation, to avenge his death. The ISPR's sequel to this video, "Mujhe dushman ke bachon ko parhana hai" (hereafter, "Mujhe dushman"; all translations from ISPR), brings this promise to fruition.[12] Released a year after the APS attack, in 2015, the music video boasts over 154 million views as of January 2021 on the official ISPR YouTube channel, where it was posted in February 2018. "Mujhe dushman" is also sung by a boy but this time the narrator is the brother of the slain child. He decides to avenge his sibling's death by becoming a teacher to the enemy's children so that they do not follow in their father's footsteps:

Mujhe maa us se badla lene jana hai
Muje dushman kay bachoon ko parhana hai

O Mother I promise, my revenge will be grand
My enemy's children will have books in their hands (ISPR translation)[13]

The child effectively shames the militant for not being a proper pedagogue to his children and for failing the responsibilities deemed appropriate for middle-class Pakistani men.[14] He cannot prepare his children to function as morally upright, religious subjects, for he himself lacks these qualities, as the video notes:

Woh jo sari hi nazaro(n) se gira tha
Na tha insan na jis ka khuda tha

He who shed every fiber of morality
He neither had a God nor humanity

Instead, the militant can only teach his children violence and destroy their futures. It is therefore up to the young male singer—a stand-in for the army—to become their pedagogue and redirect their life trajectories through education. Notice also that this construction produces the *talib* as *improperly* religious; that is, he does not understand the true nature of Islam. In this way, the ISPR can write the *talib* out of the space of *ummah* while retaining its own association as representative of proper Islam. Although the *talib* is excluded from the nation for being cowardly, immoral, and improperly religious, his children are still potential citizen-subjects who can be salvaged through reeducation.

The Talib *as Sexually Perverse*

Whereas the boy-child is rescued from the frames of victimhood through careful maneuvers, the girl-child is invoked primarily as a victim in order to elucidate the deviant sexual practices of the *talib* and, relationally, to illustrate the heroic paternalism of the *jawan*.

The ISPR's short film "Farishtay" (Angels; over one million views as of January 2021), released in 2016, features the success of Zarb-e-Azb, a military operation conducted along the Pakistan-Afghanistan border between 2014 and 2016.[15] It resulted in large territories that had been taken over by the Taliban being brought back under state control. The plot of the film revolves around a girl whose father is killed by the Taliban. They prohibit everyone from burying him in order to humiliate him even in death. The girl, though, moves the body after nightfall, digs a grave, and buries her *baba*. When the Taliban find out the next morning, they drag her out of her home and, as punishment, marry her off to one of the Taliban men. Later on, however, she is liberated by the soldiers, one of whom dies while rescuing her. The film thus follows a fairly familiar storyline in which the Taliban kidnap girls and the soldiers rescue them. In such storylines, the girl-child plays a central role, facilitating the portrayal of the *talib* as sexually perverse. Perversion in this case denotes practices that deviate from middle-class notions of heterosexuality and sexual mores.

ISPR's cultural productions almost never include explicit scenes of sexual exploitation or rape; they are only alluded to through semiotic codes, left to the viewer's imagination. This is likely due to the general unacceptability in Pakistani media cultures around featuring sexual violence.[16] Yet just because sexual violence is not explicitly featured does not mean that it is not actively conjured. Gestures, words, and colors in the video guide viewers to visualize a story about the *talib*'s sexual violence against women and girls. In "Farishtay," as the main *talib* character enters the girl's quarters, he looks drunk, sways side to side, and laughs hysterically. The girl tries to shoo him away using a wooden stick: "*hatto, choro, hatto, choro*" (move away, leave me, move away, leave me). The difference in their sizes is stark; he is at least three times her tiny build. The brooding background music evokes a sense of impending doom, foretelling the wretched future that awaits the girl. She clearly loses the fight because the following scene shows her sitting on the ground, with her head bowed down, while the *talib* sports a wide, satisfactory smile and departs.

We find yet another subtle indication of the threat that the *talib* presents to female sexuality in the ISPR music video "Ye banday mitti kay banday" (These are sons of the soil; as of January 2021, over fifteen million views; hereafter, "Ye banday"), which was released in June 2015 to mark the first anniversary of Zarb-e-Azb.[17] In the opening scene, we see a young, chubby girl, perhaps five or six years old, wearing a bright-red *shalwar kameez*. Her *dupatta* is secured to cover her hair and neck; a necklace made of brown beads sits neatly over the *dupatta*, reminding us that she is just another girl who likes to play dress-up. Around her eyes and on her chin, decorative makeup is visible. Her eyes are wide open, but her stare is blank. She is neither crying nor laughing. The camera then zooms out, and we see two gun barrels pointing at her. She now clearly looks distressed. As the frame continues to widen, we notice that she is, in fact, surrounded by two men, who are pointing their rifles at her. One of them is wearing a *shalwar kameez* and a turban. He has an extra set of bullets secured around his body. A third man—unkempt, with long, greasy hair and a beard—enters the frame and walks directly up to the girl. He also has a rifle and an extra set of bullets. As he makes his way between the other two men and toward the girl, the camera lens zooms in so that we do not see exactly what is going on or what he does to the girl. He is there only for a second or so—does he hit her? Shoot her? Kick her? Drag her? Spit on her? We have no way of knowing, but that pause is precisely the moment in which the viewer assimilates what she has seen in the video with prior knowledge about girls and the Taliban. That is how the message is sent. In discussing the production of news, Stuart Hall argues that in order to allow audiences to make sense of new information or events, reporters have to connect them to signifiers that audiences already recognize: "an event only 'makes sense' if it can be located within a range of known social and cultural identifications."[18] The girl and the *talib* are already bound into a sexualized relationship of violence; the implication is that the *talib* must have harmed her.[19]

In both "Farishtay" and "Ye banday," the girl-child is summoned to highlight the threat that the *talib* presents to girls' sexual purity. He is perverse because he forces underage girls to marry him and violates them sexually or subjects them to other forms of violence. In such cases, it is the affective economy of the girl—as a figure of innocence, purity, and protection—that is activated to construct the *talib* as perverse. His perversion is linked to his exercise of sexuality outside the realm of heteroreproductive sexuality; that is, it deviates from sexuality's primary role of reproduction. This is illustrated by his marriage practices, which privilege personal sexual pleasure over maintaining the home, either materially or culturally (recall that he is not able to discharge his responsibilities as a pedagogue to his children). This puts him out of step with normative middle-class Pakistani households that resemble the Western bourgeois nuclear family wherein sexuality is harnessed in the service of the nation-state and society. The *talib*'s breach of sexual mores is taken to be offensive, which produces him as an object of disgust. Sara Ahmed explains that disgust is a response to contact between surfaces of bodies or objects that are felt as sickening invasions.[20] In this case, the *talib*-girl encounter, or its contact zone, muddies boundaries held to be sacred and hence, transforms the *talib* into an abject, disgusting figure that must be cast out in order to restore social borders.

My reading of the *talib* as sexually perverse is different from the Western imagination of the terrorist (implicitly always Muslim) as homophobic, sexually depraved, and/or improperly homosexual.[21] Writing about the torture of prisoners in Guantanamo, scholars observe how the sexualized torture of Muslim prisoners assumed their homophobic and misogynistic propensities.[22] Elsewhere, Nivi Manchanda notes that when American and NATO forces invaded Afghanistan after 9/11, British soldiers in the Helmand province encountered men whose practices did not comport with Western understandings of manhood and homosexuality.[23] They came upon older men engaging in relations with younger men, holding hands, and wearing makeup and colored sandals. A study was conducted by a human terrain team colocated with the British forces, which explained Afghan men's relations as a consequence of separation between men and women, and inability to afford the expense of getting married due to poverty.[24] In particular, the study stated that "a culturally-contrived homosexuality appears to affect a far greater population base than some researchers would argue is attributable to natural inclination."[25] Rather than exhibiting "natural" homosexual desires, this narrative characterizes Afghan/Pashtun men as *improperly* homosexual, compromised by their deviant culture. Hence, Pashtun sexuality comes to be framed as perverse when compared to gay experiences in Euro-American contexts. In Western imagination, the Pashtun, Afghan, and Taliban militant not only aggregate into one knowable figure but also appear as either homophobic or improperly homosexual—never performing ideal heterosexuality. In the ISPR productions, the *talib* is likewise marked as sexually perverse but the perversity is linked to his performance of heterosexuality in a manner that deviates from accepted practice, conventional partners, and normative spheres. The ISPR's figuration of the *talib* then both overlaps with and departs from Western imaginations of the Taliban, constituting its own distinct kind of colonizing effect.

The Talib *as* "Pathan"

In the ISPR's cultural texts, the *talib* is often ethnicized as Pashtun and marked as backward, a discursive practice that produces tribal people en masse as bare life. In "Bara dushman," "Mujhe dushman," and "Farishtay," for instance, the *talib* often appears in the traditional Pashtun dress—which includes a turban or a *topi* (headwear resembling a calotte or skullcap), often a *coti* (waistcoat), and a shawl wrapped around the shoulders. He speaks in the Pashto language, using terms such as *jirga,* a body of Pashtun elders that decides on social matters locally. In these productions, the *talib* appears to organize his personal life according to tribal customs, which are shown to be at odds with those of the modern Pakistani nation. For example, when in Farishtay the *jirga* rules that the girl is to be married to one of the *talibs* as punishment, she appears depressed as she observes: "This *jirga* makes strange decisions. One mistake is punished by death; and another with forced marriage."[26] The *jirga's* "strange decisions" stand in implicit contrast to the modern laws established by the rational Pakistani state. Getting subjects to acquiesce to laws is the paradigmatic feature of successful sovereignty; these cultural texts clearly posit the state's own laws as rational and thus deserving of compliance.

Through these discursive strategies, the *talib* is marked as backward: backwardness, in this setting, is a placement in developmental time as well as a geographic location in areas that have not participated in the offerings of industrial and capitalist expansion.[27] Such placements affect the values one subscribes to, including claims to rationality. The *talib* is thus placed in the terrain of what Weber calls "*un*development."[28] This category is different from underdevelopment in that while those who are underdeveloped can be developed and thus salvaged, those who are *un*developed cannot be developed. The undevelopable subject is viewed as a threat to the development process itself. The *talib* is, therefore, to be either eradicated via violent wars or contained through the social construction of insurmountable difference.[29]

The contemporary slippage between the *talib* and the Pashtun has a history that can be traced to the racial politics of the British during the nineteenth century in colonial India. It is a story that is worth elaborating here in some detail given that its residue is present even today. The British colonizers considered the Pashtun (or "Pathan," a pejorative term that they used for Pashto-speaking groups) as both fanatic—hence, in need of regulation and disciplining—and martial—thus, ideally placed to fight on behalf of the empire. The Pashtuns resided in the Frontier province, which maps onto the present-day Federally Administered Tribal Areas (FATA), which have been merged into Pakistan's Khyber Pakhtunkhwa province only since May 2018.[30] The British viewed the Pashtuns as distinctive enough to require a different set of governance tactics. A number of laws, such as the Frontier Crimes Regulation (FCR) of 1901 and its earlier versions, the Punjab Murderous Outrages Act of 1867 and Murderous Outrages Act of 1877, were instituted to regulate the tribal peoples. The FCR gave political agents—intermediaries between the British government and the tribes—vast judicial powers, including the power to fine and detain hostile groups, demolish property, and even make arrests without a warrant.[31]

Pejorative and racist descriptions of the Pashtun pervade texts written by British colonial officers. For instance, in his book *The Story of the Malakand Field Force,* published in 1898, Winston Churchill represented the Pashtun as animals, writing: "These Afridi and Pathan companies of the Guides Infantry suggest nothing so much as a well-trained pack of hounds. Their cries, their movements, and their natures are similar."[32] Elsewhere, he noted, "war is in his [the Pathan's] blood; he is a born marksman, but he is dirty, lazy and a spendthrift."[33] George Curzon, the viceroy and governor-general of India from 1899 to 1905, conjured the Pashtun as simultaneously strong and child-like: "I am never so happy as when on the Frontier. I know these men and how to handle them. They are brave as lions, wild as cats, docile as children."[34] One lieutenant governor of Punjab, Denzil Ibbetson, called the Pashtun the most "barbaric of all the races," "bloodthirsty, cruel and vindictive of the highest degree," and "a bigot of the most fanatical type, exceedingly proud and extraordinarily suspicious."[35] British imaginations of the Pashtun were likely influenced by the memory of their own defeats at the hands of Afghans during the eighteenth century. In colonial imagination then, the Pashtun were animalistic, barbaric, and fanatic; while they needed to be surveilled and quarantined, their raw strength could also be harnessed for the defense of the colonial state.

Sonia Qadir observes that Muslim nationalists such as Sir Syed Ahmed Khan also conceived of the tribal Pashtun as having a unique, natural propensity for fanaticism and seem to have internalized colonial discourses.[36] Khan is reported to have said, "the Pathan tribes of the Frontier are a destabilizing influence for the Empire not so much because the Wahabi Preachers radicalise them, or because they take their Islam too seriously. They do not challenge British rule because it is illegitimate—they do it solely because they know not how else to live."[37] This formulation deposits fanaticism in those of Pashtun ethnicity and tribal locations, while shielding Islam.[38] After the political independence of Pakistan, the Pashtuns were stigmatized for siding with the Indian Congress over the Muslim League on the question of partition. The leaders of the anticolonial movement, Khudai Khidmatgar, had supported an unpartitioned India and boycotted the referendum in the Frontier province. Upon the establishment of Pakistan, they advanced a proposal for the creation of Pakhtunistan, a semi-autonomous region for the Pashtuns within the nation.[39] The proposal was rejected by the Pakistan government, and the movement's activists were termed traitors.

Contemporary representations of the *talib* as Pashtun and hence, fanatic, draw on these earlier portrayals of the Pathan. One repercussion is that the Pashtun people en masse are imagined as terrorists or pre-terrorists. The Pashtun-*talib* composite signals the possibility of a traitor within, who must be managed, disciplined, or even executed, if required. There has been widespread resistance to relocating internally displaced people from Khyber Pukhtunkhwa province into other parts of Pakistan, as they are viewed as troublemakers and a security risk. The chief minister of Sindh, in 2014, refused refugees from Waziristan for fear of "terrorists" hiding among them.[40] Likewise, mobility of Pashtun people from tribal areas to urban cities in search of employment is also often viewed with suspicion.[41] The ethnicization of the *talib* as Pashtun is widespread enough that activist scholar Ammar Ali Jan observes that the War on Terror in Pakistan appears almost to be a Pashtun problem.[42] Thus, the tribal regions and the Pashtun people, like the *talib,* have come to be viewed as out-of-time and misaligned with national rules and middle-class norms. These formulations facilitate the production of these areas and bodies as exceptions, where state and imperial violence becomes permissible.

What is interesting, though, is that in addition to depositing fanaticism and barbarism in the Pathan, the colonial and now the Pakistani state also emphasize the Pathan's warrior lineage, marking him as ideal for fighting *on behalf* of the state. After the 1857 Indian war of independence, British army administrators set out to identify new Indian recruits. They designated certain ethnic groups as martial races, among them the Pathans as well as the Sikhs and Muslims from Punjab. Hindus and Bengalis were excluded, as they were considered effeminate.[43] These imperial categorizations were based on assumptions about which "races" were strong enough to bear arms. Lord Roberts, who was the commander-in-chief of India from 1885 to 1893, and who portrayed himself as the founder of the martial race theory, argued that people living in the cold frontiers of British India—as the Pashtuns did—were more capable of fighting than those living in hot climates.[44] While these categorizations did not hold true for all the groups that the British considered well positioned to fight, according to historian Kaushik Roy the theory was influential in British army recruitment practices.[45] Its remnants can be found in the recruitment practices of the Pakistani army, which has shown a preference for Punjabis and Pashtuns. According to Hassan Abbas, this preference was the unwritten recruitment policy of the army until the 1970s.[46] Today, too, Punjabis and Pashtuns form the two largest ethnic segments in the army.[47]

When the Pashtun is employed by the state to fight for the nation, he appears as a soldier; however, when he is conscripted informally, such as when the CIA and ISI recruited volunteers to dispel the Soviets from Afghanistan, he is articulated as a *mujahid,* one who engages in *jihad.* After the Soviet withdrawal, many *mujahidin* took up the Indian occupation of Kashmir as their next cause. In that context, too, violence was deemed to be legitimate, as it aligned with the Pakistani state's ambitions. The figure of the freedom-fighting *mujahid* is yet another pathway through which the Pashtun enters national history and discourse.

This slipperiness of the framing of the Pashtun, across *talib* to soldier to freedom-fighter, is not accidental: it is a practice of power. People from the tribal areas are curated in a biologically essential way—the harsh climate and mountainous terrain are used as explanations for their ruggedness and strength as well as for their distance from modernity. These biologically essentialist framings help to construct the Pashtun simultaneously as a martial race, making them excellent soldiers and *mujahidin,* and as potential traitors/militants because they have not been completely incorporated into the polity and modernity. When the Pashtun aligns with nationalist goals, his power is harnessed to advance the nation; when he critiques or dissents, he is transformed into a fanatic, to be disciplined. The contemporary Pakistani state's fight against terrorism hinges on this delicate balance. This is not too dissimilar from the British treatment of the Pashtun, which was simultaneously dismissive and admiring.[48]

The figure of the *talib* in the ISPR cultural texts then appears as a figure of deficiency and lack—he is a coward, sexually perverse, undevelopable, and fanatic. He threatens objects of love: innocence, sexual purity, middle-class social norms; therefore, he is himself an object of disgust, even hate. These attributes and affects mark him as an aberration not only in the context of the nation but also in the contexts of manhood and Islam. Located thusly outside the political and religious community, he can be killed with impunity, without the normative strictures posed by law and religion. Said differently, these discursive moves facilitate the production of the *talib* as bare life, which, as Agamben has theorized, may be killed but not sacrificed, as it lacks sufficient worth for such a divine gesture.[49] In this way, the state performs sovereignty also through its "monopoly over sacrifice"—by determining whose life can be sacrificed and whose cannot have that particular merit.[50] Disgust, however, does not reside in a given subject or object; it is economic and envelops look-alikes, thereby expanding the scope of sovereign violence.[51]

The prevalence of everyday discrimination against Pashtuns is evidence of that expansion.

The construction of the *talib* traced thus far permits the curation of the *jawan* as an object of love. Indeed, disgust functions to maintain relations of power by hierarchizing spaces as well as bodies.[52] The *jawan* hence materializes through frames of bravery, paternalism, heteronormativity, and modernity.

The Jawan *as a* Ghazi

In the ISPR texts, the *jawan* is often referred to as *ghazi*. An Arabic term used for a fearless Muslim warrior, the term *ghazi* was historically reserved for fighters who took part in raids against non-Muslims. Later, its use was expanded and it functioned as an honorific for Muslim princes, such as those belonging to the Ottoman Empire.[53] Over time, it evolved to refer also to a successful battlefield commander. During the nineteenth-century Anglo-Afghan wars, *ghazis* were fierce, irregular fighters who used guerrilla techniques to attack the superior British armies. The British therefore saw them as a dangerous force. The Pakistani army has incorporated the term into its nationalist lexicon and harnesses this model of warrior Muslim masculinity to indicate the superior strength and training of its soldiers. In doing so it also transforms the soldier's fight into a fight for God, so that battling for the defense of the nation-state and defending Islam appear as one and the same.

Consider an article published in *Hilal Urdu* in December 2001 that provides a commentary on the "sons of country who received Nishan-e-Haider," one of the highest military honors.[54] After detailing the bravery of a number of soldiers, the article concludes with the following verses by the poet Allama Iqbal:

These *ghazis,* these determined men
To whom You [God] have given desire for power *(zoq-e-khudai)*
Desert and sea smash as they encounter him
Mountains crumble in their fear[55]

The *ghazi* is a male warrior of such superior strength that even mountains crumble before him. Not only does his might derive from a mission sanctioned by God, but also his will to fight is bestowed by God. The poem was also featured in a music video, "Ye Ghazi" (ISPR, 2018; as of January 2021, close to one million views) to pay tribute to the *jawan* from the Northern

Light Infantry (NLI) who had sacrificed their lives.[56] The NLI draws men from the mountainous northern areas of Pakistan to fight in the cold regions and until recently was a paramilitary force not fully incorporated in the armed forces. The video depicts soldiers braving the weather as they fight on for Islam. *Ghazis* in the poem appear as believing men *(momin)* who desire martyrdom *(shahadat)*. They are thus lionized as religio-nationalist heroes, as perfect men *(mard-e-momin)*. Allama Iqbal's poetry appeared at the turn of the twentieth century when independence from the British seemed a distinct possibility. He constructed the figure of the *mard-e-momin* to inform Indian Muslim men of past Muslim warriors and rally them against the colonial state.[57] The recurrence of this imagery in the contemporary ISPR discourse alludes to similar aspirations, this time to defeat a new enemy: the Taliban.

A 2016 short film entitled *Ghazi* (as of January 2021, close to ten million views) visually depicts some of the characteristics of the soldier as an Islamic warrior.[58] The film features an encounter between an army platoon and members of a militant cell. The entire six-minute span details the army chasing the militants in a jungle as the latter try to take refuge in a village. Whereas the militants scramble haphazardly, the soldiers move in an orderly, disciplined fashion. Scenes of the chase are interspersed with visuals of the command center, where senior military officers use the latest technology, including a live feed, to monitor the progress of the soldiers. By the end of the film, all three of the key suspects identified have been eliminated. Alongside the discipline and athleticism of the soldiers, *Ghazi* also features their warrior-like bravery. One scene in particular is noteworthy for it highlights the *ghazi's* almost-supranatural gallantry. During the chase, a soldier and a militant come face to face, pointing their guns at each other. The militant fires, but is out of bullets. He places his rifle on the ground, ready to be executed by the soldier. Unexpectedly, the soldier shakes his head, puts his rifle down too, and engages the militant in hand-to-hand combat. In other words, the *ghazi-*soldier is so confident in his ability that he does not need to rely on the advantage that he has suddenly gained. The fight continues for a while, the soldier and the militant attempting to subdue each other, but ultimately the soldier's superior fighting techniques grant him victory. The film breaks into a chorus, "Our name is Ghazi"; a play on *ghazi's* other meaning, "victors."

The hypermasculine moniker of *ghazi* facilitates the construction of the national soldier as a soldier of Islam, melding nation and religion. A verse in *Ghazi* makes these connections explicit: "the country is content, God is content, our hearts are content" *(Watan raazi, khuda raazi, ye apna dil bhi raazi hai).*[59] This equivalence not only binds the soldier to the country and to God but also binds God to the country. To protect the country is to protect God; to protect God entails protecting the country. The soldier thus is imagined as a bulwark of a composite I call "Islam-Country." Numerous articles in *Hilal* tie the soldier to Islam-Country. Consider "A Page from a Soldier's Diary," authored by Major Sardar Atif Habib and published in 2017.[60] He notes, "I'm the custodian of this territory, in its defense lies the survival of us all. I am the son of soil, I am a soldier! . . . I'm a guardian, saviour, defender, fighter, struggler and a warrior. My entire journey is exploring, defending, serving and fighting for the national cause." Habib goes on to explain that his bravery is due to his trust in Allah:

> Serving this country is a part of my faith. Although I do not have any apparent wealth, I am contended [*sic*] with whatever I have. His secret auspiciousness augments my few coins to meet all my needs as He fulfils my wishes before I even know, I'm always compensated by the Omnipotent in tragic times, He stands with me when I fight in the cause of His will. He never leaves his soldiers alone.[61]

This recurring theme of the *jawan* fighting for Islam-Country has a genealogy that can be gleaned from the *Hilal* magazines. The Muslim prayer and war cry *labbaik,* as well as the expression *"narae ya Ali,"* alluding to Hazrat Ali, the first Shia imam, are invoked in many issues of *Hilal Urdu,* which shroud the army's wars in religious probity.[62] We also find articles that include reflections on Muslim prayer rituals, such as *namaz,* fasting, and *hajj.*[63] Past issues of *Hilal* often describe soldiers as *ghazi,* but also include other terms that signal the religious character of their endeavor, such as *Islam ka sipahi* (soldier of Islam), *mujahid* (one who engages in jihad), *watan kay mujahid* (*mujahid* of the country), and *mard-e-Musalmaan,* which denotes the manhood of Islam.[64]

The framing of the *jawan* as *ghazi* is further cemented in the *Hilal* magazines through detailed accounts of wars that Prophet Muhammad fought during his time, as well as explications of the ethics of war as laid out in Islam. These serve as teachings for readers. In the January 1966 and November 1971 issues of *Hilal Urdu,* for instance, we find articles that describe the conquest of Mecca, and an entire issue from January 1980 is dedicated to the Prophet.[65] In addition, we find numerous references to the Quran as guide for the *ghazi's* conduct during war. The first page of the April 1980 issue of *Hilal,* for example, gives a prominent place to a chapter from the Quran that notes that war booty belongs to Allah and the Prophet, and hence people are instructed to obey them both.[66] This verse is used to educate the reader—presumably a soldier—that "the property and weapons taken from the enemies belong to the Islamic State [of Pakistan]. It is not appropriate to challenge the state's decisions . . . state decisions should be obeyed."[67] Through this transitive use of the Quran, the state acquires religious authority.

The first-person writings of soldiers included in the *Hilal* magazines also signal their affection for Islam-Country. In a letter by Akram Mulk addressed to his parents and discovered after his death, we learn his thoughts about the ongoing India-Pakistan war of 1971.[68] He writes that, "No life is precious when it comes to protecting Islam, nation, and country. It is our responsibility to present our lives for sacrifice to protect our religion and country and that is what the courageous Pakistani army is doing these days."[69] He then comforts his parents, noting that death can come to anyone at any time and that if he should die on the battlefield, then it would be a sacrifice in the path of Allah. As I will explain further below, the soldier's commitment to Islam-Country means that his death acquires meaning as a sacrifice. Dead soldiers are often considered *shahid*—martyrs—by the army, an honor that is usually restricted for those who die on the path of Islam. However, since Islam and country emerge as a composite in the army's cultural texts, the term *shahid* is liberally used for dead soldiers. The February 1980 issue of *Hilal,* for example, includes verses of the Quran that elaborate on the blessings granted to the *shahid* and *ghazi.*[70]

The articulation of the *jawan* as *ghazi* imbues his life and war-making efforts with religious sanction. However, this sanction is bitterly contested by the Taliban. As we will see in the next chapter, the Taliban too perform their own version of Islam-masculinity, hailing publics to view them instead as the current descendants of past Islamic warriors.

The Jawan *as Sacrificial Blood*

Whereas the *talib* is figured as bare life that can be killed but not sacrificed, the *jawan*'s life is sacralized through the discourse of martyrdom; in many ISPR publications he is framed literally as "sacrificial blood." In the preface to *Junoon-e-Rukh-e-Wafa* (2018), a book that features first-person accounts of soldiers, their female relations, and civilians, the then-director general of ISPR, Asif Ghafoor, notes that the price of freedom in the subcontinent has been the "blood of Muslims," and that "it is their blood that lights the candle of freedom today."[71] He then recognizes the Pakistani army's sacrifices: "we have given the price of each inch [of free land] with our blood."[72] This framing of soldiers through the semiotic code of sacrificial blood not only elevates the meaning of their lives in death but also establishes a link between present-day soldiers and Muslim warriors of the past. It was the latter's blood that fertilized the soil of the land that birthed the present-day soldier, and the present-day soldier's sacrificial blood will create possibilities for future generations.

Likewise, the soldier's life is sacralized in a poem entitled "Lahoo" (Blood), published in the November 1965 edition of *Hilal*.[73] The poet imagines creating a flag out of the sacrificial blood of soldiers and takes it to represent the sacrifice of Muslim saints, heroes, and warriors:

> *Yehi alam hai nishan-e-Haider*
> *Isi main khoon-e-Hussein Shamil hai*
> *Yehi tha aijaz Ibn-e-Qasim*
> *Yehi tha Ghauri ka rehnama bhi*
>
> This flag is the mark of Haider
> It has the blood of Hussein
> This was the blessing of Son of Qasim
> It was the guide for Muhammad of Gaur

Haider is an honorific term used for Imam Ali, Prophet Muhammad's son-in-law and the first Shia imam, known for his bravery on the battlefield. Hussein was the grandson of Prophet Muhammad and the second imam of Shia Muslims; he was brutally massacred on the battlefields of Karbala. "Son of Qasim" refers to Muhammad bin Qasim, an Umayyad general who conquered Sindh in the eighth century and is popularly credited for bringing Islam to this part of the world, and Muhammad of Gaur was the Sultan of the Ghurid Empire in the twelfth century. These linkages elevate the life of the soldier, giving it political and historical value in the universe of Islam-Country.

It is the soldier's sacrifice of his "blood" *(lahoo)* that ensures freedom for his national family. This is precisely why soldiers are popularly called the "nation's sons" or "sons of the soil." In *Junoon-e-Rukh-e-Wafa*, Muhammad Amjad Chaudhary argues that a soldier always has the option to stay in his small world and care only for his nuclear family. However, he chooses not to, for he is "the son of the *quam* [nation]."[74] In another essay, entitled "Blood's Tribute," Major Naeem recounts the life of his martyred friend, Major Khalid.[75] The piece elaborates on Khalid's bravery and gallantry on the field against militants and pays tribute to him for sacrificing his blood for the nation. Naeem also clarifies for readers that Khalid belonged to a multigenerational family of soldiers—his father was a colonel, his brother is a major, and his younger brother decided to enlist as well. Blood relations in the article appear to be both biological and metaphorical. Indeed, a key strand that runs through official publications of the army is the intergenerational transfer of the responsibility to defend the nation. For instance, in an issue of *Hilal* published during the 1965 India-Pakistan war, a column praises a boy named Zafar Javed for his courage.[76] Javed's father had recently died on the battlefield and he now wished to enlist in the army himself: "I am the lucky son of a great father. My father was blessed with martyrdom while defending the beloved country. I am proud of my country and my nation. After completing my education, I will also enlist in the army and will follow my father's footsteps by serving the country and nation." The death of a soldier on the battlefield is portrayed as a sacrifice that strengthens, rather than weakens, the resolve of others.

The connective tissue of blood erases temporal and spatial borders and binds soldiers of today with Muslim warriors of the past. This lineage elevates the political meaning of their lives and deaths, producing soldiers as aspirational figures.

The Jawan *as Protector*

The ISPR's videos cajole the viewing public to trust the *jawan:* as "Ye banday" notes, "when your difficulties overwhelm you, place your hand in theirs."[77] The *jawan,* in turn, will protect the people, carefully leading them away from danger and toward safety and happiness. To construct the *jawan* as a protector, the ISPR relies on the figure of the girl as a threatened object. Whereas the *talib* embodies threat, the *jawan* represents protection.

Recall "Ye banday," in which the small girl in bright-red clothes in the opening scene enlists audiences into experiencing the threat of the *talib.* Toward the end of the video, we see a young soldier carry the same girl in his arms, away from danger. Other girls of similar age are also being escorted by soldiers, who hold their hands and walk them out of the compound where the Taliban had held them. A similar relationship between the soldier and the girl-child appears across other cultural productions of the army as well. Consider *Faseel-e-Jaan se Agay,* a drama series jointly produced by the ISPR and a private company. The series, which aired on the national television network in 2011, traces the lives of eleven different *jawans* and officers of the army, as well as everyday people, featuring their courage "during the operation against terrorists and militants in Mingora region," according to the ISPR.[78] The aim of the series was to "unveil the real face of terrorists and militants who have been exploiting the downtrodden in the name of religion."[79] Each episode examines the story of a particular character; one specifically focuses on the figure of the *beti* (daughter). Entitled "Eik beti ki kahani" (A daughter's story), the episode tells the familiar tale of a girl who is threatened and sexually violated by the Taliban and is later rescued by soldiers.[80] The events take place in 2009 when a group of Taliban leaders began terrorizing the residents of Swat Valley. Momin Gul, the female protagonist, is courted by her cousin Najeeb Khan, but her parents refuse Khan's marriage proposal because he is not educated. They argue that Gul deserves to marry someone of a similar educational stature.

Disaffected, Khan decides to join the "Tehrik" (a reference to the TTP) because he has heard that the Tehrik facilitates the marriages of its members. He asks the Tehrik to help him marry Gul. Men from the Tehrik often kidnap the girls whom its fighters want to marry; thus, Gul is kidnapped and placed in a compound with many other girls. Instead of arranging her marriage to Khan as promised, the Tehrik commander decides to keep Gul for himself. In his custody, she is sexually violated not only by him but also by other members of the group. At one point in the series, she is referred to by the Tehrik men as "*maal-e-ghanimat*" (spoils of war, which according to some interpretations of Islamic law, are legitimate to partake in). This reference shows the distorted religious sensibilities of the Taliban. Gul is then given away as a gift to a senior commander, whose compound is eventually raided by the army. During the chaos, she escapes. She is saved by a family who offer to take her back to her parents, but on the way they are intercepted by the Taliban. This time, however, army *jawan*s at a nearby checkpoint come to Gul's aid. She is ultimately rescued and reunited with her parents.

"Eik beti ki kahani" contains many lessons for the viewing public. It teaches the audience that even though the Taliban claim to be Muslims, their practices are, in fact, incongruent with Islam. For instance, when Gul asks another woman at the compound about how they all got there, she learns that they too were abducted. She further inquires as to whether the girls are married properly, through the Muslim *nikah* (contract). To that, the woman responds, "What *nikah*? . . . They are giving a bad name to this sacred tradition [of Islam] . . . The real reason is to put a label on their own licentiousness . . . Whoever they like, they pick up in the name of *sharia*." This demonstrates that the Taliban are improper Muslims. Whereas in the ISPR music videos considered earlier, the Taliban's atrocious behaviors—in particular, killings—are not explicitly shown, in "Eik beti ki kahani," many scenes of Taliban violence are featured, including close-ups of mutilated, bloody bodies. In one scene, we observe the Taliban commander slitting Khan's throat and beating Gul. Such explicit scenes of violence are intended to offend the sensibilities of the largely middle-class, urban population that watches television in Pakistan. The *talib* thus emerges as an object of disgust. Finally, Gul's articulation through kinship bonds such as *beti,* transforms her into an elastic figure whose honor is not only her own but belongs to her family, her community, and the nation. This is made most explicit when the family that rescues her goes out of its way to ensure that she is reunited with her family, though they lose their own son in the process. The lesson here is that the violation of a *beti* is experienced as an assault not only by her but by the entire nation. Viewers of the drama are called on to empathize with her tragedy and feel proud of the courage that the *jawan*s displayed in rescuing her. The figure of the girl thereby confers the role of protector—big brother or young father—onto the *jawan* and, through him, onto the state.

To deliver on this promise of protecting the nation, the *jawan* willingly sacrifices himself and his family. The ISPR music video "Tu thori dair aur thehr ja" (Stay for a bit longer; as of January 2021, over nine million views; hereafter "Tu thori"), produced in recognition of Operation Zarb-e-Azb as a collaboration with Pakistani singer Farhan Saeed, focuses on the sacrifices of a newlywed soldier and his young wife.[81] As the story goes, the soldier is called away for duty on his wedding night and has to leave his bride behind. She, along with his mother, awaits news and communication from him, which never arrive. Meanwhile, we see the *jawan* performing his duties, valiantly fighting the militants and saving his comrades, even as he desperately misses his family. In one scene, his platoon comes under attack, and he is shot . . . he may never get to see his wife again. The *jawan* is taken to a hospital and survives. "Tu thori" begins with the following blurb, which signals the kind of resonances that the video seeks to produce in its audience: "Soldiers are humans too. They have families like we have. They share the same emotions as we do. We salute Pak Army soldiers and their families who are fighting for us day and night. We dedicate this video specially [*sic*] to Operation Zarb-e-Azb." This narrative calls on the audience to view soldiers as everyday men: they are just like us (the viewers); they are family men who have wives and mothers whom they care about. Yet they are sacrificing their families *for us.* Such storylines shorten the distance between the *jawan* and the viewing public, binding them into a relationship of intimacy and familiarity. The connection is further illuminated in "Farishtay," where the adolescent girl is captured by the Taliban and forced to marry a *talib*. As one of the soldiers enters her compound to attempt rescue, he is shot several times in the chest. Hurt and bleeding, he falls to the ground but manages to fire back and kill the *talib* in the process. As the girl attempts to revive him, she observes that he is holding onto something. She removes the bloodstained object: it is a creased photo of his wife and toddler. The soldier has willingly sacrificed his life and family for this young girl, for the nation, and for us, the viewing public. The *jawan*'s circulation as a willing sacrificial figure in and through the ISPR cultural texts manufactures a relationship of trust between the army and the viewing public; it is this felt relationship that nurtures consent for the *jawan*'s violence.

The framing of *jawan* as older brothers, husbands, and young fathers also marks them as appropriately heterosexual when compared to the *talib*. The *jawan*'s desires operate within the confines of his family as he engages in monogamous, long-term marriage. Outside of his own wife, he views all women and girls as sisters, daughters, or mothers. Through him masculinity is hitched to particular performances of sexuality, defined by heterosexual kinship relations. At the same time, the soldier's sexuality is also policed and contained, as soldiers' wives are called on to discipline themselves and ensure that their sexuality does not become a distraction for their husbands (more on this in chapter 4).[82] In short, the *jawan*'s framing as a protective kin-figure (brother/husband/father) deposits in him strength that he can use to kill and maim enemies as well as a fragility that calls forth an emotive, even nurturing, response from the populace.

ENCHANTED BY THE *JAWAN*

The ISPR's dyadic construction of *jawan-talib* accrues its affective valence as it circulates and encounters attentive publics that echo it back and, in doing so, express approval of statist practices of sovereignty. Consider a commemorative music video released on the anniversary of the APS attack by a popular Pakistani musician, Ali Azmat. Entitled "Yeh jung bhi hum hi jeetey gey" (We will win this war too), the video portrays an acute fascination with, and desire for, the soldier's masculinity.[83] In it, the singer, who is a middle-aged man, dresses up in combat gear with all the paraphernalia, including a bulletproof vest, camouflage paint, gloves, bandanas, and a Pakistani flag stitched onto the uniform. Several other middle-aged celebrities join him in the video, similarly dressed. Marketing images for the video show Ali Azmat climbing up a tree, as well as posing in an area reserved for target-shooting practice. The video plays with the militant-soldier binary and explicitly calls out the militant for being a "coward." It features scenes of militants engaged in plotting an attack and contrasts them with visuals of the counterterrorism wing, in which a team of army officials is planning a preemptive strike. While the militants work in dilapidated conditions, the counterterrorism unit is well equipped, with modern technologies at its disposal. Ultimately, the soldiers attack the militant cell and destroy it.

The music video exhibits extensive slippage between the soldier and the everyday Pakistani, which is instructive and demonstrates the elasticity of the figure of the soldier as it travels and envelops the entire nation. The video opens with the phrase "Nation fights back," and images of farmers, laborers, fishermen, children, mothers, petty vendors, donkey cart drivers, and carpenters appear, signaling Pakistan's unity in its fight against terrorism. The distinctions between the soldier, the celebrity (Ali Azmat), and the everyday Pakistani dissolve, as they coalesce on the same side, standing with (and for) each other. The quick speed with which the images rotate enhances this slippage. One can also observe this equivalence in Ali Azmat's introductory message for the video on Facebook: "Stand with Pak Army, Stand with Pakistan. #APS #16December #AliAzmat. Team Ali Azmat !!!"[84]

The *hum* (we) of "Yeh jung bhi hum hi jeetey gey" includes the entire nation. This construction seductively aligns the viewer with the *jawan;* that is, by aligning with the *jawan* the viewer too can save the nation. I see this video as a response to the army's cultural performances discussed earlier in the chapter. It not only reiterates the *talib-jawan* dyad but also transforms all able-bodied Pakistani men into potential soldiers. Such aspirations are subtly indicated in the army's videos as well. For example, in "Yeh banday" and "Farishtay," soldiers are often shown in groups, portraying collective strength. At the same time, such formations dissolve the individuality of the soldier, giving a sense that any one soldier can be replaced with another. As "Yeh banday" proclaims,

In ke apne koi naam nahi
Ik naam ke sarey pakke hain

They don't have their own name [identity]
they just abide by one name

FIGURE 2. Pakistani students at a rally in Lahore condemning the Taliban attack on APS. December 19, 2014. Credit: Reuters / Mohsin Raza.

This nameless fraternity extends to incorporate all able-bodied men of the nation. Said differently, while the nation depends on these soldiers for its protection, each soldier's individuality is meaningless to the nation; he can and will be replaced by the millions of others, such as Ali Azmat, who are ready to fight for the nation and take his place. In the army's videos, the soldier stands for the nation and in Ali Azmat's video, the citizen stands for the soldier (and thus the nation). The everyday Pakistani participates in the drama of political sovereignty by acquiescing to this relationship with the army.

This attachment to the *jawan* and the nation is palpable across multiple other public cultural performances as well, such as during the commemorative rallies that took place after the APS attack. In figure 2, we see a number of schoolboys dressed in army gear, holding up toy guns at a rally in Lahore. Similarly, figure 3 shows schoolchildren dressed as a soldier, terrorist, and mother, respectively, at a rally in Peshawar. In the latter image, the child dressed up as a soldier is pointing his gun at the child whose turban and beard signal that he is playing the part of a terrorist. Even two years later, at commemorative rallies for APS, schoolboys continue to "play" the *jawan* (figure 4) and become the bodies through which statist sovereignty is reaffirmed publicly. Through these street performances, publics reaffirm the state's power to furnish death to the Taliban.

FIGURE 3. Schoolchildren at a ceremony in Peshawar on the first anniversary of the APS attack. December 16, 2015. Credit: Metin Aktas / Anadolu Agency via Getty Images.

FIGURE 4. Schoolchildren perform at a demonstration in Karachi on the second anniversary of the APS attack. December 16, 2016. Credit: Reuters / Akhtar Soomro.

FIGURE 5. A female student condemning the attack on APS during a rally in Lahore. December 19, 2014. Credit: Reuters / Mohsin Raza.

Attachment to the *jawan* is fostered through a range of other army-civilian encounters as well. Army summer camps for children are a prime example. Growing up in Pakistan, I can still recall the summer when my brothers, as young teenagers, and several of their friends, attended one such camp at Petaro. According to my parents, this was the place where my brothers would "learn how to become men *(mard)*." More concretely, the camp would "make them tough," teaching them how to manage their time, undertake grueling daily tasks on hot summer days with a positive disposition, and become disciplined in their everyday habits. There is no equivalent camp for girls, so I never attended one. However, the idea that the *jawan* embodies a version of masculinity that is worthy of emulating, even tentatively for two months by middle-class boys who would never really end up in the military, was commonplace. This masculinity promises the best of what a man has to offer to himself, his family, his community, and the nation. The affective investment in military masculinity invites young boys to imagine themselves as future soldiers and allows middle-aged celebrities, such as Ali Azmat, to tentatively reinvent themselves as action heroes.

While it is the young boys and men who most enthusiastically take up *jawan* masculinities, there is also space for women to reaffirm the statist project by becoming soldiers. The figuration of the "army woman" becomes a focus later in this book; however, figure 5 is an illustration of women's multiple roles in the drama of sovereignty. In addition to the girl-child who requires rescue, women are also invited to tentatively experience military masculinity by becoming soldiers. This role is mostly accessible to Pakistani women of a particular socioeconomic class and ethnic background; for the majority, it remains an impossibility as, after all, the military remains an overwhelmingly male enterprise.[85]

The aesthetic productions considered in this chapter mobilize love for, and trust in, the *jawan,* while simultaneously creating distance from the *talib.* Attachment to (love for) the *jawan* and distance from (disgust for) the *talib* thus transpire concurrently. The *jawan* performs an Islamo-masculinity that brings together normative codes of masculinity, such as physical strength, with claims to defend Islam-Country against the backward Taliban. The dyad of *jawan-talib* gains affective intensity as it circulates in public culture; multiple publics reproduce it, sometimes by even embodying the *jawan* masculinity. These imitating publics are the very bodies through and upon which sovereignty is extended and reclaimed in the aftermath of a crisis. They consent to state violence in order to defend the nation against the *talib.* Violence in this case, as Foucault observes, is waged not in the name of the sovereign, but on behalf of everyone.[86] While in this chapter I have analyzed the dyad of *jawan-talib,* the national self is constructed in relation to multiple Others, including the Indian enemy and the British colonizer, as well as the imperial Other. The purpose of zooming in on the dyad is to excavate the subtle dialectical construction that emerges specifically in the post-9/11 and post-APS contexts. This dyad, like any social practice, is historically conditioned. In fact, the stickiness and durability of the *jawan* and *talib* in public culture can be described as an effect of histories of associations.[87] Thus, there is both a newness and sameness to it, as it draws on prevailing forms of essentialization while inventing new ones.

Statist cultural performances hail another audience in the Taliban. This time, however, the audience transforms itself into a counterpublic. Still, even as it takes up an oppositional stance to the state, this counterpublic often ends up mimicking the state. It is to these Taliban cultural productions that I turn my attention next.

THREE

Competing Sovereigns

THE *MUJAHID*

JAMAAT-UL-AHRAR, A FACTION OF TEHRIK-E-TALIBAN PAKISTAN (TTP), responded to the ISPR's "Bara dushman" with a video of its own, "Bara gernal bana phirta hai" (He acts as if he is some big general).[1] While the video mimics the tune and composition of "Bara dushman," no musical instruments are used. It begins with a scene in which a group of boys, about two to five years old, are working through their reading assignments, probably at a *madrasa*. One of them holds what looks like a section of the Quran.[2] The boys are in *shalwar kameez, topi,* and scarves; their scruffy clothes signal their poverty, and their rosy cheeks suggest that they are likely from the cold tribal regions of the country. A group of slightly older boys enter, walking in a queue. Some carry Kalashnikovs, often used by the Taliban militants. One of them is clearly amused by the performance aspect of this production. He struggles to maintain a serious expression and eventually gives in and giggles. Hailing the Pakistani army and the people of Pakistan, the singer, an adult, asks:

> *Kyoon meray mukhalif ho*
> *Main tau Quran ka Talib hoon*
> *Kiya rabb say jo wada tha*
> *Usi ima(n) ka talib hoon*
> *Khalil-ul-Allah ka beta hoon*
> *Muhammadi ummat say hoon*

> Why are you against me?
> I am a student *(talib)* of the Quran
> I made a promise to my Nurturer
> I am a student [or desirous] of that faith
> I am the son of Friend-of-Allah
> I belong to the community of Muhammad [PBUH] (all translations mine)

In these verses, the singer questions the hostility that he experiences, arguing that all he is doing is abiding by the primordial covenant he entered into with God. The term *talib* flags his status both as a student of the Quran (or someone who is desirous of the Quranic teachings) and as one who belongs to the Tehrik-e-Taliban. Images of the Kaba'a, a Muslim holy site in Mecca, and the word "Muhammad" flash across the screen, directing viewers to attach him to these holy symbols. He goes on to elaborate his membership in, and commitment to, the community of Muhammad (*Muhammadi ummat*):

> *Kufar ka sar kuchal diya*
> *Haan ussi ummat say hoon*
> *Main us ka khoon hoon na*
> *Is liyay batil say larta hoon*

> Who smashed the heads of the unbelievers
> Yes, I belong to that community
> I am his blood
> That is why I fight falsehood

The *talib* mobilizes the connective property of blood to secure kinship to the Muslims of the past who fought against "falsehood" by ridding the Kaba'a of idols, thereby presenting himself as the latest incarnation of those early Muslims. In the video, falsehood is symbolized by both national and imperial sovereigns, with images of Barack Obama and Pakistani generals Pervez Musharraf, Ashfaq Kayani, and Raheel Sharif flashing across the screen. The *talib* views fighting against them as a divinely sanctioned mission:

> *Wo paida hotay hi jo kaan main muj jo parhaya tha*
> *Ussi azan nay tawhid ka sabaq sikhaya tha*
> *Wahain say aman seekha tha*
> *Wahain inkar seekha tha*
> *Wahain say saber seekha tha*
> *Kufar pe war seekha tha*

> I was taught this in the ear as soon as I was born[3]
> That *azaan* [call to prayer] taught me about the Oneness of God
> That is where I learned peace
> Where I learned to decline [repudiate evil]
> Where I learned patience
> Where I learned to strike the unbelievers

The video pairs these verses with the image of a man in a black *shalwar kameez* kneeling down, aiming, then firing. This combination of text and visuals places faith alongside violence. For the *talib*, violence appears to be a key practice through which he both defends and advances Islam.

In the final stanza, the video takes an eerily mimetic turn as the *talib* responds to a specific claim in the ISPR production, in which the boy-victim informed the *talib* that his brother and father would avenge his death (see chapter 2). The *talib* now retorts that he, too, is not alone; he too has kin who will avenge the assault on Islam:

> *Meray janay kay baad is ko*
> *Mera bhai uthae ga*
> *Haywanoon per teray*
> *Islam ka percham lahraee ga*
> *Muhabbat mout say hum ko*
> *Na kuch bhi kar sako gay tum*

> After I am gone
> My brother will carry on
> He will fly the flag of Islam over animals [a state building appears as the background visual]
> We love death
> You can't do anything [to us]

The singer here posits that he is fighting not for himself but to protect Islam at the cost of his own life. He goes on to confirm his intention of hurting the army, which is deemed as assaulting the faith:

> *Tumhain aisa zakham dain gay*
> *Na jis ko bhar sako gay tum*

> We will give you such a wound
> That you will not be able to heal

Ultimately, the *talib* argues: "I belong to a nation whose gaze frightens him" *(Main aisi quam say hoon jiski wo nazar say darta hai)*, advancing a construction of nation *(quam)* that counters the one put forth by the ISPR in "Bara dushman." Here, nation is imagined not as a community bounded by the Pakistani state, but as one that shares faith and has pledged allegiance to the Taliban leaders.

By mimicking "Bara dushman," "Bara gernal" reveals how intimately connected the Taliban's performances of sovereignty are with those of the Pakistani state's. Both draw on shared cultural notions around faith, personal sacrifice, and morality to give their violence meaning. The "Bara gernal" production is more than simply propaganda: it lays out the Taliban's vision of the political, creates the sovereign space of *ummah,* and stakes control over it through performance of an Islamo-masculinity. It also delineates those who are to be excluded from this space. "Bara gernal" then circulates as a conversation of sorts in which the *talib* calls on viewers to trust him as a coreligionist and to align with his political project. In this chapter, I engage in a close reading of the cultural productions of the Pakistani Taliban, including the Urdu and English magazines published by different factions between 2011 and 2020, as well as select videos and pamphlets, to explore the discourses that they mobilize in order to fashion attachments to their political project.

TALIBAN MAGAZINES

Illustrated magazines have a long history in this part of the world.[4] Islamist parties and militants relied on this genre during the 1980s anti-Soviet war effort as a means to rally support for the *mujahidin.* The magazines published during that time included theological pronouncements, information about battlefield successes, and commemorations of martyrs. They helped fashion the religious authority of the Islamist political parties, which were often headed by neither clerics nor religious scholars.[5] Today, magazines remain a salient mode of communication for militants and political parties in Pakistan, and have entered the digital space. For instance, Jam'at-e-Islami, a political party that seeks to reform the state along religious lines, has over twenty publications, making it a major stakeholder in the country's Islamist print media.[6] Jaish-e-Muhammad, which was designated as a terrorist group by the United States and banned by the Pakistani government, and the political arm of Lashkar-e-Taiba—yet another group banned in Pakistan— also publish weekly and monthly magazines.

Several factions of the Taliban have similarly ventured into print and digital publications as a way both to respond to the cultural narratives that the state circulates about them and to advance an alternate politics. Through these cultural texts, they hope to extend their reach farther than was possible via earlier modes of communication, among them radio, CDs, DVDs, night letters *(shabnameh),* audio cassettes, and pamphlets.[7] In particular, their increasing use of the English and Urdu languages signals their desire to convey their message to a broader audience, and to transform the identity of their movement from an ethnic to a national and global one. While they also publish magazines in Pashto, for the purpose of this study, I have focused on Urdu and English magazines due to their availability, as well as their intended aspirational national/global audience.[8] These include *Ihya-e-Khilafat* (Urdu, issues 1 to 14, 2011 to 2017), *Azan* (English, issues 1 to 6, 2013 to 2014), *Mujalla Tehrik-e-Taliban* (Urdu, issues 1 to 8, 2016 to 2020), *Sunnat-e-Khola* (English, issues 1 and 2, 2017), and *Ihya-e-Khilafat* (English, issues 1 and 2, 2014). The publishers sometimes identify themselves, but at other times use descriptive phrases to keep their identities ambiguous. Therefore, I am careful to point to the provenance of the magazines when such information is available, and otherwise speculate regarding their connection to the TTP based on content. For instance, while we learn in *Ihya-e-Khilafat* (Revival of Khilafat) that it is published by Jamat-ul-Ahrar, and *Sunnat-e-Khola* explicitly alludes to its links with the TTP, the publishers of *Azan* are more cryptic, calling themselves the "Taliban in Khurasan."[9] While some scholars take this to mean that the magazine is published by the Taliban in Afghanistan, I join others, like Haroro Ingram, who argue that given the magazine's extensive references to events in Pakistan—articles chastising Malala Yousafzai and criticizing the Pakistani military, for example—it is more likely that this is a Pakistani publication.[10]

These magazines are primarily aimed at a broad Pakistani readership. However, specific publications target niche audiences such as women, or middle-class Pakistanis within the country or in the diaspora. In this respect, the *Azan* publishers' self-articulation as "Khurasani" is salient as it points to the kind of readership that they envision as well as their aspirations for the magazine's pedagogic work. "Khurasan" refers to the historic region encompassing modern-day northern/northwestern Afghanistan, northeastern Iran, southern Turkmenistan, and Uzbekistan. It occupies a unique place in Muslim history as it is believed to have been the last major conquest during the war between the Muslim caliphs and the Sassanid Empire. According to some traditions, the messianic figure, al-Mahdi, who will fight the *dajjal* (akin to the Antichrist in Christian eschatology), will appear in Khurasan. Prophet Muhammad is also reported to have said that fighters with "black flags" will appear from Khurasan to restore peace.[11] Since the Taliban imagine their mission to be a messianic one, linked to restoring harmony in a chaotic world, they attach themselves to this broader salvific project. While it is not completely clear whether Pakistan was historically included in this region, the *Azan* publishers suture Pakistan to Khurasan.[12] The connection imbues the Taliban with the symbolic authority to pave the way for the messiah. It also aligns the Muslims of Pakistan with those who currently reside in the historic region of Khurasan. Of the magazines considered for this book, *Azan* seems to be most invested in creating a global Muslim readership. Its publishers explain the magazine as "a platform for the *Muslims of the world* to see the truth for what it is and also a way for them to participate in this global effort to destroy the enemies of Allah and His Messenger. It is also a platform for the Mujahidin *throughout the world* to present the reality of their situations to the world … Azan is also a platform for the *Muslim men and women abroad* who seek to humiliate the tyrants in their own lands."[13] The editors go on to elaborate the impetus behind the launch of the magazine: "the Muslim Ummah has been targeted with the vicious propaganda of the international media that has collectively sold itself out to the dark side. The biased portrayal of international events coupled with a perspective on life that has nothing to do with the Quran and Sunnah has confused the majority of the Muslim masses with regards to their stances in this war."[14] *Azan* sees itself as a corrective for not only audiences within Pakistan but also those beyond it.

Broad ambitions notwithstanding, many of these magazines imagine niche readerships. Published in the English language and targeted to women, *Sunnat-e-Khola* (The Way of Khola)[15] sees its purpose as encouraging women "all around the world" to join the Taliban's effort by either migrating to areas controlled by the Taliban or by facilitating their conquests.[16] The editors explain: "It is need of the hour that public should be made aware of the blessings of Khilafah. Public should be introduced to the magnificent Islamic past . . . . Magazine Sunnat e Khaula is a practical effort in this direction. Ansar and Muhajir sisters of Khurasan have put together this magazine with great effort so that their voice can be heard all around the world . . . . We want to provoke women of Islam to come forward and join the ranks of mujahidin e Islam and follow footsteps of Hazrat Khaula r.a. [the honorific RA stands for *radi Allahu ʿanha* or "May Allah be pleased with her"]."[17] Khaula bint Al-Azwar was a female Muslim warrior born sometime during the seventh century. She is known to have participated in battles alongside her brother, and even to have led a group of women during a battle, in which she was wounded. She is held out as an ideal for readers who aspire to contribute to the cause of *khilafat*. The magazines use the term *khilafat* or *khilafah* to denote simultaneously the historical institutions of Muslim rule and the current regions where the Taliban reside or those they occupy. The editors of *Sunnat-e-Khola* ask women to try to migrate to lands now controlled by the Taliban, which are understood as being under a new political dispensation, *khilafat*.

In contrast to *Azan* and *Sunnat-e-Khola,* which aspire to global readership, the Urdu-language magazine *Ihya-e-Khilafat* is securely bound to a Pakistani readership. It is one of the longest-running magazines that I analyzed, with issues 1 to 8 linked to the central TTP movement and issues 9 onward identifying their connection to the Jamaat-ul-Ahrar faction. Compared to other magazines, which include colorful images, *Ihya-e-Khilafat* is spartan, often with visuals only on the cover and a few pages inside. Its English edition, launched in 2014, has global aspirations: the group realized that "there was a need to address English speaking population of the world."[18] Both editions aim to "highlight the oppression unleashed by Pakistan Army on Pakistani Muslims and to expose the un-Islamic nature of 'Islamic' Republic of Pakistan."[19] Finally, the Urdu-language magazine *Mujalla Tehrik-e-Taliban,* launched in November 2016, is also aimed primarily at a Pakistani readership. Its goal is to inform the public about ongoing activities, deliver messages from *mujahidin* leaders, respond to false accusations, and prepare Muslims for *jihad* and migration.[20]

It is difficult to determine the circulation numbers for these magazines, as most of them are banned. However, it is safe to assume that they circulate primarily within militant networks and online.[21] As I was researching for this book, I was able to locate some of the magazines (and videos) on the internet with ease; for others I had to secure access through university libraries and specialists. This ease or difficulty of access also indicates the target readership: the English-language magazines, for instance, are more easily accessible online, where middle-class Pakistanis and foreigners may find them, while the Urdu-language ones are less so, hinting that they likely circulate in tighter networks.

Needless to add, the magazines are only one element of the Taliban's public communication strategy. The TTP's official media organization, Umar Studio, produces songs and videos as well, and militants communicate with the public through leaflets, pamphlets, and night letters. Each of these communicative acts has its own peculiarities and intended audiences. Whereas the magazines and videos contain extensive citations from the Quran and hadith, the leaflets are straightforward rules or instructions that make no theological pretense. Consider, for instance, messages from the leader of the TTP Khurram Agency, distributed on May 10, 2011, to residents: "Women should be veiled. They are banned from going into the mountains and fields." "It is mandatory to keep a beard according to Islamic Sunnah. Cutting and shaving it is a big sin." "Wearing a *topi* is compulsory."[22] It is through a close reading of the Taliban's other communication materials, such as magazines, that we can understand the context of these instructions. Magazines thus offer us clues about the histories, tropes, and affects through which the Taliban advance their competing claim to sovereignty in public culture.

AMBIVALENT ATTACHMENTS:
PAKISTAN, A SITE OF BETRAYAL *AND* PROMISE

The Taliban argue that the Pakistani state was established so that *sharia* could be implemented but that this promise remains unfulfilled. They therefore express ambivalent feelings toward Pakistan. In psychoanalysis, ambivalence suggests the simultaneity of contradictory or oppositional feelings (e.g., love-hate) towards an object.[23] Freud argued that the loss of an object of love regresses into conflictual, ambivalent feelings toward that object.[24] In the Taliban magazines, Pakistan figures as such an object: it appears as a site of both betrayal and promise.

Writing in *Ihya-e-Khilafat Urdu*, Qazi Muhammad Saqib laments, "even though Pakistan was founded around the slogan 'What is the meaning of Pakistan? *La ilaha illallah*' [There is no God but Allah], today, forty-six years later the order of *La ilaha illallah* has not been implemented; whereas those people who want such an order are being eliminated."[25] In another issue of the same magazine, an author likewise distinguishes between "Quaid-e-Azam's Pakistan" and "Taliban's Pakistan," arguing that Pakistan was established so that *"khilafat-e-Islamiyya"* could be instituted.[26] He recounts the immense loss of life and honor borne by Muslims during the founding and asks, "did Muslims sustain all these cruelties so that Quaid-e-Azam's secular state could be established? No, not at all."[27] In the December 2019 issue of *Mujalla Tehrik-e-Taliban*, the editors explicitly name this feeling as "betrayal" *(dhoka).*[28] While betrayal fuels the Taliban's violence against state institutions, they explain that they engage in such violence also out of love. In *Ihya-e-Khilafat Urdu*, Mowlana Zakir begins his article, framed as a "message to ordinary Muslims from a *mujahid* of Tehrik-e-Taliban Ahrar," by noting that it is often assumed that the Taliban fighting in Afghanistan and Kashmir are legitimate, whereas those fighting in Pakistan are not.[29] He contests this logic, arguing that the establishment of Allah's order is incumbent on all lands, and therefore the struggle in Pakistan against a government that is still "British" is justified. Zakir's formulation both frames the present

Pakistani state as neocolonial, and also unites Pakistan, Afghanistan, and Kashmir in a conceptual whole, a single territory where God's law, instead of "British law," should be implemented. He defends the Taliban's motives in response to those who portray them as enemies of the state by saying that "in reality . . . we are the *lovers* of the country."[30] Zakir goes on to draw an equivalence between the Taliban's efforts and those of the Prophet, outlining how the Prophet migrated from Mecca to Medina even though he loved his home city. Accordingly, one can both love a country and migrate away from it if its social order is not hospitable. In the Taliban's discourse thus, while Pakistan appears as a site of betrayal, it remains an object of promise, as they hope to reform it one day by implementing *sharia*. Said differently, they continue to view the territory of Pakistan as a key site for the institution of *khilafat*.

These sentiments are clearly visible in a range of articles. Consider Sadiq Yarmomand's article in *Ihya-e-Khilafat Urdu,* titled "We are Pakistan and Pakistan is ours."[31] In it, he exclaims that people often believe that the *mujahidin* oppose Pakistan, but "our battle is not with Pakistan. In fact, Pakistan is our country and *we are its real protectors.*" [32] By declaring the Taliban as the real protectors of Pakistan, Yarmomand invokes a fundamental tenet of sovereignty: the protector gets to decide how to govern the territory, who to include, and who to exclude. Yarmomand's version of protection entails turning the country away from manmade law and instituting in its place *"Islami qanoon"* (Islamic law).[33] This message is repeated across multiple Taliban cultural texts. In a video message released in July 2009, TTP head Hakimullah Mehsud makes a distinction between Pakistan and its system of democratic governance: "We are not the enemies of Pakistan or the Pakistani nation. Instead we are the enemies of this current *kufr* democratic system that has been forced on us. This system is unjust and despotic. This unethical and tyrannical setup is a *kufr* system irrelevant to *sharia.*"[34] Elsewhere in another TTP video we learn that the "Taliban are not the enemies of Pakistan, its army or its administrators."[35] The video argues that "if the administrators can implement the order of the Prophet (*nizam-e-Mustafa*) then we can address the hypocrites in India."[36] The Taliban thus express an ambivalent attachment to Pakistan—while they believe that the country has betrayed its foundational purpose, it can still be reformed if they get a chance to govern it. This ambivalent attachment transforms the Pakistani army, administrators, and inhabitants into both potential brothers-in-arms *and* legitimate targets of violence.

The Sovereign Space of Ummah,
the Political Apparatus of Khilafat

While the Taliban wish to reform Pakistan, the country itself does not figure as a primary space of belonging for them; instead, they transform the *ummah* (Muslim community) into both a space of belonging and a space of control. As the editors of *Sunnat-e-Khola* remind their readers, "For them [the Taliban, the] whole Muslim *ummah* is like a single nation."[37] "Nation" in this context is defined not by territorial boundaries but through membership in a religious community. The Arabic term *ummah* refers to a people or community.[38] The Quran notes that a messenger bearing a warning has been sent to every *ummah* to direct them to God's message. Prophet Muhammad was this messenger for the Muslim *ummah*. Today, the term *ummah* is widely interpreted to mean the global Muslim community. The Taliban, however, seek to control membership in this community by defining the correct practice of Islam or Muslimness. In doing so, they transform the *ummah* into a sovereign space from which they eject those whom they deem to be improper Muslims. Indeed, while sovereignty is often linked to protection of a territory, Foucault observes that "territory is no doubt a geographical notion, but it is first of all a juridico-political one: the area controlled by a certain kind of power."[39] The Taliban thus exercise sovereignty by controlling and regulating the space of *ummah*.

While there is no agreement as to whether or not the *ummah* requires a territorial arrangement to ensure the welfare of all of its members, groups such as the Taliban draw on medieval political theorists, such as Ibn Taymiyah (1263–1328), to argue that a territory governed by *sharia* is crucial for the *ummah* to be able to realize its responsibilities toward God and each other.[40] Since the Cold War, a number of *jihadist* groups have emerged that aspire to territory so that they can institute a *khilafat*, that is, a polity that implements Islamic law. While some imagine that all lands where Muslims reside would constitute the borders of the *khilafat*, others are content with the institution of a sole Muslim polity that could function as a guide for others. Crucially, such groups see themselves as guardians or fighters in the path of Allah, who will inaugurate this system through armed resistance.[41] The Taliban in Pakistan and Daesh are among the groups that have stated the establishment of *khilafat* as a key objective. In an interview, TTP leader Hakimullah Mehsud asserted this connection between an Islamic state and welfare of Muslims: "We call on . . . the Muslim people to submit themselves to the Islamic system, which guarantees success in this world as well as in the hereafter."[42]

According to the Taliban, sovereignty belongs only to Allah, an assumption which becomes grounds for rejecting claims of state sovereignty. In a three-part serialized essay in *Azan* entitled "Destroying the Country Idol," Muhammad Qasim explains, "Islam teaches a person to bear alliance and enmity for the Sake of Allah alone because Allah is the true Sovereign, Benefactor of mankind in whose Hand rests all Power of harm and benefit. But the nationalist philosophers rejected Allah's Sovereignty."[43] He goes on to say, "The 'country' is thus an imagined area in which its people are supposed to gather under a 'sovereignty' which is not of course Allah's sovereignty."[44] In contrast, "Islam rightfully recognizes the earth as the Property of Allah and fully declares Sovereignty on it as belonging to Allah Alone who is without a partner. The Europeans rebelled against the true religion of Islam and hence had to submit to another's sovereignty besides him e.g. The king, queen and now a new idol called the 'state.'"[45] According to Qasim, only when *khilafat* is established can the sole sovereignty of Allah be recognized.[46] The editors of *Mujalla Tehrik-e-Taliban* (September 2019) therefore provocatively ask their readers, "Is the constitution of Pakistan Islamic?"[47]

Likewise, in the magazines we find extensive critiques of the nation-state as a man-made construct that displaced the Ottoman *khilafat* at the end of the Second World War. This moment is imagined as inaugurating the division of the Muslim *ummah* into separate states. Consider an article by Maulana Abdullah Muhammadi in *Azan,* wherein he argues that it was "nationalism" and "country-ism" that divided the Muslim community: "They made Muslim brothers and sisters as strangers to one another and so, Muslims began to ally and disavow, love and hate for this 'nation' instead of for Allah and His Messenger. Instead of feeling pride because of Islam, the Muslims began to feel pride because of being associated with a particular soil."[48] The author notes that allegiance is now secured through citizenship instead of being based on religious beliefs, and people are driven to fight for the nation as opposed to in the way of Allah. In the same vein, Muhammad Qasim, in his contribution to the fifth issue of *Azan,* argues that it is precisely due to the rise of the nation-state that Muslims no longer see eye to eye on many issues, as their loyalties are redirected: "The reality is that after the fall of the [Ottoman] Khilafah and the rise of the nation state, these nationalistic Armies were implanted upon the Muslim Ummah—and many of the Muslims were made to believe that Jihad was the duty of these armies and the rest of the Ummah was absolved of this duty. What this meant was that the spirit of Jihad to establish the Rule of Allah faded away from the masses and the scholars, and Islam became restricted to the Masjid and the madrassah."[49] In these narrations, the authors draw a clear contrast between the institution of the nation-state, in which sovereignty is exercised by rulers, and the institution of *khilafat,* in which only God is recognized as the sovereign and God's law, the *sharia,* reigns supreme. The ability of Muslims to enact Muslimness, including declaring the absolute sovereignty of God, is thus tied closely to the political apparatus of *khilafat.*

Islamic studies scholar Muhammad Qasim Zaman notes that while contemporary Islamists, such as the Taliban, are keenly attentive to the discussion of God's sovereignty, medieval Muslim exegetes understood God's authority as all-inclusive and its affirmation as a guidance to worship God.[50] The reduction of God's authority to political authority did not occur until the rise of European conceptions of political authority in terms of sovereignty. Zaman claims that the concept of sovereignty is therefore not indigenous to the Islamic tradition, even though it is articulated as such by the likes of the Taliban.[51] He credits one of the leaders of the Indian Khilafat movement (1919–1924), Muhammad Ali, for propagating the idea of God's authority as being distinct from that of the king's—an idea that later became a key argument for Islamists and militants. Following the First World War, a number of Muslim political leaders and intellectuals in India launched the Khilafat movement to protect the geographic boundaries and spiritual/political authority of the Ottoman *khilafat.*[52] They called on fellow Muslims to abandon relations with the British, a move that was aligned with prevailing anticolonial sentiments as well. While many intellectuals engaged in shaping the movement, Muhammad Ali's conceptualizations of the political have had an enduring effect.[53] Ali noted that there was an inherent conflict between the king's law and God's law; whereas the former directed Muslims to fight wherever it deemed fit, the latter did not permit Muslims to do so against other Muslims.[54] Ali was advancing God's authority as distinct and above a king's commands. Likely influenced by Ali, the Pakistani Islamist ideologue Abul 'ala Mawdudi (1903–1979) explicitly connected the idea of God's authority to sovereignty. In his work on the political concept of Islam, first published in 1939, Mawdudi argued that "sovereignty *(hakimiyyat)* rests only with God. God alone is the law-giver. No human being, not even a prophet, has the right to command and prohibit on his own."[55] Over the course of the twentieth century, Mawdudi's formulation of the sovereignty of God gained traction inside and outside Pakistan.

From this conceptualization of God's sovereignty emerged the call for the establishment of a caliphal state where God's law would be supreme. Mawdudi was at the forefront of this effort, with the goals of reinvigorating the *ummah* and defending Islam against colonial occupation. To reformists such as Mawdudi, the *ummah* could only survive in the modern world if it could locate itself within an Islamic state. Islamist arguments thus are paradoxically also about the modern bureaucratic state. In fact, Mawdudi founded a political party in Pakistan, Jama'at-i-Islami, and was willing to participate in formal institutional politics to advance his conception of an Islamic polity. Within this conceptualization of *khilafat,* God continues to be the sole sovereign and the sovereignty of earthly rulers is secondary.[56] In this aspect, the Taliban's aspiration for *khilafat* resonates with Mawdudi's.

The Taliban argue that to materialize God's sovereignty on earth through the institution of *khilafat* they must acquire territory, an endeavor for which they permit themselves to engage in *jihad* and call themselves *mujahidin.* Writing for *Ihya-e-Khilafat English,* Abu Rumaysah explains that since *sharia* is "a manifestation of Allah's sovereignty on the earth," the logical step is to call for the institution of *sharia.*[57] That, however, is predicated on first acquiring territory where such a law can be implemented. He therefore calls on the *mujahidin* to "pursue territory."[58] He explains, "The pursuit of territory for Muslims is thus not a mean[s] to subjugate nations—far from it—it is a method to wrestle control from tyrants."[59] Ultimately, the acquisition of territory would permit them "to implement the commands of Allah and declare Him sovereign."[60] A visual depiction of this mission is featured on the cover page of the thirteenth issue of *Ihya-e-Khilafat Urdu* (figure 6), which shows a map of Pakistan with the Taliban's flag—*La ilaha illallah* written in black against a white background—flying on a pole. The objective then is to establish Taliban rule in Pakistan. Another cover of *Ihya-e-Khilafat Urdu* (figure 7) depicts the Taliban's claims to sovereignty by pitting it against democracy. The top panel features a *mujahid* holding a gun in one hand and a Quran in the other, with the caption "My destiny, Khilafat." This is contrasted with the lower panel, where we see the Pakistani flag and what looks like a hand casting a ballot, both scorching in fire. The caption argues that democracy is a façade. Such visualities represent the *khilafat* as a viable alternate to a democratic system, and the images invite readers to make a choice between two apparently equally legitimate political dispensations. Herein, however, lies a key contradiction in the Taliban discourse—at times they imagine a *khilafat* that supersedes the nation-state, and at other times their claims are wrapped within the

FIGURE 6. Cover image, *Ihya-e-Khilafat Urdu*, no. 13, November 2016.

FIGURE 7. Cover image, *Ihya-e-Khilafat Urdu*, no. 6, May 2013.

morphology of the Westphalian order, with a desire simply to institute an Islamic state in Pakistan. Their conceptualization of the political thus both includes and exceeds the Pakistani nation-state.

Although in the Taliban magazines *khilafat* emerges as a future territorial and political order, it also appears as a lost object. References to it invoke memories of past Muslim rule, particularly of the first three generations after the Prophet as well as of the Umayyad and Ottoman caliphates. A feature article entitled "Glorious Past," in the seventh issue of *Mujalla Tehrik-e-Taliban*, for example, details the achievements of the Umayyad caliphate and contemplates the reasons for its decline.[61] Even though within Muslim history *khilafat* took on different forms, it continued to symbolize a connection to the Prophet and provided a continuity to Muslims across geographies.[62] Therefore, *khilafat* has had an emotive status, with the caliph often being viewed as a "temporal mirror of divine sovereignty."[63] This affective attachment continues to be nurtured by Muslims even today to varying degrees. While postcolonial nationalist movements curbed aspirations for *khilafat* for some time, the recent neoliberalization of the economy, sponsored by the nation-state, has imbued new energies into the project as a salvific future form of governance. Salman Sayyid has therefore argued that the political idea of the *khilafat* offers Muslims both a rooting in this world and "an escape route" from their constant subjugation and marginalization.[64] For the Taliban, the loss of *khilafat* remains psychically ungrieveable, for grieving and moving on would entail accepting a demise of God's sovereignty. This lost object is therefore preserved within the Taliban psyche where it produces new forms of identifications and political projects. All these forms display a "restorative nostalgia" that nurtures a romanticized and mythical notion of the past, mourns "the loss of an enchanted world with clear borders and values," and seeks to reconstruct it in the present without critical reflection.[65] The Taliban's claims around the institution of God's sovereignty thus have a genealogy and also are grounded in the contemporary conditions of modernity and precarity.

In fostering such forms of nostalgia, the Taliban signal the influence of other movements, such as Deobandi and Salafi. As noted earlier, a number of reform movements emerged in response to the loss of political sovereignty by Muslims during the nineteenth century in India. One such movement was led by scholars of Darul Uloom, a madrasa in Deoband, influenced by the work of eighteenth-century reformer Shah Wali Allah. This reform school, which is also an ideological orientation, remains influential even today. While the Deobandi orientation is not monolithic and scholars affiliated with it often disagreed, a key aspect of its reformist project relates to its rejection of values or practices that threaten the exceptionality of divine sovereignty.[66] The Deobandi orientation flourished during the 1980s in Pakistan under the regime of General Zia, when many madrasas with Deobandi affiliations were founded and provided sanctuary to Afghan *mujahidin*.[67] The students who formed the Afghan Taliban movement, for instance, studied in these madrasas.[68] Another key influence on the Taliban is that of puritanical movements, a major one being the Salafi movement, which started in the Arabian Peninsula in the eighteenth century. Its adherents, like the Taliban, seek to emulate the pious predecessors *(al-salaf al-salih)*, assumed to be the first three generations of Muslims. In the South Asian context, the Ahl-e-hadith school espouses and propagates the Salafi outlook. Both Deobandi and Salafi orientations are concerned with determining the correct practice of Islam in order to avoid moral decay. These ideologies have influenced the Taliban directly as well as through other routes such as through Mawdudi's conceptualization of the "Islamic state," noted earlier.

In tracing the genealogy of some of the dominant concepts that appear in the Taliban magazines, I do not intend to imply that the authors featured in these magazines have studied the work of these scholars or set out to align themselves with certain scholarly traditions. In fact, in many cases the notions of *ummah* and *khilafat* do not appear as historically grounded concepts; they are used instead for their affective valence and their ability to paint a utopic version of the future.[69] The Taliban's ideology seems to be a composite of multiple South Asian as well as Arab scholarly traditions that form their discursive milieu. Even though they substantiate their articulation of the political community through numerous citations of the Quran and the *tafsir* (interpretation), they have not produced any serious work of Islamic scholarship. What we have then, is a movement that selectively draws on a range of prevailing ideas to advance its conceptualization of the political, transform the *ummah* into a sovereign space, articulate an ideal polity for its regulation, and legitimize the violence needed to bring it to fruition. For instance, while leading Deobandi *ulama* insist that it is wrong to challenge the authority of the state, TTP factions have explicitly set out to target the Pakistani state apparatus. Yet, it is only by exploring how the Taliban mobilize the *ummah* and *khilafat* that we can get a sense of their political project. Crucially, attachment to the Taliban is nurtured both by the meanings that they ascribe to these concepts, as well as by their ongoing affective valence and accruals in Muslim collective memory.

Jihad *and* Shahadat

The Taliban call themselves *mujahidin,* laying claim to a prominent model of Islamic warrior masculinity while also elevating the political value of their lives in death. The Arabic term *mujahid* translates to someone who engages in *jihad.* While in contemporary popular usage *jihad* is understood as "holy war" or "armed struggle," it has a more complex, multidimensional, and shifting genealogy. Political scientist Roxanne Euben, for instance, notes that many of the references to *jihad* in the Quran are marked by ambiguity, including around the use of violence.[70] *Jihad* in the Quran refers to "struggle" and "striving," and *jihad fi sabil Allah* indicates striving in the path of God. However, the forms and means of this struggle vary. In early Muslim history, *jihad* was codified in at least two ways: as a struggle against oneself through restraint in order to become a better Muslim, and as a holy war to bring about a just social order. When warfare was permitted, numerous rules and restrictions were in place, including its permissibility only against non-Muslims. A few early groups (such as the Kharijites) did argue that *jihad* could be waged against illegitimate Muslim rulers, a position that was popularized again during the twentieth century by Islamists such as Mawdudi and Sayyid Qutb. These thinkers reduced *jihad* to a doctrine of warfare and deemed it acceptable against Muslim leaders who sided with the West and imperial colonizers.[71] In the Taliban magazines, *jihad* is invoked as a form of legitimate political violence aimed at facilitating the establishment of *khilafat.* The Taliban do not hold themselves accountable to historical constraints placed on *jihad* by traditional Islamic scholars. In their quest to institute *khilafat,* they believe that it is their "right to spread terror," as an author notes in *Ihya-e-Khilafat English.*[72]

The ideology of *jihad* is prominent in the Taliban discourse because it permits the sanctification of lives that would otherwise remain meaningless. When the TTP says that its slogan is "*Sharia* or *Shahadat* [martyrdom],"[73] it is pointing less to a desire to kill than to be killed for faith. The latter permits a *mujahid* to partake in the elevated status reserved in Islam for those who die for religion, making martyrdom a coveted consequence of engaging in *jihad.* In an article in *Azan* entitled "Let's understand 'suicide bombing,'" authors Ikrimah Anwar and Muawiya Hussaini explain: "The reality of the martyrdom operations is that they have turned this war on its head. A Mujahid can strap on explosives to his body or vehicle and explode it in the middle of a large gathering of the enemy and with the loss of just one life, huge losses to the enemy can be inflicted . . . the *true Muslims love death* as the Kuffar love life."[74] Political scientist Olivier Roy argues that while neither terrorism nor *jihadism* are new social formations, what is new is the pursuit of death.[75] Muslim tradition recognizes the merits of those who die in combat, but it does not necessarily have a place for those who pursue death. For the Taliban, however, death is a central part of the plan. The *mujahid* is called on to see his body as a weapon and as an instrument of establishing *khilafat*. By using his body, or more aptly by destroying it, the *mujahid* can further the cause of God's sovereignty. In this pursuit, the Taliban depart from other Islamist interpretations that condemn suicide because it anticipates God's will.[76] They also transform *jihad* into an individualized responsibility as opposed to a collective one declared by competent religious authorities. In the Taliban's ideological universe, any individual can declare himself a *mujahid* and engage in *jihad* through suicide bombing. In this respect, the Taliban also differ from the national soldier or from state armies, which aim to exercise sovereignty by exposing the enemy to death while preserving the self.

The pursuit of death by the Taliban has a local genealogy as well. David Edwards notes that with the Soviet invasion in the 1970s, death and war started to take new meanings in the Pashtun belt.[77] Before the invasion, conflicts or feuds were generally considered matters for tribes to solve, and violence was simply a way to ensure balance and parity across the parties involved.[78] Death during feuds was unremarkable. Instead, honor was linked to men's personal performances of heroism and bravery. The Soviet invasion, however, introduced a number of changes. New weaponry and technology allowed for the killing of people in larger numbers and enabled the enemy to attack from a distance, without showing itself. The conflict now involved a different kind of enemy, the state. The discourse of *jihad* gained popularity in this fight against the Soviets, and dying for faith, martyrdom, took on more meaning than individual acts of bravery and survival. That is, the locus of honor shifted from performing heroic acts of killing and surviving, to being killed.

The Taliban's assumptions about *jihad* and their pursuit of death are also influenced by the Pakistani state's history of using these ideas to rally support among Muslims. As early as 1947, when the territory of Kashmir was left unsettled after the partition of India and the Muslim majority was being oppressed by its Hindu rulers, tribal militias and other volunteers declared *jihad* with the aim of saving their brethren in Kashmir. In response, the Indian government annexed Kashmir and a full-blown war ensued between India and Pakistan. The India-Pakistan war of 1965 was also articulated as a *jihad* by the Pakistani state. In the June 1965 issue of the ISPR's *Hilal Urdu,* an article lists numerous verses from the Quran on the topic of *jihad,* and in August of that year, the same author penned a feature article entitled "A look at *jihad.*"[79] In it, he details the ethics of *jihad,* all the while convincing readers of its necessity. In another article in *Hilal Urdu,* published in September 1965, we learn about the "Benefits [in the hereafter] of *jihad.*"[80] Together, these articles emphasize the high status of those who undertake *jihad.*[81] While the discourse of *jihad* was also used during the 1971 civil war between the eastern and western regions of Pakistan, it was harder to name it as such, as the conflict was among Muslims.[82] To bypass that, the religious authenticity of East Pakistanis was cast as doubtful—a discursive strategy that resonates today as both the state and the Taliban thrust each other out of the space of *ummah.* During the 1970s and 1980s, when the CIA was rallying support against the Soviets, it too drew on the terminology of *jihad* to shroud its effort in religious probity.

Indeed, a peek into *Hilal* magazines of the past highlights the eerie similarities between contemporary Taliban articulations and the army's previous discourse. Wartime issues of *Hilal,* such as during 1965 and 1971 as the nation geared up for impending attacks from India, include articles that delineate the etiquette of *jihad,* contemplations on death, lessons from battles from the time of Prophet Muhammad, and poems of valor.[83] These issues also include extensive citations from the Quran about *jihad,* rules of life and death in war, and names and personal details of the numerous martyred soldiers awarded distinctions and medals posthumously.[84] The theme of loving death that I noted in the Taliban magazines is found here as well, though the state rarely articulates the death of its soldiers as an end in itself. For instance, in a 1971 article entitled "Love of death," the author writes about the "profession of soldiers," calling attention to the crucial role that the soldier plays in society.[85] He then notes that the ideal person for this role is not one who desires status (e.g., captain or general) for "here the only training that is given is that of loving death."[86] Drawing on the discourse of religion, the author explains that when the honor of the nation and its inhabitants is threatened, the soldier must welcome death, for death is the "pride of a *momin* [believer]," "the honor of a *mujahid,*" and "the faith of a soldier."[87] The national soldier is connected to the soldier of Islam of the past: "history is witness to the fact that Muslims are not afraid of death."[88] Another article published on December 10, 1971, entitled "Quest of life—death," makes extensive use of verses from the Quran and sayings of the Prophet to argue that death in the cause of Islam is superior to other, mundane forms of death.[89]

The Taliban's discourse on *jihad* and death then is informed by these broad social and discursive histories. Attention to these genealogies and shared cultural repertoires facilitates an understanding of how both the state and the Taliban hail publics that are already attuned to these Islamic referents. Processes of political attachment rely on simultaneously harnessing prevalent discourses and affectivities, and imbuing them with new meaning.

PERFORMING ISLAMO-MASCULINITY

Since *jihad* has traditionally been impermissible against Muslims, in order to declare their violence against the state legitimate, the Taliban dispel the state from the space of *ummah* and assert their control over this space through the performance of Islamo-masculinity. This performance entails a combination of expressions of Muslimness—through ritual acts and sartorial choices—and expressions of masculinity—through demonstrations of strength and militarism. *Mujahid* masculinity then is a specific variant of Islamo-masculinity that the Taliban perform to nurture attachment.

Soldiers of Allah

In the magazines, the Taliban portray themselves as *mujahidin* or soldiers of God, melding traditional qualities associated with warrior or militaristic masculinity with the probity of a divine mission. For this endeavor, even the Prophet is transformed into a warrior. For example, in *Azan,* we encounter stories of the Prophet in which he is reported to have equated strength with waging war without using armor.[90] Such framings conflate spiritual strength with masculine might, inviting the *mujahid* to perform Islamo-masculinity by shedding his armor.[91] The *mujahid* thus appears as a savior who will inaugurate God's rule on earth and end chaos. This salvific quality of the *mujahid* is resonant with ideas about messianic sovereignty that have long circulated in Muslim South Asia. Messianism—the notion that a savior figure will appear at the end of time to end chaos and institute a final judgement—has long influenced conceptions of rulership and authority in India. In precolonial India, messianism offered an avenue to earthly sovereignty. A. Azfar Moin traces it in the edicts of Mughal ruler Akbar (r. 1556–1605), whose reign overlapped with the end of the first Islamic millennium, when it was expected that a sacred figure would inaugurate a new universal dispensation.[92] Through new imperial codes Akbar permitted the practice of all religions and sects, positioning himself as a king with a divine spark. A confluence of divinity and sovereignty marked the Indian nationalist movement as well: in order to reject British colonial rule and inaugurate the nation as a force of welfare, nationalists linked the idea of nation to transcendental notions of moral order, justice, and divinity.[93] The national ruler was imagined as both the incarnation of divinity and a representative leader of the people.[94] Messianism as a route to sovereignty, however, became increasingly untenable during the twentieth century with the separation of state and religion. Yet the imagination that a savior figure will restore peace in an otherwise chaotic social world has remained powerful.[95] The Taliban reinvigorate these ancient grammars by framing the Pakistani and US states as the *dajjal* (Antichrist, false messiah), and positing themselves as savior figures. Theirs thus is a twist on earlier versions of messianic sovereignty—here the messiah is not a singular salvific figure but an army of God, the Taliban themselves.

The articulation of the *mujahid* as a soldier of God relies not only on the sanctity of his mission but also on the active discrediting of the Pakistani and American soldier. In the magazines, the Pakistani soldier is depicted as a coward. Referring to the ISPR's music video "Mujhay dushman" (discussed in the previous chapter), an author in *Ihya-e-Khilafat Urdu* wonders where all these young men were when the Taliban attacked Bacha Khan University in 2016; he quips that perhaps they were "afraid of the Taliban [as] they were all hiding in the caves?"[96] He then mocks the government for closing universities in Sindh and Punjab and, referring to the video again, asks, "Didn't you say you were from the nation whose children frighten the militants?"—the implication being that it is the state that is afraid of the Taliban and not vice-versa.[97] The Pakistani soldier is also constructed as ineffective on the battlefront. Writing about Operation Zarb-e-Azab, Bilal Momin in *Ihya-e-Khilafat* notes that despite all the military operations in Waziristan, the Taliban have actually spread to the entire country, which signals the military's failure.[98] The American soldier is also not spared. Consider an article in *Azan* entitled "The Drone Chain," in which the author, Jaffer Hussain, mocks Americans for waging a war from behind closed doors.[99] He scoffs at the "unmanned nature" of their attacks and asks, "Why can't they face the Mujahidin in open battle?"[100] He posits that since American soldiers are unable to defeat the "soldiers of Allah" on the battlefield, they hide behind drone technologies. He concludes by deriding the soldiers: "Certainly, not even a respectable enemy!"[101] On multiple other occasions in the magazines, we learn about a "handful of mujahidin" defeating American soldiers though the enemy had access to superior technologies and weapons.[102]

While the fighter or *mujahid* trope discussed thus far is one of the most prominent ways in which the Taliban articulate themselves, they also court the trust of their reading and viewing public through more intimate expressions. The TTP video *Bloodshed and Revenge* (2009) is a case in point. The *mujahidin* featured therein call themselves "well-wishers" and "brothers."[103] They explain to viewers, "we are your friend, not your enemy" and "we will preserve your honor (*izzat*)." In doing so, they establish a sense of closeness with the viewing public, even cajoling them to "not consider their kin as strangers." This self-reference through kinship is framed in contrast to the state, which is "not sincere to you." Likewise, a TTP pamphlet entitled "Revenge" (2012) declares: "We are tough on infidels (*kuffar*) and merciful on believers (*mominin*)." Similarly, in *Mujalla Tehrik-e-Taliban,* Ibn Hassan Khurasani describes the Taliban as men who "not only care for their own parents and siblings but even the neighbors' parents and if they see a wrong-doing they intervene!"[104] Instead of living selfishly for themselves, "they gamble their future" for the welfare of the *ummah.* They are, according to the author, "enlightened" and "moderate"—not narrow-minded and extremist, as they are often depicted. In such narrations, the *mujahid* performs a softer and caring masculinity that, unlike the discourse of doom and fear prominent in the fighter trope, works through the affective economies of fraternal bonding. It emphasizes the Taliban's destiny and future as shared with other Pakistanis and with Muslims at large. Whereas the trope of the fighter calls on audiences to trust the Taliban as protectors and saviors, here, attachment works through intimacy and familiarity.

In the magazines, the *mujahid* appears as a savior in part because he is pious. Indeed, we learn that only pious Muslims can rightfully be conferred the task of defending the *ummah.* We therefore encounter numerous exhortations in the magazines for the *mujahidin* to regularly perform their religious rituals, even on the battlefield.[105] Such performances of a pious subjectivity are intimately linked with the Taliban's claims to sovereignty. In a way, the *mujahid* is called on to perform an intense "Muslimness" in order to distinguish himself from others. He is expected to focus on spiritual reform and discipline his body to harness its strength. In the absence of territory, these bodies become the landscape onto which Taliban sovereign power is etched. Consider the cover page of the first issue of *Azan* (figure 8) which depicts a serene cloudy evening at a beach. There, we see a man with a gun

FIGURE 8. Cover image, *Azan,* no. 1, March 2013.

facing away from readers as he offers the Muslim call to prayer, the *azan*. The caption, "a call to *jihad*," in bold, capital letters, conflates the call to prayer with *jihad*. Said differently, it portrays the *mujahid*'s "call to *jihad*" as synonymous with the call to prayer. Writing about the intertwining of politics and art, Jacques Rancière notes that "images . . . are not primarily manifestations of the properties of a certain technical medium, but operations: relations between a whole and parts; between a visibility and a power of signification and affect associated with it; between expectations and what happens to meet them."[106] The image of the man praying, looking outward and toward a horizon, evokes hope and expectations of a peaceful future, one blessed with divine grace. This future however will require *jihad*.

The magazines feature extensive discussions of religious practices such as prayers, fasting, and even nightly meditation. These are both didactic and performative in that the readers are instructed to undertake such practices and their repeated mentions confirm the Taliban's religious sincerity. Articles explaining how to overpower the enemy often include stories of the Prophet that highlight how he performed nightly prayers and *ibadat* while in the middle of battle. Thus, a good *mujahid* is one who is thoughtful about his prayers, even during combat. This logic is reaffirmed through images, such as on the covers of *Mujalla Tehrik-e-Taliban* and *Azan* magazines (figures 9, 10 and 11), in which we see *mujahidin* engaged in prayer or the study of the Quran.[107] Elsewhere, images of men praying on a *tasbih* (set of prayer beads) emphasize the importance of *ibadat* (meditation) and *zikr* (remembrance) for the *mujahidin*.[108] We also find numerous accounts of Taliban leaders receiving divine guidance in their dreams or witnessing miracles on the battlefields. These stories bestow an air of sacredness—divine permission and help—to the *mujahid*'s mission, and produce him as a divinely favored subject.

The interior state of spirituality engendered through ritualistic practices is also expressed through sartorial choices. The *mujahid* is called on to perform Muslimness by visibly aligning with the *sunnah* (practices) of the Prophet. To this end, appeals for wearing a beard abound in the magazines. Issue 6 of *Azan* tells its readers, "Growing a beard is compulsory (*wajib*)."[109] This instruction is accompanied by the image of a *mujahid* (figure 12) who, in addition to wearing a beard, is also carrying a rifle and has his head covered with a keffiyeh. To add sacred weight to this practice, the following incident from the life of Prophet Muhammad is recounted: "Abu Hurayrah reported that the ruler of Yemen, appointed by the Persian emperor Kisra, sent two envoys to the Messenger. When they came into his presence, he noticed that

صبر کا معرکہ

شیخ ناجی۔

مترجم : مفتی ابو عمر بونیری حفظہ اللہ

FIGURE 9. "The Battleground of Patience," *Mujalla Tehrik-e-Taliban*, no. 5, February 2018.

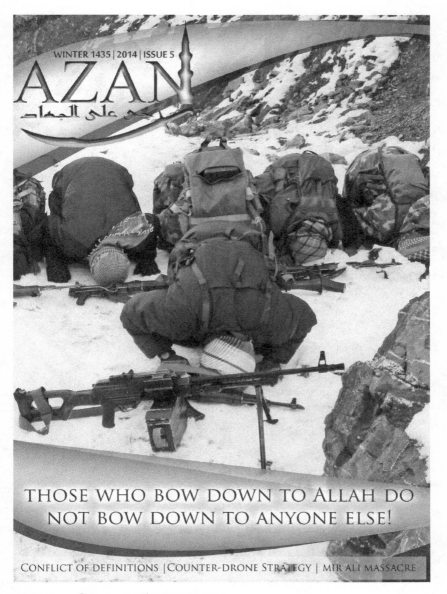

FIGURE 10. Cover image, *Azan*, no. 5, 2014.

FIGURE II. Cover image, *Mujalla Tehrik-e-Taliban*, no. 5, February 2018.

FIGURE 12. "Growing the Beard Is *Wajib*," *Azan,* no. 6, 2014.

they had shaved their beards and let their moustaches grow big. Hating their ugly appearance, he turned his face away and said, 'Woe be to you! Who told you to do so?' They replied: 'Our lord (Kisra) did!' The Messenger responded: 'But my Lord, exalted and gloried be He, has commanded me to spare my beard and trim my moustaches.'"[110]

Sartorial practices become a way for the Taliban to tie themselves to the Prophetic example and visually assert authentic Muslimness. Such choices are also presented as everyday forms of resistance against the *dajjal*. In an article entitled "Dajjal and World today," Muhammad Qasim argues that wearing a beard or donning "Islamic clothes" is the first step toward *jihad*.[111] A story about a German *mujahid* imbues these sartorial practices with further significance:

> So one day, me and some brothers were sitting and watching the videos of the Mujahidin and we felt that the Jihad was so far away from us. Then one brother said—"Maybe, we'll never reach these people." But another brother—may Allah reward him—inspired us and said, "Dear brothers! Many years ago when you were in darkness, could you have imagined that one day you will be practicing Islam in this style—that you will wear a beard, go out in the street with Islamic clothing, invite the people to Islam, pray in the Masjid, that your life will be Islam?[112]

Similarly, an article in *Azan* posits resisting cutting off one's beard when arrested by the police as a sign of immense courage.[113] The Taliban enforce these bodily norms by publicly punishing those who do not abide by them.

While the discourses of piety and sartorial practices pervade the magazines, they are presented as only in the service of inviting divine favor so that the *mujahid* can engage in his real task of securing an Islamic state. This is in contrast to other Islamic revivalist movements in which piety is in and of itself a desirable practice and can bring about reform.[114] Piety thus has a specific function within the Taliban worldview, for it is tied to victory in war and the production of a warrior masculinity. TTP leader Fazlullah explains this in a video message: "Allah has selected those He likes most for this work [to establish His rule on earth]. So who are these people whom Allah selects and raises for this work? Allah selected those people who are near to Him."[115] The *talib* thus becomes a *mujahid* with superior strength due to his piety and God's favor. Muslimness and masculinity cohere in him.

Visual evidence of the *mujahidins'* apparently supranatural strength adds potency to their performance of Islamo-masculinity. Consider the "Come to Jihad" ad from *Azan* (figure 13), which shows four fighters riding a vehicle

FIGURE 13. "A 'Come-to-Jihad' Ad," *Azan,* no. 4, 2013.

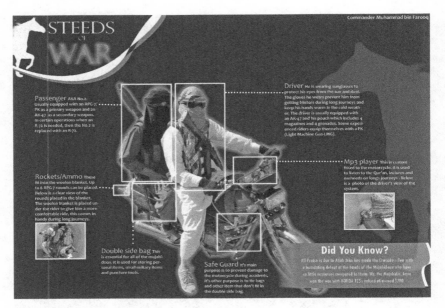

FIGURE 14. "Steeds of War," *Azan*, no. 4, 2013.

against the backdrop of what looks like explosions. They remain unfazed. Two of the fighters look straight into the camera, giving the reader a sense of certainty about their resolve. The image suggests a movie poster, following the cliché in which a hero receives a call to action—or to *jihad*—and transforms from an everyday man into a supernatural phenomenon.[116] The image is accompanied by a verse from the Quran to signal the divine source of this transformation. The *mujahid* is also shown partaking in the consumption of modern goods, in contrast with his depiction as undevelopable in the ISPR's texts. In doing so, the magazines advance the *mujahidin*'s Islamo-masculinity as contemporary. Another poster-like image from *Azan*, entitled "Steeds of War" (figure 14) is a case in point. It depicts two men, in masks, aboard a motorcycle and equipped with all the latest weapons, from rockets and ammo to grenades and RPG-7s. For entertainment these men carry an MP3 player; for protection from the sun, they wear sunglasses; for running fast, they wear trainers. Two close-up shots of the *mujahidin* are included to give a complete sense of their accoutrements. The "steeds" of the title refers both to the *mujahidin*—who are imagined as strong, muscular, and ready for action and thus horse-like—and to the motorcycles, which, despite being modest technologies, are glamorized. There is a noteworthy conflation of

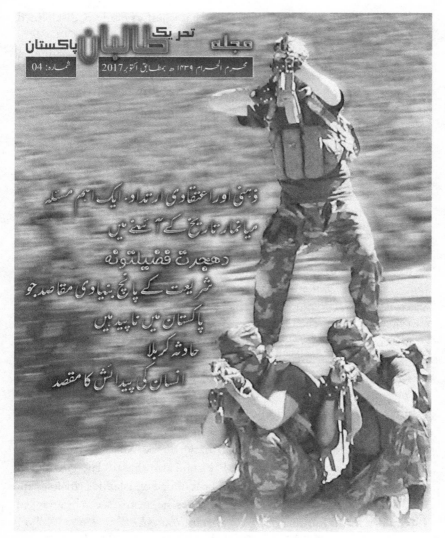

FIGURE 15. Cover image, *Mujalla Tehrik-e-Taliban*, no. 4, October 2017.

man, animal, and machine (motorcycle/MP3 player/guns) in this image, which mimics the dominant portrayal of soldiers as automatons (recall the discussion in chapter 1 about the training of soldiers). The cover image of the fourth issue of *Mujalla Tehrik-e-Taliban* (figure 15) features another portrayal of the *mujahid* as modern and strong. In it, we see three men in camouflage gear, firing at the reader. Their uniform mirrors that of the national soldiers, heralding the Taliban as a force that is just as modern, disciplined, and trained as the army.

Thus, the *mujahid*'s performance of Islamo-masculinity connects traditional notions of masculinity, related to strength and domination, with pietistic practices imagined as expressions of an authentic Islam. Through this performance, the *mujahid* invites trust in himself and the Taliban; through it, he lays claim to both normative masculinity and normative Islam. To further secure his claim to the space of the *ummah*, he sets out to eject the state from it.

Dispelling the State from the Space of Ummah

To eject the state from the space of *ummah*, the Taliban mobilize memories of past state violence against Muslims and the Pakistani state's alliance with US and NATO forces. They deploy a number of theological declarations, such as *murtid* (an apostate, one who was once a believer but is no longer), *kafir* (unbeliever), *munafiq* (a person who declares Islam publicly but at heart rejects it), *taghut* (a tyrant who rebels against God's laws, idolator), and *mushrik* (one who rejects the Oneness of Allah) to dispel the state and the army. Consider an article in *Azan* in which the author declares that, "These are not 'our armies' . . . They are 'armies of the West.' Let alone waging Jihad, they are the main obstacle in establishing Khilafah and waging Jihad!"[117] The use of "our" in this construction hails readers as Muslims, arguing that the Pakistani army does not advance the interests of Muslims but instead supports Western agendas. Another author in *Azan*, Ikrimah Anwar, contemplates the paradoxical relationship of "nationalistic 'Muslim' armies" with the West.[118] He argues that since the Pakistani army has declared that it will fight against fellow Muslims, it cannot be founded on Islamic principles and "does not stand to serve Islam."[119] Such armies, he surmises, can be attacked. Thus, when an author provocatively asks in *Ihya-e-Khilafat Urdu*, "Who is the real protector of Pakistan? The Pakistani Army or Tehrik-e-Taliban?", readers readily know the answer.[120]

The army's support of drone strikes is a key issue raised repeatedly in the magazines to cast doubts on its Muslimness. Consider an article by Jaffer Hussain in which he denounces the army for collaborating with the Americans on drone strikes in northwestern Pakistan.[121] He accuses the army of securing local spies who are asked to mark the homes of the *mujahidin* to be targeted by drones. He further notes that "as part of the secret deal that was carried out between the stooges of the Pakistani Government and Military and the US—

that the US would continue to carry out drone strikes and the Pakistani leadership would bleat out condemnation in public while being affirmative in secret. Such is the sad, sad state of the leadership of this country which has long lost legitimacy in the eyes of the Muslim Ummah."[122] According to another author in the fifth issue of *Azan,* the army's association with the West is a sign of its corruption: "one of the primary reasons of Pakistan's joining the war on terror (War against Islam) is money," for when a soldier dies, "it brings money to the pockets of Generals."[123] The TTP video "Bara gernal," discussed earlier, features a similar line of reasoning, mocking the Pakistani army generals for fighting for dollars, instead of faith or ideology. Whereas the lowly soldier battles against his Muslim brothers because he needs to survive and take care of his family, the elite officer does so because he is corrupt. In this formulation money is viewed as profane and corrupting; both the lowly soldier and the elite officer appear as misguided, for different reasons.

The authors of these articles often move back in time to draw an arc between present and past state violence, arguing that such violence is a constitutive feature of the state. Consider an article written by Adnan Rasheed in which we learn about the "massacre of Mir Ali."[124] Rasheed paints a picture of a serene landscape, where truck drivers are enjoying chai at a restaurant on a "frosty morning." This serenity is interrupted by a brutal army raid: "Innocent civilians were ... handcuffed, blind folded and shot in their heads, one after another! ... Anyone who breathed was declared an enemy combatant."[125] The juxtaposition of serenity and brutal force is further amplified as the author notes how the army then bombed a mosque in the heart of the city, killing worshippers. Rasheed connects this incident to other alleged episodes of army violence against civilians—a 1948 massacre in Babrra village in the Charsadda district, a 1953 attack during an anti-Qadyani protest, the 1970 killing of Palestinian refugees in Jordan, the 1971 killing of Muslims in East Pakistan, the 2006 airstrike on a *madrasa* in Bajaur, the 2007 attack on Lal Masjid, and the 2009 operations in Swat.[126] The army of course contests these accusations, but Rasheed's narrative is a discursive effort to construct the army as perennially anti-Muslim. He intentionally highlights only those incidents where the army engaged with other Muslims, rather than non-Muslims.

To further emphasize the cruelty of the army and police, affectively charged first-person accounts by *mujahidin* who were taken prisoner are interspersed throughout the magazines. In a letter addressed to *"mujahidin-e-Islam,"* one *talib* prisoner shares his own and his fellow Taliban prisoners' treatment at a jail in Karachi.[127] They were paraded naked, hung from the ceiling, and hit. For several days upon arrival, they were not provided any clothing and therefore could not hide their private parts. They were crammed, three to a jail cell, meaning they had to sleep while sitting. The prisoner calls on his fellow *muja-hidin* to avenge this cruelty. He notes that he does not care about his own freedom from jail; however, he does care that his fellow Taliban exact revenge for "these cruel people have challenged the *mujahidin*."[128] In this formulation, an assault on one *mujahid* takes on the proportion of an assault on all. The inability of the *mujahid* to cover his private parts is a recurring trope in such prison stories.[129] Beyond the threat of impending assault, the naked male body is also experienced as a site of vulnerability because, as J. Velleman argues, it "is unable to choose which of his impulses are to be public"—even "the unwanted erection [can be] a glaring failure of privacy."[130] This inability to control one's body further subordinates the *mujahid* to his captor, an unmaking for which he then seeks revenge. Through the publication of these pieces, the prisoner imposes a responsibility on the reader, presumably a *mujahid* "brother" or at least a coreligionist, to help him take back control from the captors.

Accounts of state violence are often accompanied by visuals that bolster the Taliban's claims. The magazines, *Azan* in particular, feature images of army generals with their foreign counterparts as well as of victims of state violence. The article by Ikrimah Anwar mentioned earlier shows images of General Pervez Musharraf shaking hands with George Bush, General Kayani alongside American commanders, and dead bodies from the 1971 civil war. A screen shot of an article with the headline "Pakistan Army has 141 Baloch women in their custody," as well as a photo of a *burqa*-clad woman with the caption "The Pakistan Army was reportedly involved in the rape of young Bengali women during the 1971 war—they were kept in a rehabilitation cen-tre afterwards because they were abandoned by their families," are included.[131] When placed alongside each other, these images from different contexts and time periods produce a coherent, uniform narrative of the army as cruel and anti-Muslim. Jaffer Hussain's article on "the drone chain" features images of collapsed buildings and a collage of the dead bodies of fourteen children; it provides no description, but the reader is called on to imagine that the chil-dren died as a consequence of CIA drone attacks, which the author believes are condoned by the army.[132] Some of the most jarring images of corpses are found in *Mujalla Tehrik-e-Taliban*—explicit photos that show severed bod-ies, burned flesh, and bodies in the midst of torture. Such images are also often included in TTP videos. Images of maimed bodies, and of people about to die or being tortured, compel the reader to engage with death and its materiality—the blood, the amputated limbs, a white shroud. The images provoke questions about who caused these deaths. Their inclusion is meant to testify to the conditions that require *jihad* as well as to concretize the TTP's arguments about the enemy.

While images of victims of state violence are shown, images of dead *mujahidin* are almost never displayed. When they do appear, they are either blurred or shown in a sanitized manner. For example, the first issue of *Ihya-e-Khilafat English* includes a poem, "O Martyr," which is accompanied by an image of a dead young man.[133] Only his face is visible; his neck is wholly adorned with garlands. The mutilated body of the *mujahid* would sit uneasily with the Taliban's claim that martyrs enter heaven and are at peace when they die; sanitized images, in contrast, bolster that claim. As the poem concludes, "Now in Jannah (heaven), Happily fly, O' lucky soul, fly," confirming the *mujahid*'s status in religious cosmology.

Together these narratives and visuals tell a story—of state violence against Muslims, alliance with non-Muslims, and corruption—through which the Taliban question the state's Islamic credentials. This allows them to extend the declaration of *kufr*, usually reserved for non-Muslims, to the army, declaring it the "*apostate* Pakistan Army" and an ally of the "*kuffar* [unbelievers]," all the while articulating themselves as believers *(mominin)*.[134] Such adjudication of faith—who is inside, who is out; who is a *momin* (believer) and who is not—and administration of punishment can be viewed as a technology of sovereign power. These gestures of sovereignty are accompanied by a range of practices through which the Taliban enforce the boundaries of *ummah*, including violent enforcement through killings, kidnappings, and public lashings.

Leaving an Opening for the Jawan

While the state and army are written out of Muslimness en masse, the individual Pakistani soldier is not discarded completely. Since he is a coreligionist and at times also shares the Pashtun ethnicity, the Taliban make an effort to convince him to join their ranks. Taliban identity construction hinges on this delicate balance between asserting difference and incorporating the Other.

We find numerous articles that plead with the *jawan* to change his ways, detach himself from the army, and align with the Taliban. These articles are softer in tone, with the authors appearing to be more understanding of a soldier's choices. Consider an article in *Mujalla Tehrik-e-Taliban* written by Khalid Haqqani, then acting *amir* of the TTP. In it, he tries to encourage the "sensitive soldier" *(ba-ahsaas jawan)* to listen to his conscience, as "these rulers are against [his] people, country, and religion."[135] Assuming that the *jawan* has joined the army to secure a livelihood, Haqqani inquires, "you butcher others' children so as to prepare kababs for your own children?"[136] The skillful wordplay is intended to both jar and shame the *jawan*. Haqqani continues: "*Fauji* [Army] *jawan!* Come! What is your compulsion? There is only one compulsion which is a few thousand [rupees] at the end of the month. Is this such a big compulsion that it prepared you to kill your own brother . . . ?"[137] Invoking kinship ties, the author binds Muslims into a brotherhood and places a responsibility on them in relation to each other. Attending to such responsibilities is presented as a moral stance superior to attending to one's own nuclear family or the interests of the nation-state. Such religiously inspired kinship ties are actively nurtured in the magazines. In an article addressed to those soldiers "who love the Prophet more than their job and uniform," a former Army major, Shamshad Hassan, who is now with the Taliban, calls on them to reflect on how their engagement in the army disproves their love for the Prophet.[138] Citing his experience, he claims that none of the generals have sufficient "*dini ghairat*" (religious honor) to risk their lives and stand up against America. While masculine honor is often linked to the protection of women, Hassan attaches it to the protection of religion as well. He asks the soldiers to join forces with the *mujahidin,* who are represented as enacting this honor.

Even though the Taliban's infrastructure is no match for that of the Pakistani army, these articles discursively conjure them as a force not only on par with the army but also possessing greater moral authority. A first-person account in *Ihya-e-Khilafat Urdu* by a former army officer, Captain Dr. Tariq Ali, details his struggle when stationed in North and South Waziristan, where the army was killing "Muslim brothers" who were often "better Muslims" than him.[139] He presents the Taliban as a morally superior, righteous force and advises soldiers still affiliated with the army to contemplate on their missions, as they are being asked to eradicate their own Muslim brothers. He calls on them to leave the army and find some other form of employment. Accounts by former army personnel such as these may very well be fictional, but they further the Taliban's exclusive claim of Muslimness and create an opening for the *jawan* to join their cause.

In targeting their writings at the *jawan,* the authors hope to weaken the soldiers' resolve and commitment to the army and raise questions about the value of their sacrifices. Major Hassan in *Ihya-e-Khilafat* asks, "Why is [it] that you die but there is never a scratch on American bodies? . . . Does water run in your veins instead of blood? And is only the blood of White people so valuable that the entire Pakistani police and army is willing to get their bodies blown up to protect them? Are only those born of American mothers human, those born of Pakistani mothers are not human?"[140] In contrast, the Taliban invite the *jawan* to engage in a sacrifice that is blessed by God. This sacrifice includes not only the sacrifice of life but also of life's luxuries. In the magazines, poverty and hardship are framed as blessings from Allah. In his address to the *mujahidin,* TTP leader Omar Khalid Khurasani instructs them to view their impoverishment and difficulties as signs of Allah's favor, for Allah tests only those who are his favorites.[141] First-person accounts from *mujahidin* acknowledge the hardships of joining the Taliban movement yet emphasize the complete trust they have in God. For instance, in response to a question about material resources, Baitullah Meshud, the founding leader of the TTP, explains that when they launched the movement they did not have any worries about how their material needs would be fulfilled: "we have complete trust in Allah."[142] Elsewhere, in a letter from a prisoner, we learn about how he left his household and luxuries to adopt the path of *jihad*.[143] However, the prisoner argues, this material hardship is necessary to bring about *khilafat.* Such sacrifices for *khilafat* are conceived of as having a higher moral and religious value than dying on the battlefield for the nation.

THE TALIBAN AS AN IMITATING COUNTERPUBLIC

Robert Asen argues that we can glean the "counter" of "counterpublics" by investigating how participants recognize their exclusion from wider public spheres and articulate themselves through alternative discursive practices and norms.[144] In this chapter, I have traced the ambivalent attachment that the Taliban express toward Pakistan, and their articulation of an alternate conceptualization of the political. By subsuming state sovereignty under divine sovereignty, advancing the *khilafat* as an ideal polity, and positing themselves as soldiers of God who will inaugurate a new sociopolitical order, the Taliban appear as a counterpublic to the state. Yet, even as they create distance from the state, they seem to be quite attentive to it—so much so that they often imitate the state, working through similar cultural repertoires, affective economies, and even performances of masculinity. For example, a specific genre of images that appears repeatedly in the Taliban magazines includes *mujahidin* standing side-by-side, in a military formation similar to that of national soldiers.[145] *Mujahidin* also often appear in the magazines dressed in army camouflage. The imitation of the national soldier curates the Taliban as a collective on par with the army. This imitation, however, is never complete, for the differences between the *jawan* and the *mujahidin* are based in both ideology and material inequalities. Yet this stance reflects how the Taliban draw on prevailing codes of masculinity, militarism, and power, and claim these for themselves. As Seyla Benhabib argues, counterpublics are not de-linked from other publics but are part of a mutually interlocking and overlapping network of opinion formation and dissemination.[146] In this respect, it is crucial to observe that the Taliban too perform Islamo-masculinity in order to stimulate consent for their violence and rule. While their performance overlaps with statist performance, it differs too, particularly in relation to how they violently police public morality, as the next chapter will show.

PART TWO

———

Stylizing Political Attachments

FOUR

Subordinated Femininities

MILITANT AND MILITARY WOMEN

IN THE FIRST PART OF THIS BOOK, I examined the Pakistani state and Taliban's conceptualizations of the political, their demarcation of who is included and excluded from the political community, as well as their performances of Islamo-masculinities, through which audiences are bound in relationships of sovereignty. The second part considers how these relations are intensified through gendered labor, kinship feelings, and memory work. Focusing in particular on figurations of women, this chapter explores military and militant women's gendered contributions to nation- and *khilafat*-building projects. The following two chapters examine kinship metaphors and affect. The analysis reveals not only how the state and Taliban hail allied publics, but also how counter- and ambivalent publics are formed. Together, they expose sovereignty as contingent and ongoing.

In August 2017, the Tehrik-e-Taliban (TTP) launched an English-language magazine by and for women. Named *Sunnat-e-Khola,* the magazine seeks to invite women "all around the world" to join the Taliban's effort as well as to share information about women who have migrated to the region of 'Khurasan.'[1] In October of the following year, the Inter Services Public Relations (ISPR) launched its own women-focused English-language magazine, *Hilal for Her.*[2] As the director general of ISPR explained it, the purpose of the magazine is to "inspire and educate our womenfolk, who can play an effective and vibrant role towards bringing a progressive change in the society."[3] These magazines share striking genre similarities, and comprise a mix of ideological writings and interviews together with articles about the everyday lifeworlds of their imagined women readers, such as caregiving, cooking, and cleaning. *Hilal for Her* also discusses themes such as makeup, hair extensions, hair color, eyebrow threading, weight loss, and home workouts, which do not appear in the Taliban magazines.[4] In addition, it includes colorful graphics and images, and its online version has a running "news" panel. Each article in *Hilal for Her* is accompanied by an image of its female author. In contrast, *Sunnat-e-Khola* has few images of women and those that are included show them in *niqabs*. It is possible that the articles are not written by women. I am, however, interested less in authorship and more in the magazines' discursive production of ideal woman-subjects for the nation and *khilafat*, as they illustrate ideal styles of political attachment.

Both *Sunnat-e-Khola* and *Hilal for Her* feature first-person accounts by women in which the writers recall their decision to align with the Taliban or the army respectively. In these stories, women leave their biological families and homes, either migrating to "the land of *khilafat*" or joining the army by conscripting or by following their army husbands. Such movements require women to establish new kinship relations, and to conform to the social codes laid out by these entities. Often, this entails taking on supportive roles so that their male relations can advance the political project. In fact, militant and military women share an uncanny resemblance. The roles available to them are linked primarily to cultural and biological reproduction and, in limited cases, active combat. They draw on similar vocabularies of religion, sacrifice, and higher purpose to assign meaning to their gendered subordination. Crucially, they view their adherence to these roles as essential for the success of the *ummah* or nation.

The chapter highlights how the *muhajira* (one who migrates) and *mujahida* (one who participates in *jihad*) of the Taliban magazines, and the army woman (a composite figure made up of the army wife, the military widow, and the female soldier) of the ISPR magazines, advance their respective political communities through similar practices of reproductive and emotional labor. Their similarity, though, does not dissolve the *dissimilarity* of the statist and Taliban political ambitions as well as the versions of normative Islam that they espouse. Indeed, women's everyday lives appear to unfold differently in each order, as the state allows a greater degree of mobility to army women than the Taliban does to the *muhajira* or the *mujahida*. What is remarkable, however, is how both claimants to sovereignty ultimately call on women to subordinate themselves in fairly similar ways and provide circumscribed, gendered avenues of participation that reinforce their specific Islamo-masculinist claims.

In the Taliban magazines, women are invoked both as *muhajira* and *mujahida*. The latter is the feminine form of *mujahid,* and the former denotes someone who has undertaken migration *(hijrat)*. *Muhajira* seems to apply specifically to women who have decided to migrate to the areas occupied by the Taliban, whereas any woman who believes in the Taliban's political stance is considered a *mujahida.* These designations, however, are fluid, and authors often switch back and forth between them even in a single article.

The writings in the magazines tend to reiterate the Taliban's assertions of disenchantment and injury. They also augment their claims to Muslimness. Specifically, we learn how women's disillusionment with the status quo drives them to join the Taliban. In an article in *Sunnat-e-Khola,* Khaula Bint Abdul Aziz writes about her "journey from ignorance to guidance."[5] Aziz, who claims to be the daughter of an army officer, grew up attending army schools, received her medical education in Lahore, and then went abroad for further studies because she wanted to "serve Pakistani people and especially Pakistan Army."[6] Over time, however, she became disaffected due to the army's secularist stance as well as its gendered and classed practices. As an example, she notes that "the free gender mixing in the school[s] . . . played a major role in my and other students moral destruction."[7] Elsewhere, she alludes to the gradual refashioning of her attachments: "What made me more *detached* from Pakistan army was the 'class system'" as "teachers used to treat students according to their fathers ranks, higher the rank of your father more luxuries and respect given to that student."[8] Later in life, even though her situation was rather comfortable, she started feeling "empty from inside."[9] It is then that she turned to the Taliban. She decided that she could not fully practice Islam in the West and thus migrated "to the land of jihad," pledging allegiance to TTP leader Mullah Fazlullah.[10]

Aziz's narrative is not unique. It, in fact, belongs to a genre that we can describe as origin stories, through which we encounter the details of many women's association with the Taliban. These stories usually follow a script whereby the protagonist is disillusioned with the ongoing affairs of the world, turns to religion in search of meaning, and finds this meaning in the Taliban's religiopolitical project. Aziz's story is particularly subversive for it shows that women from the army's own families are leaving to join the Taliban—what higher insult could there be in a context where women are closely tied to familial and national honor? In the previous chapter, I explained how the Taliban seek to expel the army from the sovereign space of *ummah* due to the army's subservience to America. Aziz's narrative points to yet another way in which the army is cast as "improperly Muslim." She articulates the army as a modernist elite whose interests, mannerisms, and dispositions are not aligned with normative religious precepts. The army is thus marked as a secular and secularizing force, which leads Aziz to detach herself from it. In her new attachment to the Taliban, she finally finds fulfillment and a sense of purpose.

A *mujahida* may also turn to the Taliban after experiencing a personal loss. She may see in the Taliban both an ideology and a physical location that provides protection and peace. The second issue of *Sunnat-e-Khola* features an account by Ummay Bilal in which she laments her husband's incarceration in a secret prison on charges of terrorism.[11] He is eventually sentenced to death in an army court; her daughter also dies of illness. These two losses ignite Bilal's support for the Taliban.[12] Over the course of the article, she recasts her daughter as a martyr and her husband as a *mujahid*.[13] The otherwise meaningless deaths become dignified through the discourse of martyrdom and *jihad*. She views their deaths as well as her ongoing economic and social difficulties as tests from Allah. In doing so, she transforms her dispossession into a sacrifice inspired by religion. Personal narratives like these are included in the magazine to explain to readers why men and women join the Taliban; as Ummay Bilal notes, the "women of Taliban want to make it clear to the world that they have happily chosen the path of jihad and are proud to be wives, daughters, sisters and mothers of mujahidin e Islam."[14]

The magazines additionally provide a medium for the *muhajirat* to fantasize about speaking to their biological families and to nurture memories of past lives. In the second issue of *Sunnat-e-Khola,* for instance, the editors fondly recount the occasion of Eid, when, as women of the Taliban community, they prepare meals for hundreds of guests.[15] The conversations that ensued signal the tensions that the *muhajirat* experience as they try to forge new kinships while pining for older relations. On one occasion when a sister "started fanning the coals in typical Punjabi style," it made others "miss our Lahore a lot."[16] We find letters from the *muhajirat* written to console fathers and other members of the family, and to inform them about their well-being under the new political dispensation. For instance, one woman recalls, "When I was embarking on hijra my father said that you would die with hunger and you would only have stone to eat in [the] valley of Khurasan.

Now I wish my father can somehow see these wonderful dishes and know the blessings I have."[17] Since these messages are mostly anonymous, the authors likely know that they will not be read by their intended recipients. They are useful, however, for their redemptive quality. Through them, the writers imagine confirming to their fathers that their marriages to the *mujahidin* are happy and that they have found their true callings. Through them, they also forge a community with other women who may also be pining for their biological families or undergoing difficulties, such as the loss of a child or *mujahid* husband. The magazines thus become a way for women to establish a sisterhood in a context where close contact is likely not possible and to engage in a fantasy of reconnecting with the kin left behind.

Olivier Roy has observed that *jihadis* often express their motives by connecting them to the suffering of others; seldom do they explain their own trajectory.[18] The first-person writings in *Sunnat-e-Khola* provide a rare glimpse into the trajectories of the Taliban *muhajirat*. Real or fictive, these personal narratives can be read as discursive strategies through which familiarity is established with the reading public. They also create the effect of a community of women—sisters—united in their hardships and grief, but also in ambition.

While the ideal woman-subject in *Sunnat-e-Khola* is one who has left her home and now resides in the land of *khilafat,* the magazine also provides guidance for women who are unable to migrate. The editorial in the first issue, for instance, explains potential ways in which civilian women can contribute.[19] These roles include publishing and distributing *jihadi* literature, writing for the cause of *jihad,* holding religious gatherings and secret meetings, arranging physical training classes, learning how to operate weapons (particularly grenades), preaching to their families, sending money, and supporting the *mujahidin* in their hideouts. The final avenue—assisting fighters in their hideouts—could entail taking food to them; helping them with transporting weapons, jackets, or other equipment; informing them about imminent raids; or even pointing out targets to be attacked. Women can hence participate in the project of *khilafat* even if they are unable to migrate.

Performing Muslimness through Willful Subordination

Two crucial ways in which women contribute to the Taliban project are by reaffirming the Taliban's claim to Muslimness through their sartorial choices and by conforming to the gendered roles prescribed for them. The latter are viewed as emerging organically from Islamic teachings and being integral to the reproduction of not only the Taliban but also the *ummah*. Willful subordination thus becomes a practice through which the *mujahida* asserts her authentic Muslimness.

Like the *mujahid,* the *mujahida* performs piety through her choice of dress, which signals her efforts to emulate early Muslims. Consider the cover image of the second issue of *Sunnat-e-Khola* (figure 16), which features a few burqa-clad *muhajirat* working on their laptops. Their black *abayas* and gloves are covered in dust, signaling the poverty of their working conditions. These women labor behind the scenes to advance the cause of *khilafat*. Elsewhere in the magazine, too, we come across images of women in full burqas, gloves, and *niqabs*. The *mujahida* also pays attention to her reproductive responsibilities. The right-hand corner of the cover image features a *dastarkhwan* (dining table), where food for the Eid festival is set out, next to a rifle. She keeps the *mujahid* content and well fed so he can do God's work. Food preparation features as a recurring topic in *Sunnat-e-Khola,* since it is a practice through which women reproduce *mujahid* communities. The magazine imagines its readers to be mothers and therefore includes articles on the care and education of children, as well as (likely fictive) accounts by children who express their desire to become *mujahidin* in the future.[20]

These gendered contributions, caregiving and reproductive labor, are articulated as emerging from the Quran and authorized by God; adherence to them then becomes a way for the *mujahida* to perform her Muslimness as well. Consider Aziz's explanation in *Sunnat-e-Khola* about the ontological differences between men and women, which have implications for their respective roles:

> Man has been given a status higher than woman but as a family leader he is the one answerable to Allah. Contrary to this woman is like an assistant to a man in household affairs. The heavy burden of responsibilities of earning livelihood, providing the family etc, has been taken off from her shoulders. Duties are less and hence in accordance to that she is given less rights, balancing them both. Man has more responsibilities and hence given more rights over wife. Woman has been kept with all sorts of luxuries. Before marriage she is under her father's strong shade, after marriage in her husband she finds a strong supporter and protector. In short love and protection is what she finds throughout her life in an Islamic household.[21]

Men and women, according to this logic, have discrete spaces of operation and distinct responsibilities. This also legitimizes limits on their rights and mobility. Indeed, when the Taliban occupied Swat and Malakand, they

FIGURE 16. Cover image, *Sunnat-e-Khola,* no. 2, 2017.

placed limits on women's mobility, their relations with men, and their access
to markets, healthcare, and education.

Such articulations of women's roles are found in other Taliban magazines
as well. For instance, in *Azan,* Shaykh Yusuf Uyyari explains the "role of
women in Ummah's Victory" as being complementary: they are to raise children according to the "doctrine of jihad," "guard the man's honor and wealth

when he leaves for jihad," and help their "husband and children to remain patient in this path."[22] Uyyari explains that "behind every great Mujahid is a woman."[23] We find numerous accounts of historical women in the magazines, cited to reaffirm this gendered hierarchy. For instance, in *Ihya-e-Khilafat Urdu* Abu-Nauman Salama writes about Muslim women who have exercised patience during *jihad* and hardship.[24] He tells a story of Prophet Ibrahim advising his son, Prophet Ismail, to divorce his first wife, who was ungrateful and complained during hardship. Prophet Ismail's second wife expressed thanks to God even in times of difficulty, and thus Prophet Ibrahim was pleased with her. The moral of the story, according to the author, is that "every Muslim woman should become a help-meet to her husband, and should only ask for things that the husband can provide."[25] Women are advised by the author to ensure domestic happiness by being obedient to their husbands, for that is also how one keeps God happy. Elsewhere, the journeys of other historical women are recounted to inform readers about the rewards that await them for enduring the difficulties of migration (to Taliban territories).[26] In this way, the authors draw on narratives from Muslim history to sacralize gendered division of labor and particular styles of political attachment.

The *mujahida* willingly aligns with these gendered responsibilities and the consequent male domination not only because doing so reaffirms her faith but also for the promise of future security. As Ummay Bilal explains, "I feel peace and happiness in looking after mujahidin. I believe that if his wish of achieving martyrdom comes true, I and my children will be looked after by mujahidin. I will be provided with shelter and food. Quite opposite to Pakistan's society where a widow is unsafe from wolves and poverty forces her to commit suicide."[27] When a woman marries a *mujahid,* she establishes kinship with others in the community as well who become responsible for her welfare. In fact, in many cases, women's marriages are decided by the local leaders; upon the death of a *mujahid,* his wife may be remarried to another *mujahid.* This practice ensures that women and their children are taken care of economically. It also gives imprisoned *mujahidin* a sense of comfort about the future of their families. Marriages in these circumstances are entered into not due to love between individuals, but for the love of the community. The object of love here is thus different. Similar marriage practices have been observed by members of Daesh as well.[28] The *mujahida* subordinates herself in certain domains of life to gain room elsewhere; through investment in new kinship relations, performance of Muslimness, and reproductive labor, she contributes to the Taliban materially and ideologically.

On the limited occasions when women are encouraged to breach gendered norms it is for participating in battle. Authors often narrate the defiance of historical women to invite readers to enact similar forms of bravery. Taliban leader Mullah Fazlullah gives the example of Hazrat Aasia, Pharaoh's wife, who aligned with Moses against the Pharaoh's wishes, despite intimidation and torture.[29] Fazlullah calls her a *mujahida* and asks his female readers to follow her example. Another author, also citing the example of Hazrat Aasia, calls on Muslim women to follow her and choose the path of *jihad,* even if it comes with difficulties.[30] In *Ihya-e-Khilafat Urdu,* Umar Shaheen Haqqani invokes the example of Hazrat Safia to permit women to perform masculine functions, such as fighting on the battlefield.[31] He narrates a time when Hazrat Safia found herself having to physically defend herself and other women. They were in a fort with only an elderly man assigned to guard them. A suspicious man was lurking around the fort, and she asked her guard to kill him. Being advanced in age, the guard declined; so she killed the man herself and threw his severed head across the fort's wall as a caution to others in his party. The author marvels at Hazrat Safia's abilities and laments that women today ignore their responsibility for advancing Islam. Instead, they are engrossed in either domestic chores or luxuries.[32] Thus, while women's most critical contribution to *khilafat* is through the support they provide to men, Taliban writers make an allowance for women to engage in combat or suicide missions when needed. For this reason, in *Sunnat-e-Khola* we find numerous images of women either practicing target shooting or simply displaying their rifles.[33] The stories of historical women defying feminine norms are told not so as to empower readers to stand up against contemporary forms of patriarchy, but as a means to emphasize women's exemplary faith, disavowal of fear and pain, and courage to rise against the *kuffar.* The *mujahida* is called on to destroy the *kuffar,* all the while submitting herself to the Taliban patriarchy.

These findings resonate with the gender relations and roles prescribed by other Islamist groups as well. Farhat Haq's study of women of the Lashkar-e-Taiba in Pakistan shows that women play a crucial role in reinforcing *jihadi* culture by adopting various mannerisms linked to Muslim societies of the past, as well as willingly excluding themselves from the public space.[34] In doing so, they "reassert and validate the difference between a Muslim and non-Muslim polity."[35] The organization, however, makes allowances for women to participate in fighting and suicide missions.[36] Likewise, studies of women's participation in Daesh point to their prominent roles as wives, mothers, and homemakers, but with allowances for the leader to decide whether women's lives are needed for suicide missions.[37] In such cases, the leader's authority supersedes that of the husband, figuring him instead as the patriarch. Female students from Jami'a Hafsa (Pakistan) furnish us with yet another example where women's entrance into the public realm and even their performance of violent acts are permitted to bring about a Muslim polity. In a speech, Hamna Abdullah, a student of Jami'a Hafsa, urges *"mujahid* daughters" to engage in combat.[38] She recounts having received divine intervention by means of a dream that conveyed permission for women's engagement in *jihad*. Dreams and miracles are an enduring element of Muslim battle narratives and play a vital role in Islamic martyrologies.[39] They transform the speaker's narrative into one that is divinely ordained. In dire circumstances then God permits the *mujahida* to subvert her gender role and engage in violence.

These contemporary articulations have a precursor in the thoughts of several Islamist reformers. In Pakistan, Jamat-e-Islami's founder Abu a'la Mawdudi's views about women remain salient. As noted in the last chapter, upon the establishment of Pakistan, he argued that an Islamic legal order can be achieved only through the political machinery of the nation-state and hence called for Pakistan to be an Islamic state.[40] He wrote a number of texts to explicate what this social and political order would look like, including reflections on women's role in a Muslim polity. In his book *Purdah and the Status of Women,* first published in 1938, he noted that for an Islamic polity to emerge, the essential biological differences between men and women had to be taken into account. He called for strict division of labor and spaces along gender lines. Muslim women were tasked with raising the next generation of Muslim men but only from within the confines of the home: "Bearing a child and shouldering the responsibility of rearing it is a decisive factor which delimits the woman's field of activity in human social life."[41] According to Mawdudi, the division of labor along the lines of gender was crucial to avoid the destruction of the social fabric of society: "A civilization that disregards this division of labour may show temporarily some sign of material progress and prosperity, but it will surely meet a tragic end eventually. For when the woman is loaded with the economic and social responsibilities along with the man, she will throw off the burden of her natural duties and thus bring social life as well as humanity to grief."[42] Over time, however, Jamat-e-Islami diverged from Mawdudi's gender ideology by permitting women to become active in the political scene of Pakistan.[43] Party members argued that by participating in state apparatuses, such as the parliament, women could help precipitate the Islamic state.

Gender ideologies that promote subordinate roles for women are also espoused by groups located outside Pakistan, as well as by non-Muslim right-wing groups. Ellen McLarney writes about Islamists in Egypt who posit women as both the biological as well as ideological reproducers of the *ummah* and who mark their labor within the domain of the intimate as "women's jihad."[44] For these women, "motherwork and homespace become ways of nurturing Islamic community outside the reach of the secular state, military intervention, and foreign ideologies."[45] Likewise, Nikki Keddie identifies Jewish Orthodox movements that also prescribe dress codes, gender segregation, and predefined roles for men and women within the family.[46] Several right-wing Christian groups also support male domination and view existing governments as undermining the family. The conflation of religion, gender, and politics thus is not unique to Pakistan or Islam; those other movements, however, deserve to be analyzed in their specificities, for they manifest locally in distinct ways, have different (but sometimes overlapping) genealogies, and produce distinctive effects.

MILITARY WOMEN

Just as establishing the *khilafat* entails sacrifices and adherence to specific gender roles, so too does defending and nurturing the nation. As I showed in my previous book, all Pakistani women are expected to contribute toward nation-building.[47] However, women associated with the army—as the mothers and wives of soldiers, and as female soldiers—take on a greater responsibility. We encounter these women in the ISPR magazines, particularly in *Hilal for Her,* as well as in other productions sponsored by the ISPR, such as television shows and e-books like *Junoon-e-Rukhe Wafa* (2018).

Soldiering Women

Similar to *Sunnat-e-Khola, Hilal for Her* includes first-person accounts of how women ended up in the armed forces. These narrations are almost always linked to the women's appreciation of the army's mission through past exposure (via their fathers, often), or to their love for the nation. In an interview, Major General Nigar Johar shares her familial impetus: "I always wanted to become an Army doctor. My father was an Army officer."[48] Commander Farah Sadia may not have been following a legacy, but she explains that she joined the armed forces because she had loved and admired them since childhood.[49] For her, "serving in the Armed Forces is not a job; it is a way of life; planned, disciplined and thrilling."[50] Captain Ayesha Khalique, on the other hand, decided to join the army to honor her martyred husband. An article entitled "Picking Up the Pieces: Walking in the Footsteps of Major Ishaq Shahid" chronicles her journey.[51] She made peace with the passing of her husband by considering his death an honor: "*Shahadat* [martyrdom] is the utmost desire of every soldier and very few are selected by Allah for this matchless bounty."[52] Using the same verses of the Quran as the Taliban do to make sense of their dead, she notes, "His *shahadat* has made him immortal as the Holy Qur'an ordains in *Sūrat Al-Baqarah* (2:154): 'Say not of those who die in the way of Allah, they are dead, nay, they are living, though you perceive (it) not.'"[53] Khalique decided to apply for the Army Medical Corps to continue her husband's mission. She went on to receive the "best shooter award," which she interprets as "an answer to the enemy that our sacrifices shall not go in vain."[54]

Once women join the armed forces, they experience close camaraderie with fellow soldiers, which transforms them into a family. These new kinships intensify their attachment to the army and the nation. In the first issue of *Hilal for Her*, Major Saba Imran reflects on her experience during a UN peacekeeping mission.[55] While her assignment took her away from her biological family, she established new kinship ties with fellow Pakistani peacekeepers: "our countrymen [became] our new family."[56] Likewise, Captain Sana Nasri recalls her days at the military academy and the "camaraderie at PMA that lasts a lifetime. Cadets learn to rely on one another and help each other rise."[57] Being a female soldier means entering a new sociality with its own sets of rules. For example, here, contact between men and women, as well as women's performance of what otherwise would be deemed masculine gender practices, becomes permissible precisely because they take place in the context of nation-building. While, for the most part, women in the army are engaged in noncombat roles, some have been invited into elite units. Ayesha Farooq is one such woman, who qualified to become a fighter pilot. In figure 17, we see her walking shoulder to shoulder with male officers; she dons the standard uniform with one modification—the head scarf. These sartorial choices permit military women to simultaneously claim military masculinity and perform Muslimness.

Like the *mujahida,* female soldiers are motivated by discourses of *jihad,* martyrdom, and sacrifice for Allah. Like the *jawan* who we encountered in the second chapter, they see Pakistan as a nation for Muslims, and by serving the

FIGURE 17. Ayesha Farooq, one of Pakistan's few female war-ready fighter pilots. June 6, 2013. Credit: Reuters / Zohra Bensemra.

country they hope to serve Allah. Humairah Shahbaz reflects on this through the poetry of national poet-philosopher Allama Iqbal, in her article titled "War and Women."[58] She heeds Iqbal's explanation of women's roles in war:

> To give the soldiers of Islam water to drink was to be your good fortune.
>
> A jihad in the way of God, waged without sword or shield!
>
> What a courage, the love of martyrdom gives!

This framing valorizes women's noncombat roles, which are also interpreted as "jihad," undertaken for the "love of martyrdom." The poem belongs to a corpus of historical narratives whereby Muslim women's performances on the battlefield in the past are taken as lessons for contemporary women.

The majority of women affiliated with the Pakistan military, however, are not soldiers. They are the wives, mothers, and sisters of soldiers, who undertake reproductive and emotional labor to sustain the army. In an article in *Hilal for Her,* Sadia Qazi wonders: "where do these soldiers derive this strength and resolve?"[59] She then proceeds to answer her own question: "mothers, wives, sisters and daughters."[60] These women, she argues, are "the strength behind the force"; it is they who, "in this saga of courage . . . are the invisible soldiers in every combat."[61] In the ISPR publications, the mothers, sisters, and wives of soldiers not only run households in the absence of men but also are the paradigmatic sacrificial figures, whose fortitude is necessary for the army to achieve its purpose. The wives of soldiers, for example, are assigned the gendered responsibility of maintaining the emotional balance of the family. They are expected to hide their worries and be ready to take over their households in the event of their husbands' death. Sadia Qazi explains in *Hilal for Her*: "When leaving home, he [the soldier] is assured by his wife that they will be *okay* no matter what, and that he should just defend the borders and safeguard our homeland, despite the fact that she knows what it means to her if he doesn't come back alive. She will be a widow to carry herself and will have to look after her children alone. She understands that she will be a single parent and will be a father and a mother both to her children and life will be a long, tiring and lonesome journey."[62] Wives of soldiers are expected to manage their affect; instead of expressing grief and anxiety as their husbands depart, they are to remain poised and in control so that soldiers are not worried about them and can focus solely on defending the borders. Such affective registers are what Jose Muñoz in another context describes as "minimalist to the point of emotional impoverishment."[63] The performance of this impoverished affect transforms these women into a distinct group; in the Pakistani public culture, there is even a specific term—"army wives"—used to refer to them.

According to *Hilal for Her*, becoming an "army wife" is a decision not to be taken lightly. In the magazine, we find an account by Hira Sagheer, a recent army wife.[64] As the child of an army officer, Sagheer thought that she would adjust well into her new role. She was mistaken: "nothing can prepare you for what is about to become your new life." Sagheer discusses the toll of her nomadic existence, in which one is expected to move every two years and thus is unable to settle.[65] However, as a consequence, the army wife becomes self-reliant and confident. She "can make any place habitable," and has her own "extra special, super power." She ultimately forms new bonds and attachments: "You will form lifelong friendships with fellow *bhabiyan* [sisters-in-law, i.e., other army wives]. These are the people who will be your family away from family." For Sagheer, being an army wife means that "patriotism will seep into your very core." Another army wife featured in *Hilal for Her*, Annum, was widowed at the age of twenty-seven.[66] She did not quite know how to engage with her loss. However, she recalled her husband's pride in being part of the army and rejected the temptation to leave Pakistan or the army, so much so that she now wishes for her young son to join the army as well. She boasts, "I feel honored for being a widow of a martyr and I want my son to serve his nation [by] joining Pakistan Army; the way his father did with pride. And it will be an absolute honor if one day in the future someone calls me a widow and mother of a martyr!"[67] Through these narratives, army wives are called on to attach themselves to the nation and continue to do so even after the deaths of their husbands.

Like the *mujahida,* military women also make meaning of the deaths of their loved ones through the discourse of martyrdom. The sister of a soldier who died in South Waziristan, Mehreen Rani, writes in *Junoon-e-Rukhe Wafa* (2018) about her brave brother's intense love for the nation and his fearlessness.[68] She clarifies that he was not afraid of death and would often tell his mother not to cry if he were martyred. The discourse of martyrdom is prominent in older issues of the *Hilal* magazines as well. For instance, addressing her brother Major Raja Aziz Bhatti, who died on the battlefield, Zaib Rani wonders in the October 10, 1965 issue of *Hilal* (Urdu): "Oh my Raja brother . . . you may have thought that I would have cried [upon hearing the news of your martyrdom]. That I would have sobbed in your memory. No, brother. I did not do that. I picked up a photo of yours, kissed it, placed it on my eyes, and the following words left my mouth: 'You have kept your sister's honor. *Bhaiyya* [brother], you turned out to be so brave!'"[69] Instead of breaking down, Rani performs the impoverished affect that suits army men's female relations. She consoles herself: "But you are alive. You were always alive and will remain alive until the end. *Shahid* never die."[70] The discourse of martyrdom as liminal death—whereby one is dead but also alive—moves death from the plane of the profane to the sacred.[71] In the same issue of *Hilal* (October 10, 1965), we come across a letter from a mother to her son, who is on the battlefield. In it, she cautions him against showing any cowardice. I have translated the letter in its entirety because it illustrates the crucial emotional labor that mothers are expected to perform to bolster the morale of soldiers. There is no way to confirm the veracity of the letter—it could have been manufactured to impart a lesson. However, its themes resonate with many gendered aspects of army service, including the figuration of mothers that I discuss further in chapter 6:

[Dear] Zulfiqar,

Everything is fine at home and I pray to God that you too are fine. I want to emphasize to you that you are a son of a brave father and a soldier of a brave nation and a staunch Muslim. Prove your bravery while maintaining your honor *(ghairat)*. Life is invaluable. Death has a time which has been determined by Allah. An honorable life of a day is better than a dishonorable life of a thousand days. I want to clarify to you that Pakistani women only trust their *jawan* to ensure that the enemy does not advance. All mothers and sisters in the country are mothers and sisters to all. To save their honor is the responsibility of each individual. I pray for your success. May Allah bring you back with victory. If you show cowardice [on the battlefield], I will consider the debt of my motherhood unpaid.

Your mother,
Zaftaan Bibi[72]

The last sentence of this letter loses some of its affective force when translated into English. In Urdu, the mother says, *"Agar aap nay buzdili dekhai tau main sheer na bakhsun gi."* A mother not forgiving a child for her care (milk) is tantamount to declaring that the child will forever remain in debt. Zaftaan Bibi is threatening her son to ensure that he exhibits bravery on the battlefield. In doing so, she performs the emotional labor required of army women—she gives her son permission to die on the battlefield without worrying about his female kin. The letter also reiterates some of the arguments presented in chapter 2 whereby all citizens, but particularly the nation's womenfolk, place their trust in the *jawan* for their safety.

These narratives produce the nation as an object of intense love and invest it with values that deserve to be protected. The emotional conflicts that a soldier may feel—between love for family and love for nation, for instance—are resolved by the army woman, who undertakes the gendered emotional and reproductive labor of intensifying the nationalist commitments of both the soldiers and the reading publics.[73]

The Everyday Female Soldier

Another female figuration introduced in the ISPR narratives is that of a woman who, while not formally enlisted, decides to take up arms to protect the state. Although rare, this figuration appears in moments when the state has been temporarily dislodged as the sovereign by dissidents. In such instances, this everyday woman becomes a soldier and emerges as a sovereign proxy. "Mehrunnisa ka Lashkar" (Mehrunnisa's Battalion, 2018), an episode of *Faseel-e-Jaan se Agay,* a melodrama series jointly produced by the ISPR and a private company, advances this logic.[74]

The episode is set during the 2009 clashes between the Pakistani state and the Taliban in the Swat Valley. A peace accord was signed in February, but by

May, skirmishes had resumed. The drama portrays the increasing encroach-
ment of the Taliban, showing how they looted property and weapons, and
harassed and terrorized the local population. On one occasion, a group of
Taliban men accost the husband of the protagonist, Mehrunnisa, demanding
his weapons, which he manufactures for a living.[75] When he refuses, they
prepare to beat him up. However, Mehrunnisa intervenes and saves her husband by shooting at one of the militants. This launches her role as a leader.
She goes on to raise a battalion of local men and women to fight the Taliban.
Dressed in a long red *shalwar kameez*, with her face covered in a black
chaddar, and a rifle by her side, she rallies her people: "[Let us] get these
people out of our valley. We have never lived a life of dishonor and slavery,
and will not live one now," she exclaims.

While Mehrunnisa's actions could be read as an assertion of local
sovereignty—after all, she is engaging in violence, seeking control of territory,
and deciding on who gets to live and who must die—she is rearticulated in
the drama as a sovereign proxy. She picks up weapons only to support the
state: "We will not let the government weaken; we will give support," she
explains. We also learn that an army captain has been visiting and advising
the battalion on how to engage the Taliban. Even as the battalion fights
under her guidance, the army continues to figure as the ultimate savior.
Indeed, the battalion members find comfort in knowing that the army is
aware of the atrocities of the Taliban and will rescue them. The logic is that
the army will attack the Taliban from outside the valley, and Mehrunnisa's
battalion will take them on from the inside. She and her troops operate as an
extension of the army. Purnima Mankekar, in her analysis of representations
of nationalism and Indian womanhood in melodramas, observes that characters often exist as metaphors for certain existential states rather than as
autonomous individuals.[76] In *Faseel-e-Jaan,* Mehrunnisa, like the female
soldiers, represents a rare form of womanhood that is permitted to breach
masculine societal codes, but only in the name of facilitating statist
sovereignty.

STYLIZING IDEAL POLITICAL ATTACHMENTS

The figurations of *mujahida* and army woman perform multiple functions in
extending Taliban and statist claims to sovereignty. First and foremost, by
performing subordinate femininities and Muslimness, they demonstrate

ideal styles of political attachment to the state and the Taliban. These styles reiterate the Islamo-masculinist claims of these entities. Relatedly, tales of women's labor bestow probity on these political projects. Second, by narrating their stories, women writers in the magazines carve a place for women in the *khilafat* and in military projects. In other words, they bring into effect the very womanhood(s) that they write about. Finally, the magazines address a public of presumably female readers on ideal ways of contributing to these projects. In doing so, they also circulate as public pedagogies of sovereign attachments.

We find uncanny resemblances between the *mujahida* and the army woman. Both are nomadic, often leaving their homes and families of origin to support their political cause. They perform crucial reproductive labor to sustain their respective political communities, including affective labor to keep up the morale of male fighters. They are called on to establish new kinship networks, to stand firmly by the *mujahidin* or soldiers, and to adjust quickly to new circumstances in the event of the deaths of the latter. This adjustment entails a brief period of mourning, followed by continued political allegiance to *khilafat* or nation. The *mujahida* and the army woman perform Muslimness for their respective entities not only by making careful sartorial choices but also by aligning with prescribed gender hierarchies that are posited as divinely ordained. While women are expected to contribute primarily as wives, mothers, and sisters, in some cases, they are also permitted to break gender norms when their help is needed for combat or its support. However, their participation in this realm is often short-lived and limited.

The similarity of their gendered subordination, however, as I noted earlier, does not dissolve the dissimilarity of the *mujahida* and the army woman's political projects and normative Islams. Indeed, the latter influences the degree, intensity, and forms of subordination experienced by women, especially as they unfold in everyday life. For example, while both sets of women are called on to be prepared for the deaths of their male relations and both rely on their communities—*mujahidin* and army—for support, the widowed *mujahida* is presumably quickly married off to another fighter. In contrast, the army woman is encouraged to rely on a more amorphous patriarch—the army—which provides welfare and support, leaving her with some space for personal autonomy. Likewise, whereas the Taliban's normative Islam steers them to place limits on women's education and mobility, the army's modernist bent translates into more everyday freedoms for army women. Hira Sagheer's writings, noted above, provide a glimpse into the kind of personal empowerment that army women experience. Articles on work-life balance, entrepreneurship, online businesses, and international leisure travel in *Hilal for Her* also point to women's active, public everyday lives.[77] Images of female authors, their heads uncovered, with full makeup and jewelry, likewise signal different assumptions about embodied Islam and the performance of piety when compared to the Taliban. These representations in turn reiterate how the Islamo-masculinities of the state and the Taliban rely on different normative Islams (more on this in the concluding chapter).

Even as the state and the Taliban stylize the ideal forms of political attachments, there is always affect that escapes—the *mujahida* who misses her biological family, or the soldier's mother who remains haunted by the ghost of her dead son, refusing to move on (more on this in chapter 6). Thus, while sovereign attachments rely on women's reproductive and emotional labor, this relationship also has room for renegotiation and can even unravel.[78] In the next two chapters, I develop this inquiry further by examining how kinship metaphors and affect are mobilized by the state and the Taliban to interpellate allied publics, as well as moments when publics refuse or modify these attachments.

FIVE

Kinship Metaphors

THE *BETI* AND *BEHAN*

IN 2017, THE ARREST OF NINETEEN-YEAR-OLD NAUREEN LAGHARI became a national news sensation in Pakistan. She had left home on the morning of February 10 to attend classes at the Liaquat Medical College in Hyderabad but did not return. Her parents filed a missing persons report with the police. A few months later, four militants were arrested in Lahore for planning to bomb a church on Easter; one of them was a woman later identified as Laghari.

It was found that Laghari had travelled to Lahore with the hope of eventually migrating to "the land of *Khilafah*," as she explained to her brother in a text message.[1] She had married a militant, Ali Tariq, joined his network, and at the time of her arrest was expected to blow up a church in a few days.[2] During the military raid, Tariq was killed, and while Laghari engaged in a shootout with the police for about an hour, she was eventually captured.[3] Surprisingly, she was released a few days later. The representative of the Pakistani army disarticulated her from terrorism and rearticulated her as a "*quam-ki-beti*" (nation's daughter) who had been duped by the terrorists. Laghari therefore deserved protection and not punishment; she was ultimately forgiven.

This chapter surveys a number of cases to illustrate how the state, the Taliban, as well as "the people," draw on kinship feelings to create and expand the scope for sovereignty. In particular, threats to the *beti* (daughter) and *behan* (sister)—who are imagined as proxies for the honor of men, the *ummah*, and the nation—stir up feelings of care and humiliation, providing the affective environment for the sovereign functions of violence, rescue, rebuke, and forgiveness. I begin with a consideration of Laghari's case to point to how, through the metaphor of *beti*, she is cast as the daughter of not only her parents but the entire nation. The ISPR utilizes this figuration to furnish itself as the patriarch, binding the nation into a paternal public. This public then legitimizes state violence in the name of protecting the *beti*. This kinship feeling is so powerful that even women who attack or plan to attack the state but then decide to reform their ways, such as Laghari, are forgiven and folded back into the national family.[4] Women who critique the state, however, are not offered such possibilities; they are disciplined. The case of gang-rape victim Mukhtar Mai illustrates how women who do not abide by patriarchal scripts of compliance, which are interlinked with ideal styles of political attachment, are reprimanded. These women become what I am calling the "unruly daughters."

The Taliban also articulate women through kinship metaphors to cultivate a public that legitimizes their violence. Here, the feminine subject of rescue and protection is the *behan,* and sometimes the *beti,* who has been violated, often sexually, by the *kuffar*—a category that includes both national and imperial Others. Her violation recruits the magazines' readership as a fraternal public that views it as a breach of the *ummah's* honor and therefore coheres together as a humiliated collectivity. To avenge this injury and forestall future ones, retaliatory and preemptive violence become permissible. In the Taliban magazines, we also encounter figurations of female kin who have gone astray—I call them "wayward sisters"; they become objects of ridicule even as they are constantly cajoled into aligning with the Taliban.

While these paternal and fraternal publics are instantiations of allied publics vis-à-vis the state and the Taliban, kinship affects also produce additional publics—those that express an ambivalent attachment to the state but are also not allied with the Taliban. The final case in the chapter dwells on such a public, one that emerges during protests. Judith Butler reads protests as "provisional versions of popular sovereignty," wherein "the people" contest statist hegemony over meanings of life and death.[5] I consider the demonstrations that occurred around the arrest of Aafia Siddiqui, a Pakistani woman who has been incarcerated in the United States. Here, protestors used the kinship metaphors of *behan* and *beti* to establish affinity with Siddiqui against both the national and imperial sovereigns. They expressed care for their incarcerated "sister" and shamed the state for not fulfilling its role as patriarch. At times protestors also sought to displace the state, casting themselves as the sovereign actors who would undertake the functions of protection and rescue.

These cases illustrate how kinship feelings can both foster and impede sovereign attachments. Hitched to performances of Islamo-masculinity, sovereignty in these instances is advanced through feelings of care, humiliation, and shame in relation to fictive sisters or daughters. Such feelings then orient the publics into attachment with, or against, sovereign power. In the process we also learn about attachment styles that are considered appropriate by the state and the Taliban, as well as those that are deemed inappropriate; the latter emerge in the figurations of the unruly daughters and wayward sisters.

PATERNAL PUBLICS, THE STATE'S DAUGHTERS

In Pakistan, women occupy a paradoxical status. On the one hand, as symbols of familial, communal, and national honor, they command respect; on the other, these same relationships are deployed to constrain their rights as citizen-subjects. The Pakistani state plays a crucial role in advancing this paradox.[6] Through its laws as well as its cultural productions, it articulates women primarily as subjects of masculinist protection. This paternalistic relationship to women is often expressed through the kinship relation of *beti* (daughter), which permits the state to both discipline and forgive women. Naureen Laghari's story illustrates these dynamics.

The news of Laghari's arrest and later release quickly became a media sensation. Her story, however, was carefully scripted. Much of what we know about her comes primarily through the recorded confessions and press conferences of the ISPR and from interviews with the arresting police officers. The heavy scripting of these events transformed them into a theatrical performance, with a plot line, a twist, good and bad characters, and a benevolent patriarch. That is precisely why Waseem Badami, a news anchor for the ARY television channel, called Laghari's journey a "film story" *(filmy kahani)*: "It is a film story: there is a girl-child *(bachi)* who studies at the Liaquat Medical College; her father is the head of a department at another university. The girl-child disappears overnight; parents complain; a message is played on TV [it is a message about her having reached *khilafat* territory]; parents deny it; police say that this is indeed the case. In a raid in Lahore, a terrorist is killed, a girl is found, and it turns out to be that same girl! And now her views are on display."[7] It is this theatricality that I consider worthy of study, as it discloses the affective appeal of vulnerable middle-class femininity in the fashioning of sovereign attachments. The kinship feelings that cohered around Laghari fastened strangers as a feeling paternal public that acquiesced to state practices of violence and forgiveness in the name of protecting her.

Laghari's confession was recorded and played for journalists during an ISPR press briefing as well as aired on television. Before playing the video, the director general of the ISPR, Asif Ghafoor, introduced her as "our own girl-child, the nation's girl-child" *(hamari apni bachi hai, quam ki bachi hai).*[8] Upon the conclusion of the video, he noted, "The reason for showing you this video confession is that these children are our children. The youth surge is our strength."[9] Later, in another press briefing, Ghafoor framed Laghari as everyone's daughter, and through the use of "we," installed the army as well as the national public as the patriarch: "Now, if she were my daughter *(beti)* or your daughter, and if we save her from being used per the design of terrorists . . . then should we punish her like a terrorist? Or should we give her a chance to go out and tell the rest of our young generation about how she was provoked . . . and how she was used wrongly . . . . parents should be aware, institutions [need] to be aware and we [should] use her in our society for correction. We shouldn't punish her."[10] The terms *beti* and *bachi* are used synonymously by Ghafoor to denote a subject in transition, requiring the paternalistic protection of those who care for her. Ghafoor validates the state's decision not to punish her by calling on viewers to imagine Laghari as their own daughter: surely, if she were their daughter, they would forgive her transgression. In doing so, he not only forges the state as the patriarch but extends this paternalism to those watching the televised press release. He explains, "Naureen Leghari was on her way to becoming a terrorist. She was not a terrorist."[11] Laghari is thus transformed into an abstracted daughter-subject, everyone's daughter, who deserves the forgiveness and protection of both the paternalistic state and the paternal nation at large.

Ghafoor shifts blame to social media and the terrorists, both of which emerge as corrupting forces. He alludes to her as "*kam-umar*" (of young age) to signal her immaturity and inability to form her own judgments about joining the militant group.[12] Through this frame of youthfulness, Laghari is denied political subjectivity, including the possibility of possessing antistate and pro-Daesh views. Instead, she is viewed simply as a tool in the hands of the terrorists who have "brainwashed" her.[13] Laghari is also desexualized, a framing that intensifies her articulation as a subject that requires protection. We find almost no mention of Laghari's marriage to Tariq in the ISPR and media discourse. If it were acknowledged that she had married a terrorist—which she could legally do since she was over the age of eighteen—then her status as a *bachi* (girl-child), a condition that is imagined as innocent, pure, and devoid of any sexual desire and political agency, would be threatened.

While the term "woman" carries with it ideas of social personhood and legal status (albeit limited), the concept of "girl" is culturally and socially associated with dependency, protectedness, and legal incapability.[14] Erasing Laghari's marriage in public culture was a deliberate strategy to pursue her articulation as a subject in need of rescue by the state and nation. What we are left with is a vulnerable, immature girl-child, who was provoked by the terrorists; she is the nation's daughter and therefore deserves to be forgiven.

These dominant articulations of Laghari as immature and gullible are contradicted, to some extent, by other information that circulated about her. She was repeatedly invoked in the media as a bright student who was serious and thoughtful about her coursework. In an interview, the vice chancellor of her university explained that she was regular in her attendance and obtained good grades.[15] In Pakistan, gaining admission to a medical university is a high achievement; Laghari must have been an organized and deliberate student, not quite the immature girl that the ISPR made her out to be. This is also apparent in her interviews and in reports about her activities just prior to her departure for Lahore. In a *Neo News* report, we learn that she had started wearing a *burqa* some time ago, used to talk to friends about *jihad,* kept in contact with those linked to the *khilafat* via the Internet, and posted pro-*jihad* messages on Facebook, due to which her account was suspended twice.[16] When a television anchor asked her whether she was "compelled *(majboor)* to go to Lahore," she indicated her own desire to undertake the journey.[17] At one point, she even noted that the vision of an Islamic territory appealed to her exceedingly. We also know that she was not kidnapped but bought the bus tickets to Lahore herself. When the television anchor asked her whether she had tried to escape her (presumed) captors, she replied, "No . . . " then quickly corrected herself, "I guess I must have. But I was trapped."[18] These elements of her story are overlooked because Laghari can only be forgiven by the national public on the condition that she is seen as gullible, pure, and ignorant.

By recuperating Laghari from those who brainwashed her, the state and its allied public are able to perform the sovereign function of protection. Ghafoor declared in a press conference, "we saved her in time."[19] Crucially, this event enabled the state to expand its surveillance of families in order to avoid such mishaps in the future. For instance, in the aftermath of the arrest, much of the discussion by the ISPR and in the media focused on the role of parents in thwarting the radicalization of youth by terrorists. Political commentators discussed parents' responsibility for the proper upbringing of children, including greater monitoring of their movements as well as their use of social media.[20] Such narratives transform parents into agents of the state who are expected to detect terrorist proclivities in their children and report them to the police. Laghari's figuration as *beti* thus created an alliance of sorts between the state and the family in which sovereign powers of surveillance, punishment, and forgiveness are shared.

The shared practices of sovereignty visible in Laghari's case are the latest episode in a long history wherein the Pakistani state and the family have entered into an alliance to regulate women. Through a range of apparatuses, the state has codified women as mothers and daughters, suturing women's legibility to their relationships with men. This alliance materializes in women's intimate lives through its many administrative and legal arms, and in relation to a range of issues such as marriage, sexuality (including definitions of rape and adultery), inheritance, and child custody. The idioms of protection, care, and security play a central role in both creating and limiting possibilities for women.[21] There is a class dimension to this as well, as I have explained in my previous work.[22] The state is interested in preserving the respectability and purity of the middle-class heterosexual family. Since women's bodies and movements have been sutured to expressions of respectability, they have become targets of surveillance and regulation. Thus, another way to understand the intimacy of the state with women is to reinterpret it as the sovereign's interest in preserving, protecting, policing, and regulating middle-class women because they symbolize the ideal, patriotic heterosexual family upon which the sovereign relies for legitimation. Saima Waheed's court case from 1997 is an example of this. It shows how the state is invested in reproducing certain gender ideals, and particularly in extending the privileges of the father. The case also brings to light the tension between women's figurations as daughters and as citizens.[23] It shows how Laghari's case contains residue from the past and also is subtly different, given the post-9/11 context.

Waheed, a twenty-two-year-old woman, had married Arshad Ahmad, a man whom she liked. Her father, Hafiz Abdul Waheed, filed a case to annul her marriage stating that since he had not given his permission, the marriage was not legal. The case rose to national prominence, eventually ending up at the Lahore High Court. Whereas the father argued that the marriage was illegal, Waheed's lawyer contended that she was *sui juris* (entitled to act for herself) and therefore could marry anyone she liked. While the court eventually upheld the validity of Waheed's marriage, a close reading of the judges' opinions provides a glimpse into how concern for women binds the state (courts, in this case) and the family into one paternalistic formation. The judges imagined their role as more than legal interpreters of the law; as one of the judges, Justice Chaudhry, stated, "We are national judges and as such custodians of the morals of the citizens."[24] Drawing on the Quran and *hadith* (sayings of Prophet Muhammad), he argued that marriage was not simply a contract but also a religious duty; therefore, obedience to parents could be legally enforced.[25] This, however, contrasts with how Muslim jurisprudence often interprets marriage as a civil contract and not a sacrament, indicating that the ascription of "religious duty" by Justice Chaudhry was a specific interpretive move.[26] Through recourse to religion he argued that marriage was crucial for the welfare of the family and in doing so, cleared the path for parental authority and consent to be enforced by the courts:

> Islam being religion of nature and covering all human activity from cradle to grave, has taken special care of the integrity, upkeep and preservation of family. In Islam family unit is fully oriented. The *nikah* [i.e. marriage] is uniting/ linking not only two individuals but also two families. The rights and obligations in Islam are not according to the sex but according to its contribution to the family .... The parents are responsible for marriage of the children generally and girls particularly .... It is amply clear from the above instance that the obedience [to] the parents could be enforced by the Courts.[27]

Justice Chaudhry further delineated the precise legal mechanisms through which parental authority could be administered, proposing amendments to the Muslim Family Courts Act of 1964.[28] He also called for the state to regulate or ban avenues such as marriage bureaus that encourage men and women to choose their own spouses.[29] In his statements then we can detect an alliance between the state and the family for the regulation of children, particularly girls, that resonates in Laghari's case as well.

The mechanisms for regulating women were more concretely laid out by Justice Ramday, who, while upholding the validity of Waheed's marriage, still argued that marriages arranged by family elders were the ideal. He condemned interfaith marriages, claiming that they were entered into on the basis of "sheer momentary impulses which . . . are patently not in their interest and which are also a cause for shame and disgrace to the whole family."[30] In the case of contested marriages, he argued that "the aggrieved person shall have a right to initiate proceedings in the competent Court seeking annulment."[31] The judgment described "aggrieved person" as parents, or in their absence, brothers, connecting male honor with women's marriage preferences. Through the weight of his opinion Justice Ramday cleared the path for a closer scrutiny of the familial realm and ultimately awarded control of women's bodies and sexuality to male members of their families. He also called for the state to intervene in social relations between men and women. Specifically, he argued that secret friendships or marriages, and courtships, should be made into penal offenses.[32] He further suggested a prohibition on women "using perfumes when going outdoors lest the fragrance attracted some men towards them."[33] Veiling, staying indoors, and using a mild tone are all invoked in the judgement as practices through which women could shield themselves from the outside/outdoors/men.[34] In this narrative, the outdoors is constructed as a place of corruption, and it is the responsibility of the patriarch, from the father to the judge (a representative of the state), to ensure that women are protected from such sources of contamination.[35] Thus, Justice Ramday's opinion called for the codification of paternalistic attitudes into law, thereby consolidating the articulation of women as daughters (of their fathers and the state) above and beyond their other subject positions (such as that of a citizen). It is clear from this brief examination of the judges' opinions that through the articulation of women as daughters, sovereignty over their bodies is assigned to the family and the state.

Laghari's case is the latest episode of such sovereign practices. However, while linked to Waheed's case, it is also subtly different. Whereas the family and the state share the responsibility of monitoring and surveilling daughters, the family is now increasingly cast as lacking the necessary ability to forestall radicalization by terrorists. It must, therefore, rely on the state to protect children. Television anchor Saadia Afzal of *92 News,* for instance, concludes an interview with Laghari with the following message for her audience: "Viewers, the reason for showing you this conversation with Naureen Laghari is so that you can keep an eye on your children in your homes, children who are immature *(na-pukhta zahain),* young *(kam-umar).* Just like Laghari, who is nineteen years old . . . and this girl-child's thoughts and concepts . . . and how these children are manipulated, used and radicalized."[36] Once children are identified as being in danger, parents are to report to the police. Girl-children thus are brought into tighter circuits of familial and state surveillance.

That Laghari was forgiven is also tied to another, newer, global discourse of youth fragility that is specific to post-9/11 global counterinsurgency efforts. In recent years, a number of policy prescriptions based on the US government's countering violent extremism (CVE) strategy have taken on a hegemonic status globally. This strategy assigns a major role to youth in addressing terrorism. It includes efforts to empower local partners within and beyond the United States to prevent terrorist acts through community engagement programs, often aimed at youth. A joint Department of State and USAID strategy document from May 2016 elaborates this as follows: "State and USAID will expand and enhance programs targeting youth who are identified to be at high risk of radicalization and recruitment to violent extremism. State and USAID will support programs that build a sense of belonging, community and purpose. USAID will design programs to support youth empowerment, nurture networks, skills development, and civic and economic opportunities. State and USAID also will support programs that train and mobilize youth to serve as leaders in their communities and globally in the work of CVE."[37] As a key US ally in its fight against terrorism, the National Counter Terrorism Authority of Pakistan has set out to empower marginalized youth, reform madrasas, and create a new national narrative. The US State Department, USAID, and US Institute of Peace (USIP) are all active in Pakistan, managing projects with local partners, many of which focus on youth.[38] Alongside the paternalistic discourse that marks all women as *betis* to be protected, the discourse on CVE provides yet another framing of youth fragility, one that informed the Pakistani state's engagement with Laghari. In this framing she becomes not a terrorist but a *beti* who will help facilitate the deradicalization goals of the state. In a press briefing, the director general for ISPR, Ghafoor, explains the future that awaits her:

> Let me tell you more. In Swat, when radicalization and extremism was underway, Taliban had also taken young children there and brainwashed them. We took many of those children later on when they were free [after the military had rescued them]. If we send them to jail then afterwards will they become good citizens or will they work against Pakistan? We sent them to a deradicalization center, we brainwashed them positively, told them about *Pakistaniyat* and today, after three to four years, they are good citizens, they earn for their parents, go to school, go to colleges, and contribute to Pakistan. So with regards to Naureen, I would like to say [the same] . . . to tell our male and female children about threats they face, how her brain was damaged.[39]

Ghafoor transforms the proper noun *Pakistan* into an ideology, *Pakistaniyat*. To be Pakistani then is not simply to have an association to territory but to adhere to an ideology that produces an affective attachment to Pakistan. It is a set of sensibilities and dispositions that confirms one's social membership in the nation. Laghari is therefore conscripted to play a crucial role in the state's pedagogical project of nurturing such an attachment in others. Through a retelling of her story as one of being misguided and then saved or rescued by the state, she is to help engender this ideal disposition, moral virtue, and character—or *Pakistaniyat*—in other youth. Encounters with her and her story may become the means through which new publics, youth publics in particular, attach themselves to the state.

My intention here is not to assign either blame or innocence to Laghari. Instead, it is to call attention to the ways in which the state enrolls women in performances of sovereignty. In this case, feelings of kinship with *betis* are mobilized to forge a paternal public that acquiesces to statist sovereign performances, from protection to policing. *Betis*, however, are not always compliant; those who strike a different relationship to the state become "unruly daughters." These daughters are incorporated into sovereign projects through practices of disciplining. Mukhtar Mai's experience is a case in point.

Unruly Daughters

In June 2002, Mukhtar Mai, a thirty-year-old woman, was gang raped in Meerawala, Pakistan by a group of men belonging to the powerful clan of Mastoi. The rape was retribution for alleged sexual advances by her twelve-year-old brother toward a woman from the Mastoi clan. Police investigations later revealed that her brother was in fact kidnapped and sodomized by Mastoi men and that the accusations were a cover-up. Mai filed a police report against the men and fourteen of them were arrested. Six were sentenced to death by hanging and the remaining eight were acquitted. While the convicted men appealed the decision, Mai filed an appeal with the Lahore High Court against the acquittal. In March 2005, the Lahore High Court overturned the death verdict of the convicted men and released five of the six, citing insufficient evidence. The court also commuted the death sentence of the sixth man to life in prison. The government of Pakistan, however, came under intense international scrutiny and, as a result, appealed the decision of acquittal to the Supreme Court of Pakistan. Mai's case, which had been pending since 2005, was finally reopened by the Supreme Court in January 2011. In April of that year, the Supreme Court upheld the verdict of the Lahore High Court and acquitted all but one of the defendants. The lone convicted man received a sentence of life imprisonment.

What interests me in this case is how the state moved from helping Mai (albeit under international pressure) to disciplining her as she became more vocal about the injustice. In 2002, Mai received $8,200 in compensation from the Pakistani government; however, by 2005, as she began speaking about her assault outside Pakistan, she was viewed as a threat.[40] Mai's case started receiving extensive media coverage abroad. The *New York Times* columnist Nicholas Kristof wrote about her, noting that he had "come across someone even more extraordinary than Osama [bin Laden]," alluding to Mai's courage in taking on her rapists. He described Mai as "the Rosa Parks for the 21st Century."[41] The BBC covered her efforts to establish a school for girls, and she was named "Woman of the Year" by the US magazine *Glamour*, and "Person of the Week" by ABC news.[42] She was invited to speak in Chicago, New York, and Washington, and her story was mobilized in these spaces to illustrate how violence against women goes unchecked in Pakistan.[43] She, therefore, soon became an object of the sovereign's wrath.

When Mai was invited to speak in the United States in 2005, the then-president, Pervez Musharraf, barred her from traveling abroad. He reasoned that her presence abroad would damage Pakistan's image and explained that his decision was "in the best national interest."[44] This was at the time when Pakistan was positioning itself as a key ally in the US War on Terror. Musharraf later explained: "I truly believed that the invitation would have tarnished Pakistan's international image rather than help improve the lot of women folk in Pakistan or elsewhere in the world. I believe there was a strong ulterior intent of maligning Pakistan by vested interests, rather than sincerely helping Mai out."[45] The travel ban was later lifted when Musharraf came under pressure. He was also censured when, during an interview with the *Washington Post*, he said that the accusation of rape "has become a money making concern. A lot of people say if you want to go abroad and get a visa for Canada or citizenship and be a millionaire, get yourself raped."[46] Musharraf maintains that he was misquoted.

Musharraf's disciplining of Mai was uncharacteristic since his government had tied its reputation to advancing women's status in Pakistan. Not only were more seats than ever before or since reserved for women at all levels of legislature during his tenure, but women were also appointed to senior government positions and a range of laws were modified to remove discrimination towards women. Mai's case is interesting precisely in this context as it shows the intersection of the benevolent and disciplinary dimensions of sovereign power, as well as the interaction of state and imperial sovereignty. The *quam ki beti* becomes a liability and an unruly daughter when she displeases the (national) patriarch either through disobedience or by seeking the help of another (imperial) patriarch. Statist sovereignty in such cases is performed through acts of discipline and reprimand—cancelation of visas, ban on travel, insinuation of lying—that reassert statist control over bodies. These performances of sovereignty are undertaken for the benefit of the national family. While the violation of Mai's body was upsetting to the state, it was more upsetting that she failed to tie herself to the state through the normative idealization of a compliant daughter. In light of this, her embodied violation was overlooked.

Laghari and Mai's cases show how the kinship metaphor of *beti* is mobilized in the service of statist sovereignty. Kinship feelings of care and protection produce paternal publics that tie themselves to the state; in doing so, such publics permit state performances of sovereignty ranging from rescue and forgiveness (Laghari) to reprimand and discipline (Mai). Crucially, the paternal public itself becomes a sovereign actor through policing women in intimate spaces as well as on the streets.[47]

FRATERNAL PUBLICS, THE TALIBAN'S SISTERS

While the Taliban magazines recall multiple instances of national and imperial violence—such as colonial and imperial occupation, torture of prisoners, and drone attacks—a recurring figure that personifies the viscerality of this violence is the figure of the violated (often sexually) Muslim woman. Memories of violence against women have been shown to play a critical role in the formation of national and religious, including militant, publics.[48] In the case of the Taliban, such violence is used to bind magazine readers into a fraternity. The violated Muslim "sister" is simultaneously historical—as stories of specific women are told and retold—and metonymic—a stand-in for all Muslim women, perpetually at risk of being assaulted by the *kuffar*. Islam's honor congeals in her, and her violation therefore stirs up collective humiliation. While the sister is the most prominent kinship figure in the magazines, we also find mentions of daughters and mothers.

Kuffar *Violence, Humiliated Brothers*

One of the female victims of *kuffar* violence most frequently discussed in the Taliban magazines is Aafia Siddiqui. A Pakistani neuroscientist and graduate of MIT and Brandeis University, Siddiqui was tried in New York City in

2010 for the attempted assault of an American soldier in Afghanistan in 2003. She is currently in an American prison, serving an eighty-six-year sentence. While she was convicted for assault, Siddiqui had been wanted by the American authorities for her involvement with Al-Qaeda after having been implicated by one of the 9/11 masterminds. Siddiqui and her family maintain her innocence, insisting that she was abducted by Pakistani intelligence and handed over to the United States. They also allege that while in American custody in secret prisons, Siddiqui was abused and sexually assaulted. While some onlookers believe that Siddiqui was indeed involved in terrorist activities, others point to the fact that she was never charged with or convicted of terrorism. They claim that the assault case was a cover-up for her forced abduction, torture, and illegal detention by the Americans. As with Laghari's example, adjudicating the case matters less to the inquiry at hand than tracking how her cause was (and is) taken up by the Taliban to contest the Pakistani state.

In the Taliban magazines, Siddiqui's story is narrated to outline both the Pakistani state's shortcomings in relation to protecting its own citizens and the ongoing imperial assault on Muslims. She is often invoked through gendered and familial idioms, which produce a sense of intimacy between her and the readership. For instance, in an article in *Azan,* Khattab Ismail mobilizes the same kinship metaphor of "daughter" that the state uses to describe its relationship to women, to question the Pakistani regime's treatment of Siddiqui: "the hypocritical Pakistani regime handed their own daughter to the Kuffar . . . the local traitors sold their own daughter."[49] He then alleges that "she was tortured and raped for five years" and humiliated in other ways, such as being "treated exactly like a man." For a woman to be treated as a man suggests an undoing of her gender and the protection that she should be afforded. In light of this violation, Ismail asks his readers, "Oh my beloved Ummah! Where is the honor of Islam? Where is our dignity? Our Muslim sister has been abused and tortured! Her honor has been violated. Isn't it obligatory upon us to rescue our prisoners from the oppression of the Kuffar?"[50] He hails readers as brothers due to their shared membership in the *ummah* and invites them to rescue their siblings. A fraternal public is similarly hailed in *Ihya-e-Khilafat Urdu,* where an author humiliates and reprimands the "sons of Ayesha" for allowing the assault of Muslim women and for not abandoning their comfortable lives to save them.[51] Hazrat Ayesha was one of Prophet Muhammad's wives, and is known among Sunni Muslims as the "mother of believers." In calling his readers "sons of Ayesha" the author not only imagines his audience as predominantly male but also establishes kinship across them, as brothers. Muslim men thereby are collectively humiliated for permitting the assault of their sisters. The editors of *Mujalla Tehrik-e-Taliban* too invoke violence against women as an "insult" *(bay-izzati)* toward the Muslim community.[52]

Another prominent instance of *kuffar* violence that is recalled time and again in the magazines is the Pakistani army's siege of a women's seminary, Jami'a Hafsa, which was affiliated with Lal Masjid in Islamabad. The mosque and its associated men's and women's madrasas started clashing with the government in 2005. Earlier, they had enjoyed close relations with the state. The first imam of the mosque, for instance, was appointed by General Zia ul-Huq to the Majlis-i-Shura, an advisory body that the general had set up to emulate early practices of Muslim governance. During the 1980s, Lal Masjid was used by the US-Pakistan alliance for the recruitment of volunteers to fight the Soviets in Afghanistan.[53] After the exit of the Soviet Union from Afghanistan, the mosque maintained its relations with the *mujahidin* and had connections with Taliban leaders, such as Baitullah Mehsud and Mullah Fazlullah.[54] When the Pakistani state decided to align with the United States in its War on Terror, the Lal Masjid leadership saw it as a betrayal, and the mosque became a center for antistate and anti-American activities.

In 2007, during General Musharraf's tenure, the teachers and students of Lal Masjid and Jami'a Hafsa called for the institution of *sharia*. They started an antivice vigilante campaign, which included kidnapping a woman who was accused of running a brothel, and stopping shopkeepers from selling "un-Islamic" music and movies.[55] Things came to a head when some students attacked the Ministry of Environment, kidnapped a few police officers, and called for a revolt against Musharraf. The government engaged in mediation efforts, which failed. Thus began the army siege of Lal Masjid and Jami'a Hafsa, Operation Sunrise, which lasted from July 3 to July 11, 2007. The students and teachers put up a rigorous fight. In all, more than one hundred students and teachers and eleven army personnel died in the encounter. The mosque and the women's seminary were damaged. This event provoked public outcry and functioned as a catalyst for bringing together otherwise disparate militant groups under the umbrella of Tehrik-e-Taliban Pakistan, which was officially launched five months after the encounter, in December 2007. In the following year, the Taliban and al-Qaeda attacked a number of military and intelligence sites, including the base of the elite commando unit of the army responsible for Operation Sunrise.[56]

The siege of Lal Masjid is taken up in Taliban magazines to promote a distrust of the state. The storming of the women's seminary in particular is construed as both unbelievable and memorable. Images of armed military personnel surrounding women clad in black *burqas* are included to visually convey a sense of the siege. Often the authors assume that the readers know about this particular incident and therefore mention it in passing, sometimes even referring to it implicitly. For example, in an article addressed to Malala, Muhammad Qasim asks her, "Where were you when scores and scores of Muslim women, pious, honorable were slaughtered inside a mosque of Allah in your own capital city? Answer! NO! You were from the perpetrators."[57] At other times, the reminder is more explicit, such as in an article written by Ikrimah Anwar for *Azan,* in which he mentions the "army massacre of Muslim women of Lal Masjid Islamabad in 2007."[58] Through this repetition, the event is kept alive as a wound that fails to heal. It embeds deeper and deeper in the Taliban collective memory, where it loses its specificity and becomes a symbol. The purpose of such memories, however, is less to accurately depict the past than to convey affect and forge a sociality in the present. The assault on Muslim sisters at Lal Masjid provokes outrage and binds the readership as injured brothers who must align with the Taliban to avenge this wrong.

Rape has a central place in this archive. In *Ihya-e-Khilafat Urdu,* Mufti Umar Zaman writes about the "mass rape" *(ijtama-i zina)* of "pure Muslim women" by "animal-like Americans" who "do not let them wear clothes."[59] He exclaims, "our sisters were sold for a few dollars [to Americans] and they were violated."[60] The March 2006 gang rape and murder of fourteen-year-old Abeer al-Janabi by American soldiers in Iraq is specifically invoked to frame the imperial *kafir* as the true "terrorist." Popularly known as the Mahmudiyah rape and killings, the incident involved the gang rape and killing of al-Janabi, as well as the murder of her mother, father, and six-year-old sister by five American army soldiers. In the first issue of *Azan,* we find an excerpt from a court speech by Tariq Mahenna, an American pharmacist who was convicted of conspiracy to provide material support to al-Qaeda.[61] In the speech, he contests his marking as a terrorist and argues that "if we were to somehow bring Abeer al-Janabi back to life in the moment she was being gang-raped by your soldiers, to put her on that witness stand and ask her who the 'terrorists' are, she sure wouldn't be pointing at me."[62]

While the events surrounding the arrest of Aafia Siddiqui, the siege of Jami'a Hafsa, and the rape of Abeer al-Janabi are specific, they facilitate the creation of the figuration of "the violated Muslim sister." This figure becomes an interpretive lens through which the Taliban understand the state of all Muslim women, past and present. For example, they ponder the conditions of the "141 Baloch women" whom the Pakistani army allegedly has in its custody and the "1350 women from Swat whose even *duptta* (scarf) was not seen by outsiders, [but who now are] in jails, secret shelters, and black sites."[63] Baloch women are more purposefully mobilized in a recent December 2020 video circulated by the Taliban, where they are shown protesting against the (alleged) state-backed abductions and disappearances of their family members.[64] This mainstream footage of women is coopted by the Taliban to advance its own antistate agenda. The figuration of "the violated Muslim sister" is again activated as writers imagine the conditions of Muslim women in Syria and Burma. M. Umar in *Azan* laments, "The sisters and the daughters of the Sunnis [who] have been taken away and subjected to horrible abuses in the jails [in Syria]."[65] Here the abuser is not only the non-Muslim imperialist but also the Shia Muslim, who appears in the Taliban worldview as a nonbeliever. Similarly, Aasim Umar, writing in *Ihya-e-Khilafat Urdu,* hints at the rape of "Sunni sisters and daughters" and announces the "funeral of *dini ghairat*."[66] The author's use of the phrase *dini ghairat* (literally, religious honor) is illuminating because it melds masculine and religious honor into one formation: religiously inspired male honor. Likewise, an author in *Azan* addresses former US President Obama and exclaims, "you've raped Muslim women, you've violated honor."[67] The rare women authors featured in the magazines also imagine the pain of their sisters. Umm Khurasan pens "A letter from a *mujahida* in Khurasan to a *mujahida* sister in Syria" in *Mujalla Tehrik-e-Taliban,* in which she forges a sisterhood across borders on the basis of their shared pain.[68] She notes that while women are experiencing hardship in Syria, their sisters in Khurasan are not unaware of their difficulties and feel their sorrow: "while your blood flows and your honor is violated, our hearts are bursting with sadness too, our lives become heavy too."[69] Such accounts by women augment fraternal publics, as the pain of these sisters stokes humiliation and becomes an alibi for retaliatory violence.

Humiliated, the "sons of Ayesha" set out for *jihad* and enact the salvific *mujahid* masculinity discussed in the prior chapter. Indeed, Roxanne Euben argues that "what's mobilized by humiliation discourse is not some universal standard of manhood but rather a normative masculinity still widely constituted in terms of the power to provide, protect, and control."[70] We encounter this masculinity in an article in *Azan* in which Allama Ibn Jawzi wonders, "Where are the Men?" He asks, "Oh people! What has happened to you? You have forgotten your religion and have deserted your honor."[71] He chastises Muslim men for not defending the *ummah:* "Woe to you! Are you not hurt by the fact that Allah's enemy and your enemy has become a threat to your lands—those lands which drank the blood of your ancestors? This enemy will humiliate you and enslave you."[72] He goes on to embarrass readers who refuse to fight, by feminizing them: "Oh people! Indeed the flames of war have erupted and the call to Jihad has been made and the doors of the heavens have flung open! So, if you do not take your place in the war, then let your women go so that they may do battle. And go and cover yourselves in perfumes and antimony, oh women of turbans and beards!"[73] Since men are unable to perform their manly duties, women have had to leave the realm of the private to protect themselves: "Do you know what bridles and ropes are made of? They are made out of the hair of women because they didn't have anything else to give! I swear by Allah! This was the hair of those pious and righteous women whom even the sun never glanced upon."[74] Women's entrance in the public is viewed as a source of immense insult by the author and he hopes to provoke that feeling in his readers in turn. Indeed, the author concludes, "tremble with fury . . . because the men have lost their manhood."[75]

Performing *mujahid* masculinity entails both preemptive and retaliatory violence, not necessarily against the specific men who have dishonored Muslim sisters but against the state and imperial *kuffar* that make this violation possible. In *Ihya-e-Khilafat Urdu* an author urges readers to ensure that "each and every sister's and each and every mother's tears are avenged."[76] Such forms of retaliatory violence often have to be *visible,* even spectacles, in order to compensate for past humiliation. The quote from Osama bin Laden featured on the back cover of the sixth issue of *Azan* makes this clear: "The roots of humiliation cannot be crushed except with a hail of bullets . . . without a shower of blood, shame cannot be wiped from the faces."[77] The violated Muslim sister gives affective force to her brothers, buttressing them to engage in *jihad.*[78]

The Wayward Sisters

Just as the state identifies and disciplines "unruly daughters," the Taliban too demarcate sisters who have gone astray, whom I call "wayward sisters." In the magazines, this subject position is occupied by women connected to the Pakistani state or those who explicitly reject the Taliban. Like the *jawan,* these sisters are not written off; they are called on to reconsider their attachments, reform their ways, and join the *jihad.* We find discussion in the magazines of two "wayward sisters" in particular: Malala Yousafzai and Ayesha Gulalai, both of whom are identified as breaching not only Taliban-prescribed norms of ideal womanhood but also the tenets of faith. Yousafzai and Gulalai are both Pashtun women from the tribal areas who do not fit the subject positions that the Taliban make available for women—that is, they are neither the victims of *kuffar* violence nor do they align with the Taliban project (like the *muhajira/mujahida,* whom we met in chapter 4). Instead, both have publicly spoken up against the Taliban. Yousafzai was the victim of a shooting by the Taliban in 2012 and since then has become a global icon for girls' education. Gulalai boasts the honor of having been the first female member of the National Assembly of Pakistan to represent the Federally Administered Tribal Areas, from 2013 to 2018. While other Pakistani women have engaged in such activism, these two women have drawn the Taliban's attention, perhaps because both hail from areas where the group had established strongholds.

Between 2007 and 2009, Mullah Fazlullah's faction of the TTP swiftly took over the valley of Swat, where Yousafzai lived. As part of their brutal campaign, they kidnapped and beheaded people, closed shops, and destroyed property. They also prohibited girls from attending school. Yousafzai spoke out against these atrocities and wrote an Urdu column for the BBC entitled "Diary of a Pakistani Schoolgirl." Consider the following entry, where she reflects on the Taliban's campaign against girls' education:

> I was in a bad mood while going to school because winter vacations are starting from tomorrow. The principal announced the vacations but did not mention the date the school was to reopen. This was the first time this has happened. In the past the reopening date was always announced clearly. The principal did not inform us about the reason behind not announcing the school reopening, but my guess was that the Taleban had announced a ban on girls' education from 15 January. This time round, the girls were not too excited about vacations because they knew if the Taleban implemented their edict they would not be able to come to school again.[79]

Yousafzai's writings eventually led the Taliban to attack her.[80] However, she continued to publicly contest their brutality. She is therefore marked in the magazines as misguided and is infantilized. In *Azan,* Muhammad Qasim refers to her as the "not-so-young 'peace icon' who has seemingly managed to charm the entire world with her 'heroic' antics."[81] He blames "world media" for making "a criminal young woman into an 'international superstar' soon on the way to 'Nobel stardom.'"[82] Qasim questions Yousafzai's and her father's credentials as Muslims, chastising the father for allowing Yousafzai to appear in documentaries without the veil and to speak to male journalists. Even as authors like him question Yousafzai's Muslimness, they leave the door open for her to join them. In an "Open Letter to Malala," Adnan Rasheed, whom we encountered in chapter 3, tries to explain the Taliban's viewpoint to her, noting in particular that they are not against education.[83] Instead, he states that it is a particular type of westernized education that the Taliban contest. After extensive explanations, Rasheed advises Yousafzai to "come back home, adopt the Islamic and Pushtoon culture, join any female Islamic madrassa near your home town, study and learn the book of Allah, and use your pen for Islam and the plight of the Muslim ummah and reveal the conspiracy of the tiny elite who want to enslave the whole humanity for their evil agendas in the name of 'New World Order.'"[84] In another message to Yousafzai, published in *Sunnat-e-Khola,* a student from Madrassat-e-Sharia likewise invites her to reform her ways and pursue the path of *khilafat:* "Come back home Malala and lets join me and other sisters in this madrassa in Khurasan and make the word of Allah supreme even if kuffar hates it."[85]

Similar sentiments are directed toward Gulalai, whose involvement in politics is viewed as a breach of normative Taliban codes of womanhood. In an article in *Sunnat-e-Khola* entitled, "Muslim Woman a political tool," Khaula Aziz lists the various ways in which women have been instrumentalized in Pakistan, from the entertainment and financial industries to politics.[86] Aziz expresses displeasure at the sexual harassment complaints that Gulalai filed against Imran Khan, the chairman of Pakistan Tehrik-e-Insaf (PTI) party. She is careful to note that she is in no way a fan of Khan and in fact does not agree with his "secular ideology." Her contention is only with how Gulalai is being utilized as a "political tool" to distract votes away from PTI and toward its rival party. Ultimately, Aziz argues that Pashtun women like Gulalai should not engage in politics at all. In addition to being misused by the state, according to Aziz, their involvement in politics also takes them away from divinely sanctioned and tribally prescribed gender roles: "Why are you not obeying your Creator Allah Almighty and keeping yourself with in the four walls of your house as Allah commanded Muslim women in Quran ... Why you are not covered in proper veil as commanded by Allah Almighty ... Why are you freely mixing with other men sitting with them, softly speaking to them, especially such provocative closeness with your 'abuser' Imran Khan is questionable ... Why are you not respecting 'Pukhtoon' traditions in which a woman is meant to be hidden not exposed, and respected not humiliated."[87] According to Aziz, then, Gulalai deserves no sympathy for her sexual assault court case for, in a way, she invited the assault. As with Yousafzai, Gulalai is not written off. Both are called on to refashion their attachments, and to orient themselves to the divinely sanctioned sovereign proxy, the Taliban.

More recently, the Taliban also assigned the subject position of "wayward sisters" to women who participate in the Aurat Azadi marches, which are local variants of the global Women's March organized annually on March 8. In a recent (December 2019) issue of *Mujalla Tehrik-e-Taliban*, Mukaram Khurasani argues that the popular slogan of the march, "my body, my choice" *(mera jism, meri marzi)*, spells disaster for society.[88] Women's autonomy, according to Khurasani, would lead to vulgarity and obscenity in society. Instead, he calls on women to recognize the status afforded to them by Islam: "Islam has given women respect through the status of sister, wife, and mother."[89] He strongly objects to women who reject this status, noting that such women should be reprimanded lest their actions lead to the "defeat of Islam."[90]

Both the state and the Taliban thus mobilize kinship feelings to hail paternal and fraternal publics. These feelings bind strangers to the political entities, creating and expanding the scope for sovereign practices, which range from forgiveness and rebuke to violence. In the final section of the chapter, I consider yet another public—estranged from both the state and the Taliban—that performs popular sovereignty through recourse to the same kinship metaphors. I examine protests that emerged around the arrest of Aafia Siddiqui; this time, it is "the people" who mobilize kin feelings to stake a claim on Siddiqui's life and to fashion attachments away from the state.

THE PEOPLE'S SISTERS AND DAUGHTERS

For a number of civil society and religiopolitical groups, including the Taliban, Aafia Siddiqui's case highlights imperial brutality during the War on Terror and the Pakistani state's shortcomings in relation to protecting its citizens. The case has garnered attention in the Pakistani public culture for a number of reasons: first, as an upper-class, highly educated woman, Siddiqui belongs to a segment of society that is normally shielded from state and imperial violence; second, since her case was adjudicated outside Pakistan, it has invigorated fears about the disposability of Pakistani lives; and finally, allegations of her mistreatment in American prisons provides evidence of imperial assault. Therefore, numerous groups that otherwise do not share similar politics—from Islamists to human rights activists—have converged on the issue of her detention. She has been transformed into an icon of sovereign gendered violence and a rallying cry for the defense of Islam.

Siddiqui's arrest and trial in New York prompted a number of public demonstrations. Such gatherings continue to take place on her birthday and on International Women's Day. During these demonstrations, participants question what it means to be a Pakistani citizen and what the state's status is in relation to imperial forces, all the while lamenting the torture of a fellow "sister" and "daughter." They reject the statist and imperial marking of Siddiqui's body as disposable and make a performative claim on her life on behalf of "the people." Siddiqui thus becomes a palpable, intimate figure, as opposed to a woman whom they have never met. A close reading of posters and banners that have appeared during rallies for Siddiqui illustrates how her body and story are taken up both to contest the sovereignty of the state and to assert popular sovereignty through the intimacies of kinship.

Consider figures 18 through 20, taken at protest rallies in Karachi, Islamabad, and Lahore, respectively. Figure 18 shows supporters from the Ladies' Wing of the Muttahida Qaumi Movement (MQM), a secular political party, invoking her as the "nation's daughter." Similarly, the protestors in figure 19 identify her as *quam ki beti* and call for her release. In figure 20, we see PTI supporters describe her as their "innocent sister."[91] These protestors establish kinship with Siddiqui, a position from which they launch their critique of the state and enter into an ambivalent relationship with the sovereign. The complete slogan in figure 19, for instance, reads: "For selling the daughters of the nation to the Americans, Musharraf should be hanged." Feelings of care for their sister lead the protestors to seek the death of the sovereign, Musharraf.

Protesters similarly shame the state for being unable to protect its womenfolk. Consider a poster displayed at a rally in Lahore hosted by the Insaf Student Federation (ISF), the official student wing of PTI. It reads, "Have shame, have decency. Release Dr. Aafia" *(sharam karo, haya karo, Dr. Aafia ko riha karo).*[92] The phrase *sharam karo* (have shame) is a taunt that simultaneously humiliates the state and questions its masculinity for failing to protect its womenfolk. Likewise, the term *haya,* which means modesty and decency, alludes to middle-class notions of respectability linked to women's bodies. In other instances, explicit equivalences are established between women and the nation—both betrayed by the rulers. At a protest by

FIGURE 18. Supporters of MQM at a protest in Karachi condemning the verdict against Aafia Siddiqui. September 28, 2010. Credit: Rizwan Tabassum / AFP via Getty Images.

FIGURE 19. Pakistani civil society activists in Islamabad protesting Aafia Siddiqui's arrest. February 4, 2010. Credit: Aamir Qureshi / AFP via Getty Images.

FIGURE 20. Supporters of PTI demonstrate in support of Aafia Siddiqui in Lahore. February 6, 2010. Credit: Arif Ali / AFP via Getty Figures.

FIGURE 21. Aafia Siddiqui's portrait displayed at a demonstration in Karachi. March 7, 2010. Credit: Asif Hassan / AFP via Getty Images.

Pasban—which until the 1990s was the youth wing of Jamat-e-Islami, a right-wing religious party in Pakistan, but is now independent—we find an image of an emaciated Siddiqui locked inside a cage, left to die (figure 21). The banner reads, "A woman in prison, a nation in chains." The locked-up woman represents a locked-up nation, weakened and emasculated by American aggression.[93] One popular style of posters places an image of a youthful Siddiqui—with a chubby face—alongside one of her in prison (see figure 22). Often, no explanation except "Before" and "After" is provided, the juxtaposition itself being didactic. With her face tilted downwards, eyes closed and darkened, mouth half open, and disheveled hair, this ghost-like figure of Siddiqui haunts the nation. It produces public feelings of fear—"it could have been me"—prompting strangers to seek her freedom through and against the state.

Even as the protesters hold the Pakistani and American states responsible for violence against Siddiqui, their kinship with her paradoxically also means that *they,* too, failed to protect her. Therefore, we also find instances where protesting publics express feelings of shame. During a demonstration in Lahore held by ISF on January 22, 2010, a poster reads, "Sister Aafia, we are ashamed *(sharminda)*" (figure 23). Eve Sedgwick argues that shame "attaches

FIGURE 22. Jamaat-e-Islami supporters protest the detention of Aafia Siddiqui, Karachi. August 17, 2008. Credit: Rizwan Tabassum / AFP via Getty Images.

FIGURE 23. PTI supporters protest in Lahore. January 22, 2010. Credit: Arif Ali / AFP via Getty Images.

FIGURE 24. PTI supporters protest in Lahore. January 22, 2010. Credit: Arif Ali / AFP via Getty Images.

to and sharpens the sense of what one is . . . [it] is the place where the question of identity arises most originarily and most relationally."[94] Shame is thus productive and tied to subjectivation, the becoming of a subject. Siddiqui's incarceration is construed as a personal assault, and is cemented as such—these young virile men have admittedly failed in their duty to protect their sister. Indeed, in some posters Siddiqui is imagined as making a direct appeal to her "brothers": "Save me, for the sake of Zahra's *chaddar*" (figure 24). Az-Zahra is an honorific title given to Prophet Muhammad's daughter, Hazrat Fatima, and the long scarf *(chaddar)* here represents her honor. Such emotive appeals, albeit fictive, simultaneously incite shame and jolt her "brothers" into action, fraying their attachment to the state. Indeed, in response, her brothers proclaim: "Dr. Aafia Siddiqui, Nation's sons are with you," as a poster at another PTI rally held in Lahore asserts.[95] The nation's sons will step in, in place of the sovereign, and save their sister.

Feelings of fear, care, and shame then pave the way for diverse actors to form a counterpublic to the state and stake a claim on Siddiqui's life. This intimacy is simultaneously singular (for her) and plural (for all women, as they are historically subjectivated as daughters/sisters). Such localized expressions of popular sovereignties, as Amahl Bishara's work shows us, do not rely on juridical apparatuses of laws or acknowledged rights.[96] Instead, they work through affect. While the excess of feelings and emotions during protests is often viewed pejoratively as the coming together of irrational masses, Deborah Gould argues that we should instead consider political emotion as *nonrational,* since it moves crowds in ways that are "beside, or to the side of, rather than within, conscious, cognitive sense-making."[97] Studying the intersections of emotion and protest illustrates how nonconscious but felt affective states influence political behavior.[98] The affective force of kinship fashions attachment to Siddiqui and moves the protesting publics into ambivalent attachment with the state, such that at times they call for state intervention and at others times seek to displace the state.

These protests were by no means representative of majority opinion in Pakistan, but the performance of popular sovereignty is not contingent on the popularity of an opinion. Such performances function as tentative moments of disruption that call forth additional performances of statist sovereignty. Indeed, against this pressure, the Pakistani state called for Siddiqui's release. In 2010, during her trial in New York, the then-president of Pakistan asked the American envoy to repatriate her under the Pakistan-US prisoner exchange scheme. The prime minister termed her the nation's daughter, saying: "We all are united, and we want the daughter of the nation to come back to Pakistan."[99] The opposition leader also demanded her release.[100] During his election campaign in 2018, the current prime minister, Imran Khan, promised to bring Siddiqui back.[101] And, as I was first drafting this chapter, in March 2019, a member of the Punjab provincial assembly moved a resolution to award her the title of "Daughter of Pakistan."[102]

KINSHIP FEELINGS, MASCULINE PUBLICS

Drawing on the kinship feelings linked to the figure of the *beti,* the Pakistani state articulates itself and hails its male citizens as paternal protectors. It performs sovereignty through forgiveness and reprimand, respectively, in the cases of Laghari and Mai. These cases are public pedagogies for they delineate appropriate and inappropriate styles of political attachment to the state. The ideal attachment advances what the ISPR director general called *Pakistaniyat,* which is both a nationalist ideology and an affective disposition that binds one to the state. Siddiqui's case, however, highlights how the same kinship feelings can be mobilized to fray these attachments. Expressing the will of "the people," protesters signal displeasure with the state and call for their sister's freedom. The Taliban also invoke kinship metaphors to hail and humiliate a fraternal public that readies itself to avenge the violation of Muslim sisters by the *kuffar*.

The dynamics that I have traced in this chapter are possible due to the prior troping of women as subjects of masculinist protection.[103] Not only do the army and the Taliban express domination in and through the trope of the daughter/sister who requires rescue, but the protestors too ultimately call on the state (or themselves) to perform masculinist responsibilities in relation to Siddiqui, and in doing so, reaffirm masculinity's privilege. In these cases, violence against women gets reduced to a violation between men rather than an embodied violation against the women in question.[104] Even rape is transformed into a political sign that stirs up affect deemed to be useful for performances of sovereignty. Ultimately, the paternal and fraternal publics cast women's bodies as proxies for the honor of men, nation, and religion. Women writers and protestors, too, participate in the production of these masculine publics, and in doing so, they too become members of those publics. However, their entry into masculinity is tentative, for it is premised on alignment with the underlying gendered sovereign project.

SIX

Managing Affect

THE MOURNING MOTHER

THE INTER SERVICES PUBLIC RELATIONS (ISPR) music video, "Mitti de ye maan" (This mother of the land, 2015), recounts the sacrifice of a mother whose son, Captain Ali, was killed during a military encounter with the Taliban.[1] The video shows the mother, lost in her thoughts, gazing at the playground and gardens where she used to spend time with her son. Her flat and somber affect is juxtaposed with scenes from the past where she is joyfully playing with her young child. Images of Captain Ali fighting valiantly are interspersed throughout; Ali is eventually shot and killed. The song creatively invokes *maa(n)* (mother) to denote both Captain Ali's mother and the motherland:

> *Mitti de ye maan*
> *Tera haal maan nay poocha hai*
> *Kaisay khoon bahaya main*
> *Sawal maan nay poocha hai*
>
> This mother of the land (motherland)
> mother is asking about your condition
> How I sacrificed my blood for you
> mother is asking about it (translation mine)

The video progresses to show how this mother deals with her loss. Instead of getting disillusioned with the army, she becomes more resolute and proudly welcomes her younger son into military service. She thus performs her duties as an ideal citizen-subject of the state, which require reinterpreting the death of her son as a sacrifice for the national good. This mourning mother continues to tie herself to the state and circulates as a public pedagogy for viewers.

The figure of the mourning mother is often employed during wartime and crises to signify loss.² While in some cases the suffering of the mother can be a forceful appeal for peace, in others, the same suffering is used to fan the flames of war or to legitimize counterinsurgency operations.³ Feminist studies scholar Swati Parashar urges us to pay attention to how states ascribe emotions to the bodies of their citizens, for it is through such utterances that they exercise control over both compliant and deviant subjects.⁴ In this chapter, I follow the figure of the mourning mother to examine the political and affective work that she performs in Pakistani public culture. I pay particular attention to how this figure has been invoked in the aftermath of the APS attack as well as during the state's counterinsurgency operations.

For the state, the mourning mother performs multiple functions: she is didactic in that she teaches appropriate affect management to mothers whose children may have died on the battlefield or during terrorist attacks; like the *beti* and *behan* in the previous chapter, the mourning mother too activates the protective impulses of the masculinist state and male citizens, producing the ideal affective landscape for counterinsurgency; and finally, in the aftermath of crisis, through her the nation materializes as a mourning collectivity, binds itself to the state, and readies itself for revenge. What is remarkable is that this figure also appears in the Taliban magazines, where she helps to reframe the *mujahidin's* suicide attacks as sacrifices for religion. In both cases, mourning, followed by detachment from the lost object and reattachment to the sovereign, is prescribed as the normative affective trajectory for mothers.

The state, however, is sometimes met by a counterpublic that coheres not through mourning but through politicized melancholia. I examine the political critique of some mothers of APS students who declined the nationally prescribed ways of managing their grief. Instead, they kept the memory of the lost objects (their slain children) alive, and mobilized it to critique the state. Such mothers emerge as "melancholic mothers." In his earlier work, Sigmund Freud posits mourning and melancholia as two distinct reactions to the loss of a beloved object.⁵ With mourning, the lost object is eventually released and the bereaved ego transfers attachment to another object; it thus becomes "free and uninhibited" again.⁶ With melancholia, however, the ego develops a pathological attachment to the lost object and is unwilling to let it go. The melancholic ego internalizes the loss in order to preserve it. Whereas mourning propels one forward, melancholia entails subsisting in the loss. Queer theorists have resisted the pathologization of melancholia, arguing that it can be a creative political force.⁷ It is precisely by rejecting nationalist articulations of their loss, and thereby refusing to perform emotional labor for the state, that melancholic mothers simultaneously contest *and* rework sovereign attachments. Instead of facilitating paternalistic attachments to the state, they perform affective agency that blocks positive collective affectivities toward the state.[8]

EMOTIONAL LABOR FOR THE NATION

In the aftermath of the Taliban attack on APS, article after article, song after song, op-ed after op-ed, and painting after painting represented the attack through the figure of the mourning mother. The front page of the December 17, 2014 issue of *Nawa-i-waqt,* an Urdu-language newspaper in Pakistan, featured nine images—four of them showing injured children and the rest displaying mothers in various stages of mourning. The image most prominently placed shows a woman wailing over a coffin (figure 25). Kneeled on the ground, in the midst of many other coffins, she stretches her arms out as if appealing to God in sheer helplessness. Her *dupatta* has slid off, showing her hair; there are large water stains on her *kurta,* perhaps from kneeling on the

FIGURE 25. Image on the front page of *Nawa-i-Waqt,* December 17, 2014. Credit: Reuters / Fayaz Aziz.

FIGURE 26. Painting by Rahat Masud, 2015. Reproduced with permission from the artist.

wet ground or from wiping away her tears. Other women and men surround her, but we cannot see their faces. The caption reads, "The mother of a child martyred during the attack on Peshawar school crying next to the coffin."[9]

Mourning mothers were invoked in other popular cultural representations of the attack as well. A painting by artist Rahat Masud displayed at an exhibition entitled "Massacre of Innocents" at the Alhamra Art Galleries in Lahore in March 2015 (figure 26) follows the genre conventions of the *pietà,* in which the Virgin Mary is seen cradling the slain body of Jesus. Here, we see the

FIGURE 27. Students from the Imamia Students Organization, in Karachi, protest the Taliban attack on APS. December 17, 2014. Credit: Asif Hassan / AFP via Getty Figures.

mother of an APS student *as* the Virgin Mary. The image captures the perenniality of the mourning mother, fusing Virgin Mary and an APS mother and uniting them in their grief. The pain of a mother mourning her son thus features as a transhistorical, known emotion. Whereas the *Nawa-i-waqt* photo represents the more dramatic, high-intensity state of this grief, the stage of wailing, screaming, and sobbing, the painting depicts a subdued state of depression and listlessness. That the painting was later acquired by the Army Museum in Lahore signals the nationalist investment in the latter portrayal.[10]

Marta Zarzycka views the mourning mother as a "strong image" that can guarantee its own identity, regardless of its location, time, and context.[11] Together with the slain child, it forms a cluster that accumulates affective and symbolic power with each new iteration.[12] The power of this image lies not in conveying specific information about an event but in its portrayal of the emotions of grief and loss to its multiple publics.[13] The image featured on the front page of *Nawa-e-waqt* is actually from an attack on a church in Peshawar in September 2013. The woman it depicts is mourning the loss of her brother, who was killed during the attack, along with over fifty other people. For a major newspaper and several other smaller outlets to publish this photograph and link it to the APS attack, reframing it as an image of

FIGURE 28. Mian Ijaz ul Hassan, "Massacre of the Innocents," 2015, oil on canvas. Reproduced with permission.

maternal mourning, shows how abstracted yet useful the figure of the mourning mother can be for the representation of grief. The same image was reproduced as a poster at a rally against the Taliban after the APS attack (figure 27) and made its way into a painting exhibited at an APS commemoration event (figure 28). The strong image of the mourning mother can travel from tragedy to tragedy, city to city, abstracted from its specifics while still stimulating grief and loss.

Affective Pedagogies of Mourning

The mourning mother offers a vital affective pedagogy to mothers who have lost their children. She encourages them to reinterpret their loss as a sacrifice necessary to keep the nation safe, to perceive this sacrifice as an honor, and to continue to participate in the nation-building process. Captain Ali's mother is a case in point. She mourns the loss of her son but correctly interprets it as her sacrifice for her country, one that she remains willing to undertake again. By contributing the right feelings to the collective, the mourning mother performs emotional labor for the nation. Sociologist Arlie Hochschild defines emotional labor as the effort undertaken "to induce or suppress feeling in order to sustain the outward countenance that produces the proper state of mind in others."[14] Through their emotional labor, mourning mothers sustain the nation-state as an object of love, bolstering attachment to it, especially in times of crisis.

To facilitate the channeling of the mothers' grief toward reaffirming the nation, the Pakistani state assigned the title of "martyr" to the APS children. In the hierarchy of deaths, martyrdom is the highest form. Originally reserved for those who die in the cause of Islam, it is now also used by the state to refer to soldiers who die on the battlefield. By extending this status to the APS children, the state assigns a meta meaning to the mothers' loss and gives it a distinguished place in the national and religious cosmologies.[15] The children now reside alongside the brave soldiers and Muslim warriors of the past. They were not victims of a state unable to secure its own school but willing martyrs who sacrificed themselves for the state. Their mothers are assimilated into the same national cosmologies as "mothers of martyrs."

The success of this pedagogy is evident through its echoes in public culture, where the APS children were interpreted primarily through nationalist frames. Consider an article entitled, "Mother, forgive me," in *Jang Urdu,* which is one of Pakistan's largest Urdu-language newspapers.[16] The author paints a picture of the events that must have transpired during that day at the

APS: as it did every other morning, the school assembly began with the recitation of the Quran. This was followed by the singing of the national anthem, through which, the author imagines, "the children expressed not only the stature of their homeland but also announced their strength, courage, and steadfastness."[17] The students then dispersed to their classrooms, where their teachers took attendance. The author imbues religious and national connotations to the students' responses to their teacher:

> as the children respond with, "present, sir" or "present, madam" they were actually saying: "O homeland, we are present. We will nurture you with our blood and will protect you." The children go on to say: "Oh Allah, we are your believers, we are at your behest. We will give blood and our lives. And we are present for this country of Pakistan that you have given us. Oh Allah, our small lives are insignificant in your magnanimity. But, accept our gift and keep our homeland prosperous. And keep my friends, my parents, my elders, and each particle of my homeland in your safety. Vanquish the enemies of our homeland." While the children were expressing their determination and sacrifice with each utterance of "present, sir" or "present, madam," at home their mothers were getting restless as if aware of the impending disaster. They had sent their beloved children off after feeding them breakfast, after combing their hair.[18]

In this extract, trust in Allah, sacrifice for the nation, and the love of the mother coalesce to establish a connective chain of sorts: love for Allah is to be expressed through love for the nation, and love for the nation calls on the children and their mothers to sacrifice for it. Reliance on religious and national symbols transforms these ordinary deaths into sacrificial ones. The author then envisions how anxious the mothers must have been upon hearing about the shooting. They must have run towards the school, praying for the safety of their children and trying to sneak a peek inside against the sounds of guns and ambulances. They must have seen their children's disheveled hair, the same hair they had combed earlier that morning. They must have witnessed their neatly pressed uniforms and polished shoes now drenched in blood. But the children must have had smiles on their faces, as they (posthumously) say: "Mother, don't cry. We have sacrificed our lives for our nation, for our religion *(din)*. Mother, tell historians that we are continuing the tradition of sacrifices that those before us had given for this nation. Don't let anyone say that innocent children and students have made no contributions for this country . . . . Mother, tell *abba* (father) that he should be proud that his son gave his life for the homeland. But ask for his forgiveness too because

I gave my life without seeking his permission."[19] According to this narration, the mother and *abba* should transform their mourning into pride, for their son has achieved martyrdom.

The APS mothers were praised in public culture for being resilient and for tolerating immense pain for the good of the nation. A *Dawn* news opinion piece published a few days after the APS attack awards the title of "Woman of the Year" to "the Pakistani mother": "Nearly 150 of them buried their children in this the last month of the year, and no assessment of women can be complete without saluting the courage of these mothers. If war has defined Pakistan's politics in 2014, the resilience of the Pakistani mother has been its least saluted constituency."[20] Similarly, on the occasion of International Women's Day in March 2015, a blog entry in *The Express Tribune* listing "14 Pakistani women who help us hold our heads up high" reserves the "top spot" for "The mothers of APS' murdered children."[21] The author explains that "their children were taken from them by a war which had absolutely nothing to do with them and these mothers are now making the ultimate sacrifice; trying to move on."[22]

It is assumed that after a period of mourning, the mothers will move on for the sake of the nation. In doing so, they also facilitate others in moving forward in national time. Even fictive children are enrolled in this enterprise. For instance, in a popular song, "Mother, who will you swing on the swings" *(Maa kisko jhulao gi jhoola)*, the child advises his mother not to punish herself with grief.[23] Likewise, in a poem in *The Express Tribune* portraying the viewpoint of a slain child, the child tells his mother not to cry since his scars and wounds have healed.[24] He is not haunted by the monsters anymore; he rests in heaven under the wings of fairies; he is cared for like a royal, fed with desserts and sweets. He no longer weeps when he recalls his mother and *baba*, his teachers, his school and his books, so:

> ... wipe off your tears,
> And worry not,
> O' Mother, cry not.[25]

Articles in the ISPR's *Hilal* similarly cajole mothers to move on. In a piece entitled "Beyond the Day of APS Tragedy," Amir Zia praises a slain child's parents for not crying during his funeral but instead "being proud of their sacrifice."[26] Effectively, they are called on to emulate the parents of dead soldiers.

There is a fairly well-established affective script for mothers whose sons, as soldiers, have died on the battlefield. Cynthia Enloe notes that militaries often rely on the cooperation of mothers and must win them over if they are to sustain their recruitment efforts.[27] Therefore, "the militarization of mothers—and the very idea of motherhood—has been crucial for any successful manpower formula."[28] The Pakistani state is not any different. The storyline of "Mitti de ye maa(n)" can be found in numerous other ISPR productions as well. In the video "Chaddar hai Maa(n) ki" (Mother's shawl; released in 2012), we encounter a young woman whose soldier-husband dies, leaving her to raise their son by herself.[29] Even though she misses her husband terribly, she soldiers on. In the final scene, we see her predictably proud when her son decides to join the army. The video uses the figure of the woman-parent to signify both the motherland and mothers themselves, and in doing so stresses one's responsibilities to both maternal entities:

> Chadar hai maa'n ki arz-e-watan
> Yeh na bhoolna
> Aye taza waridaan-e-chaman
> Yeh na bhoolna
>
> Treasure this motherland my children
> Hold it close to your hearts forever
> O' new comers never forget your motherland (official ISPR translation)[30]

Yet another ISPR music video, "Khak jo khoon main milai hai," which aired in 2017, features a mother whose eldest son dies while fighting off terrorists.[31] At his funeral, when she receives the Pakistani flag and her son's army cap, her younger son grabs the cap and wears it, as the mother looks on affectionately. These videos, which appear year after year with an almost identical storyline, show that attachment to the nation has to be nurtured repeatedly and is an ongoing process.

A similar narrative is also pursued in the ISPR *Hilal* magazines. *Hilal for Her*'s "Mother of a Martyr—A Hero in Her Own Right" portrays the life of Sadia Rehman after her son dies during an encounter in Swat.[32] Rehman is introduced in the text as "a valiant mother" and "a compassionate and courageous soul." We are told that even though she misses her son terribly, "she is reminded that martyrdom is an answer to all her prayers, because a martyr never dies." These mothers are role models, for they correctly interpret the violent deaths of their sons. As the author explains, "there is no woman who has a stronger character than a mother who embraces her son's martyrdom with pride."[33] Rehman, in fact, is now also on her way to healing. In her son's memory, she has taken the initiative to organize events that bring the families of martyrs together. She explains, "the idea is to pave way for martyrs' families to come together as one. We are a family knitted together by the sacrifices of our sons, fathers and brothers."[34] Here, kinship ties are produced through a shared sense of loss and sacrifice, and the mourning mother, Rehman, plays a key role in forging these ties ideologically, as well as materially, through her labor.

While the mourning mother is a dominant figure through which the loss of soldiers is portrayed, we encounter a few instances of the mourning father in the ISPR archives as well. In the video, "Yaaro mera yaar na raha" (Friends, my friend is no longer, 2015), for instance, we see a father roaming around the house, then wandering though parks, beaches, and a graveyard, lost in thought.[35] He is restless. Ultimately, though, he too reconfigures the death of his son as a sacrifice:

> *jis matti kay sath wo khela*
> *Us matti ko day aaya hoon*
>
> The soil that he played with
> I have returned him to that soil

The father compares his son to a flower whose loss is needed so that the garden can grow. It is this engagement with grief—mourning followed by healing or moving on—that is desired by the nation.[36]

Affective Atmospheres, Grieving Publics

The mourning mother is a remnant through which the nation fathoms the loss of the APS children. Her proliferation in public culture produces the nation as a feeling, grieving public. As people rally around her, they begin to affectively engage with her loss and feel it as their own. Eventually, she produces an atmosphere in which the state is invited to expand its counterinsurgency operations to avenge her and the nation's loss.

Affective atmospheres are salient in the production of attachment to the state. Cultural theorist Ben Anderson notes that "it is through an atmosphere that a represented object will be apprehended and will take on a certain meaning."[37] In the post-APS atmosphere, the mourning mother not only symbolized the assault on the nation but also harnessed publics that sought retaliatory violence from the state. Even a cursory look at posters displayed during rallies in the aftermath of the attack reveals this appetite for revenge: "An eye for an eye. Hang them all. Hang them high. MQM (Pakistan)," says a poster at a rally in Karachi.[38] We see similar sentiments from Lahore: "Hang the terrorists."[39] Although the implicit actor being asked to take revenge here is the state, the political act of the rally itself is a performance of sovereignty by the people, one which assigns death to certain bodies and places them outside the space of the nation. Similar calls for state action appear in the ISPR magazines. In an article entitled "They are not from us," published in *Hilal Urdu,* the author notes, "We will avenge the blood of these children. After all, they are our children."[40] In another article also in *Hilal Urdu,* an author narrates the grief of a mother as a way to call on the state to take further action: "[Even though a year has passed, the] wound is still fresh . . . the mother's lap is still shivering, she still visualizes the dangerous scenes . . . she still has hatred for those terrorists who ruthlessly killed innocent children but *alhumdullilah* [praise be to God] she has the ambition to root out terrorists from the country . . . . On December 16 many mothers lost their children and now these mothers want a safer Pakistan for their remaining children."[41] The mourning mother unites political parties that otherwise disagree on multiple fronts. Speaking at a gathering of parents, the information minister for Khyber Pakhtunkhwa province explained, "the Dec 16 attack has left every house grieving and in agony . . . . It was the APS incident, which forced the government to launch Operation *Zarb-i-Azab* and accelerate military operation in other tribal areas."[42] Needless to add, it is a quick slide from a discourse of revenge to a discourse of war. An article in the ISPR's *Hilal English* is one of many such calls in which the nation appears to be at war: "Pakistan is at war. It is at war with the internal enemy which is being propped up and sustained by the external forces. These are not the normal times and there cannot be business as usual . . . . These are times to form a united front and supplement one another's efforts to win this internal war, which is far from over. This we owe to our country and the future generations. Pakistan must win this war—the sooner the better."[43] The figure of the mourning mother thus generates an affective atmosphere within which the state can launch counterassaults with wide leeway.

The mobilization of the mourning mother that I have traced thus far resonates in other contexts as well. During the Nicaraguan Contra war, the state drew on the mothers of fallen soldiers as a way to channel public grievances away from the state.[44] Similarly, in the case of the United States during the First World War, the "good mother" was one who did not impede the conscription of her son. As Lorraine Bayaard de Volo puts it, "the message was that mothers must not put 'selfish,' 'unreasonable,' and even 'hysterical' emotional attachments to sons above duty to the nation."[45] Mothers thus perform crucial emotional labor to advance political attachments. Yet there are mothers who refuse to undertake this labor. A case in point are the APS mothers who mourned differently and reworked ongoing attachments to the state.

AFFECT ALIEN: THE MELANCHOLIC MOTHER

Photographs from the funeral of APS student Mohammad Ali Khan, in particular those of his mother, Gul-e-Rana, and his grandmother, were perhaps some of the most circulated images in relation to the APS attack.[46] In one instance (figure 29, from the front page of the Urdu newspaper *Daily Express Lahore*), we see Gul-e-Rana holding on tightly to her son's coffin, hunched over it as if speaking to him. Other women surround her and are visibly distressed. A boy of six or seven years has climbed onto something to sneak a peek at the dead body over the shoulders of the women. In another image (figure 30, from the front page of the European edition of the *Wall Street Journal*), we see Khan's grandmother wailing.[47] The constellation of women surrounding a coffin is immediately recognizable as a representation of mourning mothers.

There were, however, several other images of Gul-e-Rana taken by the same media company (Reuters) that were not selected to represent the APS tragedy. These noniconic images advance a different reading of mothers. In figure 31, for instance, we see Gul-e-Rana engaging with Imran Khan, then a member of the National Assembly and chairman of PTI, the party that governed the province where the incident took place. She has a determined expression and gestures assertively, as army men and Khan look on. In figure 32, we see her addressing journalists. She extends her arm to show them a photo of her slain son, seeking to reach a wider audience. She is adamant in her resolve to ensure that he is not erased from personal and collective memory. As Roland Barthes states, "photography has something to do with resurrection . . . . [The photograph presents] reality in a past state: at once the past and the real;" in these terms, the photograph's subject—Gul-e-Rana's son—is always simultaneously present and absent.[48] In figure 33, we see Gul-e-Rana almost a year later, joining other APS mothers in a protest. They were raising their voices against the state's failure to deliver on the promises made after the deaths of their children. These pictures evidence Gul-e-Rana mobilizing the memory of her son

FIGURE 29. Gul-e-Rana, the mother of APS student Mohammad Ali Khan, mourns her son. December 17, 2014. Credit: Reuters / Zohra Bensemra.

FIGURE 30. The grandmother of APS student Mohammad Ali Khan mourns her grandson. December 17, 2014. Credit: Reuters / Zohra Bensemra.

FIGURE 31. Gul-e-Rana with Imran Khan, chairman of PTI. January 2015. Credit: Reuters / Fayaz Aziz.

FIGURE 32. Gul-e-Rana holds up a picture of her deceased son for journalists. December 22, 2014. Credit: Reuters / Fayaz Aziz.

FIGURE 33. Gul-e-Rana protests along with other mothers at Aman Chowk in Peshawar. February 2016. Reproduced with photographer's permission.

to mourn differently. Her loss registers on her face as determination; there is a certain doggedness about her. She resists moving on as is expected of mourning mothers. By staging sit-ins and engaging with journalists and politicians, she keeps the conversation about her slain son open and public. In this way, she figures as an "affect alien" who "ruin[s] the atmosphere" by exposing the bad feelings that are supposed to stay hidden.[49]

Resistance to forgetting, often viewed as melancholia, is frequently considered as an unhealthy response to loss. Queer theorists, however, have retheorized it as a force for creative politics. It is a type of mourning that David Eng and David Kazanjian describe as active rather than passive, militant rather than reactionary, social rather than solipsistic.[50] It is an affective energy that enables social transformation.[51] Instead of renouncing the loss and detaching from it, melancholia is a relationship to the lost object that offers political potential. As Catriona Mortimer-Sandilands explains, "melancholia is not only a denial of the loss of a beloved object but also a potentially politicized way of preserving that object in the midst of a culture that fails to recognize its significance. Melancholia, here, is not a failed or inadequate mourning. Rather, it is a form of socially located embodied memory in which the loss of the beloved constitutes the self, the persistence of which identification acts as an ongoing psychic reminder of the fact of death."[52] Melancholia is what Sara Ahmed contends causes blockage in our collective orientation towards hegemonic structures.[53] I view Gul-e-Rana and other mothers like her as "melancholic mothers." Their melancholia manifests in their refusal to perform statist scripts of mourning.

In January 2016, Gul-e-Rana participated in a press conference held outside a hospital at Charsadda, where victims of yet another Taliban attack were being treated.[54] This time, four gunmen had opened fire at Bacha Khan University, killing at least twenty people and wounding another twenty. Speaking to a group of reporters, she compares the grief of the mothers whose children were killed at the APS in 2014 to that of the mothers who lost their children at Bacha Khan University. She calls out the government for not instituting proper measures after the APS attack. Had they done so, she argues, the events of Bacha Khan would not have happened:

> Kill us once so that we are finished. Instead of dying each day, it's better that we die once ... you are running after official electoral seats *(kursi)* ... and the national action plan [which was devised as a response to the APS attack] ... where is it? Who is implementing it? In the past mothers were crying, and one year, one month, and six days later, again mothers are crying. ... How long will mothers continue to be left without support? How long will our generations die? Our lineage is ending. Who will take our name? How long? Tell me how long?
>
> Are we paying the ransom for being Pakistanis? Or is it for being Muslims? ... What should we do? Where should we go? Tell me, should we leave Pakistan? Become displaced? At least that way we will stay alive ...
>
> ... [They tell us to] send children to school. Today schools are open to show the terrorists [that the nation is strong]. We did this earlier too last year [referring to the APS attack]. What did we get? Again, we received corpses. Again, our sons died. Again, parents are left without support ... the elderly fathers who pick up the corpses of their young sons, they know [the pain]; the ones who bury their loved ones, they know [the pain]. You [addressing Imran Khan] don't know because your children study abroad. Your children do not study in Pakistan's Khyber Pakhtunkhwa. Tell Imran Khan to enroll his sons in schools here. Why doesn't he? Let them study here. Tell them to study in APS. Tell them to study in Charsadda University. Then you will know.[55]

Gul-e-Rana also rejects her articulation as a national sacrificial figure through the epithets of "brave" *(bahadur)* and "great" *(azeem)*, and interrogates the use of honorifics such as "martyr" *(shahid)* for the slain children: "[They call us] brave . . . we are not brave. [They call us] great . . . we are not great. They keep calling us great. They say, he was martyr. You told this to mothers yesterday, that [their sons] were martyrs. How was he martyred? Is this a joke? Every day you feed us that they are martyrs, they will be in heaven . . . that they are martyrs, they will be in heaven."[56] Gul-e-Rana finds the reduction of her son's killing to martyrdom comical: "Is this a joke?" In popular imagination, a *shahid* becomes a *shahid* not only due to the cause that he fights for but also because he is chosen by Allah for that special cause and hence is rewarded with heaven. By rejecting the title of *shahid* for her son, Gul-e-Rana contests the statist and social resignification of her son's killing as a sacred sacrifice and grounds it back in the profane. She shifts the focus to suffering, enduring loss, and ongoing state and nonstate violence. Her rejection of the honorific is also a rejection of the state's sovereign right to assign meaning to life and death.

Gul-e-Rana is not alone. Mothers whose children have been killed, as well as those who have been injured, have sought accountability from the state. They have held commemorative events and met at each other's homes.[57] They have staged sit-ins featuring large photographs of their slain sons as well as mnemonic objects such as T-shirts, glasses, books, and backpacks. They have cursed politicians and tried to engage the media. Their protests however have remained on the margins of public culture; their statements often appeared in citizen-generated media, lesser-known publications, and on social media, including amateur videos on YouTube. These mothers both refuse nationalist interpretations of their loss *and* utilize them to critique the state.

For instance, during the first anniversary of the APS attack, one mother, Farahnaz, exclaimed, "People say I should be proud because my son is a martyr; would any mother willingly trade places with me so she would feel this 'pride'?"[58] Mothers protested the sluggish pace of police investigations and the delay in disbursement of medical funds, and called for the institution of a judicial inquiry. When Imran Khan visited APS in January 2015, protestors did not let him enter the premises as planned; he had to use a different entrance. A mother criticized him for announcing and celebrating his marriage a mere month after the attack: "You were busy getting married without doing anything about my child who died less than a month ago."[59] During a "peace conference" organized by state officials in May 2015, a mother exclaimed, "We do not give a toss about the Tehreek-i-Taliban Pakistan, the Islamic State or the Afghan Taliban. We only want the perpetrators of the December 16 Peshawar carnage to be produced before us."[60] Another mother,

Shahana Ajoon, even mocked the state's effort to rename a road after her son: "What good is that?" she asked.[61]

Melancholic mothers often rearticulate themselves as citizens who deserve redress instead of glorification. When interviewed by Aaj News in 2014, a mother addressed the prime minister of Pakistan directly, calling him out for delaying justice and causing additional suffering:

> If Nawaz Sharif's daughter, Maryam Nawaz had been shot, would he be sitting [idle]? Would he be sitting like this? If Kulsoom Nawaz [Nawaz Sharif's wife] had been shot, would he be sitting like this? Your speeches, all your efforts, how much pain can they address? What can you do? Because of you four more people died. Because you came to visit, all roads are blocked, ambulances cannot enter. Why? *Ji, Vazir* is coming. President is coming. All roads are blocked. The people who were trying to find their kids, they also died. Is this our government? How will you show your faces? ... One time, one time if only one of their kids gets shot ...[62]

In other cases, mothers asked for details of the efforts that the state had undertaken to arrest the terrorists. Falak Naz, who lost two sons during the attack, queried: "I want answers. Who have they prosecuted and hanged? I don't know who these men were or what they did exactly. When were they caught? From where? How do we know these men were not already in jail? ... What about the facilitators? The men who led the terrorists to our children, to my sons, where are they?"[63] Another mother of a child who was disabled as a result of the attack speaks in a bystander video about the lack of support from state officials and the delays in releasing the promised medical funds.[64] Standing outside what looks like a government building, she speaks to a group of men who have gathered. Her video seems to have been taken by one of them and later posted on YouTube. The mother's displeasure is palpable in her loud voice and elaborate gestures:

> The people who reside in these big big bungalows ... and take bribes and *haram* [something that is forbidden under Islamic law] ... this is our children's blood money, which they have taken .... Why has my son been disabled for over a year now? When I bathe my adult child, he cries with shame. When I see my son, he tells me, *"Ammi,* it would have been better had I died." I tell him, "No, I am your mother, I have taken care of you before too, and I can take care of you now too." Don't they fear God? Won't they die? ... *Baighairatoon* (without honor), we are not begging. We are asking for our rights ...[65]

Disabled children, like this mother's son, have an ambiguous presence in the nation since they simultaneously represent the horrors of militarisms and are mobilized by the militaristic state as icons of sacrifice.[66] Instead of viewing her son's injuries as a willing sacrifice, this mother demands compensation in the form of medical aid, asserting herself as a citizen who has certain rights. She details her encounter with a bureaucrat who was supposed to approve medical funds for her son but instead called her "difficult" and a "burden": "our children, Pakistan's children, are a burden on these dishonorable men?," she asks.[67] This mother repeatedly uses the term *baighairat* to shame the bureaucrats into action. As discussed earlier, the term *baighairat* has specific meanings in relation to men in the Pakistani context—*bai* means without and *ghairat* means honor, shame, modesty, and self-respect. To call a man *baighairat* is to insinuate that he lacks honor and is unable to perform his gendered responsibilities. As representatives of the state, these bureaucrats were deemed *baighairat* not only for being unable to perform their professional responsibilities but also for not enacting the manhood of the state. She therefore angrily points to the state's duplicity in calling the slain children, "Pakistan's children": "Weren't our [disabled] children the children of the nation [too]? They were shot inside their school, inside an *army* school [she emphasizes *army*]. Our children also wanted to study. Our children also wished to be officers. Why don't they get their rights? Why are they taking away their rights? Should we forever stay uneducated, ignorant, tribal?"[68] In these scenes, we also observe the powerful role that media technology plays in facilitating the travel of narratives that interrogate ongoing attachments to the state. Through amateur videos, as well as private channels and independent journalists, mothers forge a counterpublic. This media—the media of the street, the one that relies on cell phones, and evades censorship—works as a kind of countersurveillance of the state.[69]

Some mothers use the state's own rhetoric of martyrdom to take it to task. For instance, during an interview for ARY Digital, a popular Pakistani television channel, an APS student's mother, Seema Atiq, demands that her son be awarded the state's highest military honor, *Nishan-e-Haider*, a distinction normally reserved for soldiers.[70] She argues that her son "has sacrificed for his country. That is why we are saying that our children have the right to *Nishan-e-Haider* so that we can get assurance that their lives were not wasted, that their blood was not wasted. We want their names to survive even after our lives." Hearing this, the father adds, "We don't want to forget this incident, and neither should our rulers." Such demands for awards from the mothers, while numerous, have often been dismissed for they do not fit the somber sacrificial image of the mourning mother. Crucially, the state is also invested in keeping some distance between fallen soldiers and fallen citizens as it relies on the former for its war-making efforts. The television anchor is therefore seen consistently redirecting the conversation with Atiq to memories of her son, Aiman: "Your son is beautiful, good-looking, like a hero." Pointing to a photo where Aiman seems to be posing, she asks, "Was he very interested in styling his hair like this and taking photographs like this? What did he want to be?" Later, the anchor asks the mother about what it feels like to lose her oldest son: "In our society when a mother bears a son, she feels a sense of support . . . she becomes proud. In our society, this happens. And when the firstborn is a son, he secures the mother." Other questions and comments include: "Did he share his secrets with you?"; "Were you a strict mother or a friendly one?"; "When would you get mad at him?"; "He is a hero-like child"; "Did he ask you to feed him sometimes with your hands? When children grow up sometimes they ask for affection like this from their mothers"; "Do you remember his last words as he left for school?" The constant probing and corralling ultimately results in Atiq breaking down and crying. In that moment she becomes the sacrificial mourning mother and performs the kind of affect that she was invited to perform on national television in the first place.

In these examples, we observe evidence of melancholic mothers, mothers who refuse to let go. While some contest statist ascriptions, others mobilize the same ascriptions to demand concessions. In both cases, mourning persists as melancholia. The lost object changes the mother; it reshapes her. As Mortimer-Sandilands notes, "melancholia is a form of preservation of life—a life . . . that is already gone, but whose ghost propels a *changed* understanding of the present."[71] Melancholia even transforms the body at a cellular level. Shahana Ajoon, whose son died at APS, notes, "there are times when I look into the mirror and I don't recognize myself. I didn't talk like this. I didn't look like this. I didn't even think like this."[72] The melancholic mother rises in anger to disarticulate her son's killing as a sacrifice for the nation and rearticulates it as a consequence of state negligence. Asserting sovereignty over the dead child's body through the intimacy of her relationship with him, she rejects the conditions that mark his death as permissible. She thus forges an ambivalent, even oppositional, attachment to the state.

While mothers are minor characters in the Taliban archive, we do encounter them there as well. For the mothers of the Taliban *mujahidin,* mourning begins when their sons or daughters decide to join the Taliban, as this often entails them leaving their biological families. This mourning mother, like the mother in state archives, is called on to manage her emotions and reinterpret the loss of her children as a sacrifice, in this case for the *ummah.*

In a poem entitled "Oh my Mother!", which appears in the fourth issue of *Azan,* Abu Salamah al-Muhajir addresses his mother, whom he left behind when he migrated to the "lands of *jihad.*"[73] The poet appeals to her not to lament for him but to understand that he has set out on the path of Allah and will be rewarded accordingly:

> Your son's a *mujahid* so do not bereave
> Would you cry for me as I may be killed?
> For if that occurs, Allah's promise will be fulfilled
> Of our Lord's promise, are you aware?
> Let me inform you, some of what's been prepared
> For your very son, if accepted in this path
> Don't cry my mother, rather smile and laugh
> With the first drop of blood all my sins disappear

He asks his mother to smile through her loss and reframe her mourning into pride:

> So be joyful oh mother, and say this aloud
> My son's a *mujahid,* for this I am proud

The biological mother, however, continues to haunt the *mujahidin,* especially those who leave without parental permission. This ghost—the mourning mother who did not give her permission for *jihad*—is taken up in numerous articles. Her affect is cast as improper as it hinders the *mujahid*'s mission. The *mujahid* is therefore called on to disregard her wishes. For instance, in an article aimed at the "daughters of Hawwa" in *Sunnat-e-Khola,* the author admonishes readers: "don't be ignorant of your obligation. It is your duty to fight *taghoot* [idols or demons]. If parents are obstructing your way then leave them . . . . Inshalla[h] you will be blessed with such a mother that will make you forget the sorrow of abandoning your own mother."[74] Here the author tells readers to look forward to establishing new, nonblood, kinship bonds upon joining the Taliban. In another article in *Azan,* addressed to the "jihadis in the West," the author contemplates the many reasons young men and women might hesitate to join the Taliban, including a "concern for parents."[75] He notes that although seeking permission from parents, particularly from mothers, is crucial, when *jihad* becomes an individual responsibility as opposed to a collective one, such permission is not required: "In fact you must fight even if it is against your parents' wishes."[76] Disregarding the mother's wishes in such instances becomes acceptable. Here, attachment to family is pitted against attachment to the Taliban, and the latter is privileged over the former. The *mujahid* is encouraged to leave behind an aging mother, and by extension other relations, for his cause is greater than any worldly attachment.

The mothers whose children have been killed by the state, in contrast, have a central place in the Taliban cosmology and cultural texts. Their grief is transformed into a battle cry for the *mujahidin.* In *Azan,* Maulana Asim Umar highlights the "pain of Syria" through the figure of the mourning mother: "The flowing tears and stoned eyes of our mothers and daughters betray hope that maybe some Muhammad bin Qasim or Mua'tasim would come and free them."[77] These mothers—and daughters—await the *mujahidin* rather than the state. The same author draws again on this trope in another issue of *Azan,* but this time to mobilize "Muslim brothers of India" for *jihad.*[78] Editors of *Sunnat-e-Khola* ask "How many Ismaels have our mothers sacrificed to raise [the] flag of *La ila ha illala!*" and express sympathy for the mothers who receive the disfigured bodies of their sons.[79] The mourning mother in these instances functions as evidence of state atrocities and authorizes revenge. She fosters feeling publics and thus, operates in a way similar to the threatened sisters and daughters discussed in the previous chapter.

Needless to add, the figurations of the mother considered in this chapter—as either mourning or melancholic—obscure the heterogeneity and complexity of how grief manifests. Yet it is important to account for how the mother appears in public culture and the affective work that she is made to do in the service of stylizing political attachments. This exploration shows that mourning and melancholia are different ways of engaging with loss; the former is the preferred nationalist and Taliban affect, and the latter is a refusal to let go of the lost object. Melancholic mothers speak of personal experiences of loss and depart from the collective scripts of sacrifice that both the state and the Taliban rely on to intensify relations of sovereignty. In doing so, these mothers illuminate the affective dimension of sovereignty.

Conclusion

IMBRICATED SOVEREIGNTIES

IN THIS BOOK, I have told a *particular* story of sovereignty—one that is situated in a discrete time and place, focused on specific actors and their performances. The project's point of departure are the myriad gendered figurations that appear in statist and Taliban texts, each tied to a particular temporality of emergence and carrying the residue of the past. These figures are both symbolic and material, as they represent deeply felt realities within sociocultural and geopolitical formations. My examination of these figurations—the discourses that produce them, the affective publics that cohere through them, as well as their circulation and reiteration—allows for a theorization of sovereignty as an ongoing attachment between claimants of sovereignty and their publics. These attachments are nurtured through performances of Islamomasculinity and intensified through kinship feelings, affective atmospheres and pedagogies, and memory work.

Specifically, through a range of cultural texts, the state and the Taliban recruit strangers into relationships of trust, protection, fraternity, and even love. These relationships become the structure of feelings that permit the classic and everyday acts of sovereignty that we immediately recognize: violence and governance. Accordingly, the book demonstrates the salience of affirmative attachments—of brotherhood and sisterhood, of care and intimacy, of religious or national belonging—as pathways to sovereign violence. In doing so, it also illustrates that political attachments (to the state and Taliban) are shaped by attachments to particular scripts of gender and sexuality, assumptions about normative Islam, conceptions of the family, and imaginations of the past and the future.

Political attachments, however, are not always in the service of power. We also encountered moments when subjects forged a counterpublic. Attachments to the same object (Pakistan, a lost son, martyrdom) or kin-relation (*beti, behan,* brother, mother) were mobilized toward alternate political ends, producing estrangements. Rather than certainty, there is an indeterminacy in sovereign attachments that leaves room for the emergence of alternate politics. Sovereignty thus remains an ongoing and contingent project, never fully accomplished. It is performative, for its claimants must repeatedly engage in practices in addition to violence, such as the production of the cultural texts considered in this book, to give the appearance of their absolute and unqualified claim to it.

The relationships of attachment highlighted in the book could never exhaust the heterogeneity of relations, discourses, and affects that shape political subjects in Pakistan. Indeed, no single story is adequate to understand the complex dynamics of sovereignty. Each story, however, does offer us some clues about the processes through which subjects attach themselves to the sovereign. Together, they highlight how the Pakistani state and Taliban's performances of sovereignty rely on shared cultural repertoires, affective pedagogies, and collective memory, suggesting a complicated imbrication. In particular, the reliance on Islamic referents signals that postcolonial sovereignty in Pakistan continues to be tied to a transcendent reference, even as specific actors draw on it for different effects. Historically polyvalent notions of *jihad, khilafat, kufr,* and *shahadat,* as well as hypermasculine models of Islamic masculinity, *mujahid* and *ghazi,* are invoked to sacralize contemporary political projects. As both the state and the Taliban invoke Muslimness to claim religious legitimacy, they also transform it into a necropolitical discourse, exposing those deemed beyond it to death.

The state and Taliban are decidedly not juxtaposed here in order to draw equivalences between the two. Instead, their juxtaposition is meant to highlight the cultural and affective dimensions of sovereignty across evidently antagonistic entities. Indeed, the differences between the state and the Taliban are abundantly apparent—the Taliban's conceptualization of the political both includes and exceeds the normative boundaries of the modern state, and while both the state and the Taliban perform Islamomasculinity, their underlying vision of normative Islam differs. This difference has material implications for those who live under their political dispensations. As mentioned in this book's introduction, when the Taliban governed parts of Swat and the Malakand region, they implemented their vision of Muslimness through brutal and vicious violence. Furthermore, for all its claims to and mobilization of Islamic categories and symbols of legitimacy, the Pakistani state ultimately operates within the conceptual confines of the modern nation-state and enjoys international recognition on that basis. The purposeful reading of the cultural texts of the two entities side by side is therefore aimed at shifting the discussion of sovereignty away from questions around absolute dominance to ones about entanglements, overlaps, and co-constitution.

While the dynamics highlighted here are particular to the Pakistani cultural scene, the insight that sovereignty is performatively forged through attachment processes may resonate in other contexts as well. In this final chapter, I review the salient themes that we encountered in the book and linger on the kind of world that they conjure.

CORRESPONDENCES *AMIDST* DIFFERENCES

It is not a coincidence that kinship metaphors and religious vocabularies emerge so prominently in both the state and Taliban performances of sovereignty. While assumptions of absolute sovereignty and territorial wholeness were already precarious before 9/11, the Pakistani state and its inhabitants have since experienced a further unraveling of this fantasy. Both imperial US military power and global markets have impinged on expectations of sovereign autonomy, and the Global War on Terror has brought Pakistan into ever-tighter circuits of control, as the United States stretches and diversifies its imperial practices. Against this background, family life and religious communities have emerged as crucial sites for intensifying the fantasies of belonging and authority.[1] We therefore observe renewed efforts by the state to reestablish its relationship of sovereignty by drawing weight from these social relationships. The Taliban similarly draw on religious and familial attachments to advance themselves as sovereign. Each thus vies for a semblance of absolute sovereignty in a landscape marked by fluidity.[2]

The Pakistani state and the Taliban posit the nation and *ummah,* respectively, as primary spaces of belonging and control, or sovereign communities. Both argue for the need for territory in order to guarantee the wellbeing of their members. While in statist cultural texts, Pakistan (or Islam-Country, as chapter 2 notes) appears as such a territorial formation, for the Taliban, territorial aspirations include and move beyond the Westphalian boundaries of Pakistan. Theirs comprises a global territorial domain governed by a different political formation, the *khilafat.* However, the state's and the Taliban's conceptualizations of the political are not radically disconnected. The Pakistani state often relies on Islamic concepts—such as *jihad, shahadat, ummah,* and models of Muslim masculinity—in order to affirm its own legitimacy as a nation-state for Muslims; and Islamist groups such as the Taliban imagine the Pakistani state as an ideal site for the materialization of an Islamic polity. Both permit themselves to engage in armed struggle to secure and defend these fantasies. To invite trust in their abilities as ideal protectors, they mobilize what I call Islamo-masculinity, a performance that simultaneously draws on and crafts prevailing hierarchies of masculinity and normative Muslimness.

In the ISPR's music videos and short films, for example, we encounter the figure of the *jawan,* which is sacralized against its foil, the *talib.* The *jawan* is strong and brave; he is willing to sacrifice his life and family to defend Islam-Country and its inhabitants. He invites the nation to trust him: "When your difficulties overwhelm you, place your hand in theirs."[3] In the *jawan* we encounter the latest incarnation of Muslim warriors, *ghazi,* a discursive melding of masculinity and Islam that transforms the *jawan* into an object of intense love. He thus circulates in public culture as an affective glue that binds the national public to the state. The creation of such allied publics around the *jawan* is evident in the citizen-generated media and public rallies that we encountered in chapter 2. Here, both young as well as middle-aged men imitate the *jawan* and, in doing so, reiterate statist claims to sovereignty.

While the *jawan* is a prominent personification of sovereign power, the head of the state is another salient one. A close reading of the autobiographies of three state leaders in chapter 1 provides a glimpse into how they assign themselves, and through them the state, the right to govern and engage in violence. Like the *jawan,* they too locate threat in other bodies, often those of militants. While the idiom of masculinity remains salient in these performative acts as well, it is intensified through claims to normative Islam. Each leader advances a version of Islam that they believe can improve the welfare of the nation. Attachment to state leaders thus proceeds not only through their performance of dominant masculinities but also through their claims to an Islam that accords with the nation-state. Islamo-masculinity again emerges as salient in binding the reading publics to the sovereign.

The Taliban also perform Islamo-masculinity and in doing so surface as a counterpublic to the state but one that also imitates it. They furnish an alternate political vision by contesting statist claims to Muslimness and advance their political project as divinely sanctioned. Yet in delineating such alternatives, they draw on the same cultural repertoire, Islamic referents, and collective memories as the state. The Taliban rework prevailing attachments to the nation-state by pointing to how the Pakistani state has failed to fulfill its originary promise of instituting an Islamic state. They posit themselves as the soldiers of God who will now undertake *jihad* to bring this promise to fruition. They stake a claim on the space of *ummah* by performing piety exemplified by their sartorial choices and ritualistic practices. At the same time, they dislodge the state from this very space through careful memory work. This includes recalling past alleged violence by the army against fellow Muslims, as well as the army's ongoing facilitation of the American invasion of Afghanistan and military operations in northwestern Pakistan. These episodes of violence are narrated in the Taliban magazines to discredit the army as a defender of Muslims.

Given the Taliban's vociferous claims of Muslimness, the Pakistani state has had to shift its narrative in this regard. In the past, the enemy in the nationalist discourse was assumed to be Hindu; the question was never about Muslimness (proper or improper practice of Islam) but about the threat from the non-Muslim Other. Islam was mobilized by the state to rally all Muslims against this non-Muslim enemy. Indeed, Islamic discourse played a central role in the establishment of Pakistan. The leaders of the Pakistan Movement defined Muslims as a community *(quam)*, distinct from Hindus, that needed a homeland to practice its faith. Muhammad Ali Jinnah, the leader of the Muslim League, is reported to have described the flag of the party as the "flag of Islam."[4] He often used Islam and Pakistan, and Muslims and nation, interchangeably.[5] After partition, religiopolitical parties such as the Jamat-e-Islami persistently called for the establishment of an Islamic republic in Pakistan. Islam has a salient place in the national imaginary, and continues to inform state practices and culture. In particular, the state has partnered with certain religious groups—Deobandi *ulama,* for instance—at various times to augment its religious credentials. During crisis moments, such as during wars with foreign entities, Islam has been mobilized to make meaning of death. The discourses of *jihad* and *shahadat* have enjoyed prominence in the army's narratives for they increase the moral-political value of the life that perishes on the battlefield. In the current moment, however, as the state encounters an enemy that loudly lays claim to Muslimness, we find it participating in the production of normative Muslimness as well. It does so by tying Muslimness to discourses of modernity, development, and middle-class social norms. From this lens then the Taliban emerge as improper Muslims, as they are unable to interpret the Quran according to modern sensibilities. Of course, this is not the first time that the state has invoked normative Muslimness; during the 1971 civil war as well, distinctions were created among Muslims whereby East Pakistanis were marked as improper Muslims for being closer to Hindus. In these sovereign contests, Muslimness is transformed into a site of control and regulation, as both the state and the Taliban pronounce their respective normative boundaries and dispel the Other from it.

Intensifying Relations of Sovereignty

Sovereign attachments that rely on Islamo-masculinities gain intensity through women's figuration as kin-in-danger. From the *quam ki beti* mobilized by the ISPR to the violated sisters who appear in the Taliban magazines, women are conceived of as the repositories of the honor of both Islam and the nation. Their violation not only testifies to the conditions of chaos unleashed by the enemy, but also stirs up collective feelings of humiliation, which produce paternal and fraternal publics (recall chapters 3 and 5). These feeling publics view retaliatory and preemptive violence as permissible, and align with the political claimants who are willing to undertake this rescue effort, either the state or the Taliban.

Women also appear in state and Taliban texts to outline the emotional and gendered labor required to nurture political attachments. The figure of the mourning mother, for instance, teaches mothers of slain soldiers and APS children about appropriate ways of managing grief (chapter 6). While mothers can mourn their losses, they are ultimately pressured to reframe them as sacrifices for the nation and to regenerate attachment to the state. Through this figure the state exercises necromantic power, infusing new meaning into the dead (as sacrificial lives) to advance nationalist attachments.[6] Mourning mothers in the Taliban archive, too, perform similar functions, facilitating the reframing of departed family members as an expression of divine favor. The *quam ki beti* in state archives emerges as yet another pedagogic figure, instructing women to perform appropriate styles of political attachment or risk being reprimanded and disciplined. As female soldiers, army wives, *muhajira* and *mujahida,* women represent the gendered labor needed for nation- or *khilafat*-building projects (chapter 4). On limited occasions they are even called on to participate in active combat. Such figurations of women display the affective dispositions and the emotional labor through which attachment to the state and Taliban are both strengthened and corroborated.

While kin feelings are often mobilized to boost sovereign attachments, we also encounter moments when the same feelings fashion attachments away from the state. Protestors who mobilized kinship relations with Aafia Siddiqui, and the mothers of slain APS children who refused state-prescribed affect are examples of publics that emerge from the breakdown of normative political attachments. Such estrangements not only signal the performativity of sovereignty but also provide a glimpse into potentially different arrangements of power.

My findings build on and extend earlier feminist contributions that highlight how women form the moral economy of nationalism. In these studies, the central concern has been to show how women—as symbols and reproductive bodies—become the material through which national identities, culture, and difference are advanced.[7] In this book, too, we observe that women's figurations are invoked to construct national selves; however, they do much more than that. These figurations produce the affective atmospheres and feeling publics that foster attachment to claimants of sovereignty. Crucially, the book contributes to the field of gender and politics by paying attention to masculinities: figurations of men—as sovereigns or proxy sovereigns—emerge equally as salient as those of women in performances of sovereignty, fanning the flames of militaristic passions.[8] Men's bodies also turn into material through which sovereign attachments unfold. Finally, while in previous studies the state has been appreciated as a key agent in the production of political sentiments, this study reveals a dynamism between competing sovereigns as well their multiple publics. This dynamism appears both in scenarios when sovereign performances are reiterated as well as when they are rejected.

Specifically, the analytic of Islamo-masculinity, as a performance of masculinity that interlinks with normative Islam, enables us to detect affinities between the state's and Taliban's performances of sovereignty. Yet, statist and Taliban assumptions about normative Islam differ vastly. The Taliban, for instance, imagine a version of Islam that they believe emulates the Prophetic *sunnah* (practices of Prophet Muhammad). Their arguments for implementing *sharia* are based on the interpretations of select scholars. Importantly, they also use these interpretations to police public morality, oftentimes violently. The Taliban's interpretations are contested by many who also take the *sunnah* as their guiding principle. In the case of the Pakistani state, while Islam influences legal codes and cultural norms, these codes and norms are also shaped by colonial legacies. Both the Pakistan Penal Code and the Code of Criminal Procedure are legacies of the British colonial period and are based on British common law. During the 1980s, President Zia-ul-Haq set out to "Islamize" these laws.[9] He established a federal Shariat Court that was empowered to review any law and decide whether or not it aligned with a Deobandi version of Islam. If not, the government was compelled to amend it. Through this measure certain scholars' interpretations of the Quran made their way into Pakistani law. An example is the Qisas and Diyat Ordinance of 1990, which was linked to other laws relating to murder and bodily harm that the Shariat Court had found to be contrary to Islam. This ordinance in particular has been used to forgive perpetrators of violence against women, and only recently has an amendment been introduced to close the loophole.[10] The incorporation of *sharia* however has neither been systematic nor consistent. Indeed, many heads of state, including Musharraf and Bhutto (whom we encountered in chapter 1), as well as the army have chosen to distance themselves from it and to align explicitly with democracy and moderation, in hopes of ensuring that Pakistan is not viewed through the same lens as the Taliban.

The different normative Islams of the state and the Taliban also inflect their performances of masculinity and articulation of ideal women-subjects. Even as we observe their similar marshaling of kinship feelings and calls for women's reproductive and emotional labor, the specific ways in which the state and the Taliban regulate women differ. The Taliban, for instance, are notorious for constraining women's physical mobility, interactions with the opposite gender, and access to education, markets, and healthcare. The state regulates women too (as is clearly apparent in chapter 5), but with varied strategies and intensities that align with their version of a "modern" Islam. Thus, even though in the book I draw attention to their shared repertoire in order to work against the common assumption that sovereignty is an absolute quality of the state alone, there are salient differences between the modalities of state and Taliban violence.

This book's examination of political attachments and estrangements through the analytic of Islamo-masculinity, kinship feelings, and memory work would be useful in other contexts too. Indeed, this book supplements other studies on masculinity, militarism, affect, and sovereignty that are often written from the perspective of the US empire, by reversing the gaze. It zooms in on a postcolonial scene where assumptions of absolute sovereignty remain a fantasy, where imperial sovereignty continues to make its presence known through drone strikes, threats, and incarcerations, and where ideas of Westphalian sovereignty sit, often uneasily, alongside notions of divine sovereignty.

The violent clashes between the state and the Taliban are perhaps the most immediate, visible effects of sovereign contests. Such contests, however, have a cultural life too, and this book attempts to elaborate on that. The statist and Taliban claims to sovereignty produce, through their reliance on gender and Muslimness, a range of precarities, from the subordination of women and the hierarchical ranking of masculinities to the designation of some bodies as backward. Both set of claims mythologize women as bearers of communal, national, and familial honor, and men as defenders of that honor. They advance rigid definitions of Muslimness, and acceptable versus failed performances of piety. Such moral binaries further calcify gender and religious difference. Indeed, Victoria Bernal reminds us that while violence is destructive, it is also formative.[11] It lives on, leaving a mark on individuals and communities, as well as on arrangements of power.

The discourses that I have traced are not limited to the realm of high politics. They move sideways, reverberate, and iterate gender, sexual, and ethnic difference. While an ethnographic account of how individuals make meaning of the figurations studied in this book is beyond its scope, we do not have to look too hard to find such evidence of multiscalar reverberations.[12] For instance, in 2010, when floods ravaged the Swat Valley, assumptions about women as bearers of familial honor meant that their mobility was restricted.[13] State and NGO funds were often made available to men but not to women. The widespread articulation of women primarily through their relationships to men also has legal implications, as women are unable to assert their rights as citizens. Likewise, the ethnicization of the *talib* as Pashtun reinforces discrimination against Pashtuns, seeded during British rule. What we have then is the enervation of life in many forms due to sovereign contests—from the decimation of bodies and the destruction of the built environment that sustains life, to the symbolic violence of masculine hierarchies, female subordination, and hardened religious identities. The latter is what Mbembe describes elsewhere as the "small doses" of death that structure everyday life.[14]

While the attachment forces unleashed through the performances of sovereignty considered in the book seem to reproduce ongoing inequalities, they can also be redirected toward different patternings and arrangements of the world. The lifeworlds that I have traced are not a given: any figuration contains within it seeds that can unravel it. In the course of repetition, there is a possibility that subjects may undo or redo figurations in unexpected ways.

We see examples of such instances when subjects forge new attachments. Mothers of slain APS children rebuff the offer of nationalist epithets like *shahid ki maa(n)* (mother of martyr) and instead critique the state and ask for compensation. They protest both state neglect and Taliban violence. They take over public spaces and demand to be recognized not as passive mourning subjects, but as citizen-subjects whose claims for justice should be heard. They persist, create posters, and express their right to appear. These melancholic mothers act from and against the vulnerability introduced into their lives by both terrorism and counterterrorism. When protestors rework the kin feelings attached to *behan* and *beti* to shame the state for letting one of its *beti*s, Aafia Siddiqui, remain incarcerated in the United States, they stake a claim on her life and death against national and imperial sovereigns. By occupying public space, they use their bodies to express care for their sister. They also showcase their own right to exist without being subjected to state and imperial sovereign injury. The state's unruly daughters are yet another case in point. These daughters, such as Mukhtar Mai, deviate from established conventions of political attachments by speaking up when subjected to indifference by the state.

The melancholic mothers, the pro-Siddiqui protestors, and the unruly daughters are all publics that signal the potentiality of affect to escape nationalist and militant attachments. Through these estrangements new attachments can be formed. Of course, the refashioning of attachments does not necessarily lead to more capacious forms of living. For example, the attachments forged by the Taliban, while they invest in a new political world, also bring subjects into tighter circuits of control and violence. There remains, however, the potential that such estrangements may lead to more expansive ways of living; they may point to pathways away from violence. At the same time, redirecting attachments toward nonmilitaristic relations and gender-egalitarian lives requires material and affective infrastructure through which new publics, socialities, and politics can be forged and sustained. The critique offered in this book is a step in that direction.

NOTES

INTRODUCTION

1. Kamran Ghoraeya, "December 16 Pakistan's 9/11," *Jang*, December 29, 2014, https://jang.com.pk/news/18020.

2. HNGN Staff, "Pakistan Prime Minister Nawaz Sharif: 'These are my Children and it is my Loss,'" *HNGN*, December 16, 2014, http://www.hngn.com/articles/52971/20141216/pakistan-prime-minister-nawaz-sharif-children-loss.htm; Ismail Khan, "National Inaction Plan?," *Dawn*, August 28, 2016, https://www.dawn.com/news/1280318.

3. "Pakistan PM Nawaz Sharif Heads to Peshawar, Calls the Attack a 'National Tragedy'" *Times of India*, December 16, 2014, https://timesofindia.indiatimes.com/world/pakistan/Pakistan-PM-Nawaz-Sharif-heads-to-Peshawar-calls-the-attack-a-national-tragedy/articleshow/45534367.cms. Emphasis added.

4. As cited in Timothy McGrath, "3 Reasons Why the Pakistani Taliban Attacked the School in Peshawar," *PRI*, December 16, 2014, https://www.pri.org/stories/2014-12-16/3-reasons-why-pakistani-taliban-attacked-school-peshawar. Emphasis added.

5. On sovereignty and violence see Max Weber, *The Vocation Lectures*, edited by David Owen and Tracy Strong (Indianapolis: Hackett Publishing, 2004).

6. Accounts of sovereignty as bounded by the nation-state and its institutions appear, for the most part, in the disciplines of political science and international relations. For indivisibility as a defining characteristic of state sovereignty, see Hans J. Morgenthau, "The Problem of Sovereignty Reconsidered," *Columbia Law Review* 48, no. 3 (1948): 341–65; this articulation of sovereignty as singular and indivisible draws on Jean Bodin, *On Sovereignty: Four Chapters from Six Books of the Commonwealth* (Cambridge: Cambridge University Press, 1992); for an overview see Caroline Humphrey, "Sovereignty," in *A Companion to the Anthropology of Politics*, ed. David Nugent and Joan Vincent (Oxford: Blackwell Publishing, 2007), 420. For further elaboration of the concept, including its internal and external features, its legislative and constitutional dimensions, and discussions on the scope of the

sovereign, as well as arguments about the decline of state sovereignty, see Wendy Brown, *Walled States, Waning Sovereignty* (Brooklyn: Zone Books, 2010); Alan James, "The Practice of Sovereign Statehood in Contemporary International Society," *Political Studies* 47, no. 3 (1999): 457–73; Daniel Philpott, "Sovereignty: An Introduction and Brief History," *Journal of International Affairs* 48, no. 2 (1995): 353–68.

7. Sara Ahmed, "Communities That Feel: Intensity, Difference and Attachment," in *Affective Encounters,* ed. Anu Koivunen and Susanna Paasonen, 10–24 (Turku: University of Turku, 2001). For more on the intersection of affect and sovereignty, see David Gullette and John Heathershaw, "The Affective Politics of Sovereignty: Reflecting on the 2010 Conflict in Kyrgyzstan," *Nationalities Papers* 43, no. 1 (2015): 122–39; and Ann Stoler, "Affective States," in *A Companion to the Anthropology of Politics,* ed. David Nugent and Joan Vincent, 4–20 (New York: Wiley, 2008).

8. Cynthia Weber, "Performative States," *Millennium* 27, no. 1 (1998): 77–95; Michel Foucault, *The History of Sexuality,* trans. R Hurley, vol. 1, *The Will to Knowledge* (New York: Pantheon Books, 1976), 136.

9. Robert Hariman, *"Public Culture,"* in *Oxford Research Encyclopedia of Communication,* ed. Jon Nussbaum, 1–16 (Oxford: Oxford University Press, 2017).

10. See for instance Nick Meo, "Taliban Recruits Teenage Suicide Bombers for Revenge Attacks," *Telegraph,* May 30, 2009; Mukhtar Khan, "The FM Mullah's and the Taliban's Propaganda War in Pakistan," *Terrorism Monitor* 7, no. 14 (2009).

11. Roxanne Euben calls on scholars to undertake such interpretive efforts in "Spectacles of Sovereignty in Digital Time," *Perspectives on Politics* 15, no. 4 (2017): 1007–33. In doing so, I am also responding to Cynthia Weber's call for the study of the particular practices that confer sovereign status onto states or other claimants; Weber, "Performative States," 92. See also Enrique Galvan-Alvarez, "Performing Sovereignty: War Documentaries and Documentary Wars in Syria," *European Journal of English Studies* 22, no. 2 (2018): 204–16, on how the medium of the war documentary provides a unique opportunity for militia fighters in Syria to appear as competent governing agents.

12. Achille Mbembe, "Necropolitics," *Public Culture* 15, no. 1 (2003): 11–40.

13. Raymond Williams, *The Long Revolution* (London: Hogarth Press, 1961), 47.

14. See Lila Abu-Lughod, *Remaking Women: Feminism and Modernity in the Middle East* (Princeton, NJ: Princeton University Press, 1998); Nira Yuval-Davis, *Gender and Nation* (London: Sage Publications, 1997); Deniz Kandiyoti, *Women, Islam and the State* (Basingstoke: Macmillan, 1991); Jyoti Puri, *Sexual States: Governance and the Decriminalization of Sodomy in India's Present* (Durham, NC: Duke University Press, 2016); Swati Parashar, Ann Tickner, and Jacqui True, eds., *Revisiting Gendered States: Feminist Imaginings of the State in International Relations* (Oxford, UK: Oxford University Press, 2018); Wendy Brown, "Finding the Man in the State," *Feminist Studies* 18, no. 1 (1992): 7–34; Anne McClintock, "Family Feuds: Gender, Nationalism and the Family," *Feminist Review* 44 (1993): 61–81.

15. See Saadia Toor, "Moral Regulation in a Postcolonial Nation-State," *Interventions* 9, no. 2 (2007): 255–75; Moon Charania, *Will the Real Pakistani Woman Please Stand Up?* (New York: McFarland, 2015); Rubina Saigol, "His Rights/Her Duties: Citizen and Mother in the Civics Discourse," *Indian Journal of Gender Studies* 10, no. 3 (2003): 379–404; Neelam Hussain, Samlya Mumtaz, and Rubina Saigol, eds., *Engendering the Nation-State* (Lahore: Simorgh, 1997); Maleeha Aslam, "Islamism and Masculinity: Case Study Pakistan," *Historical Social Research* 39, no. 3 (2014): 135–49.

16. Other useful studies include Adi Kuntsman, "The Soldier and the Terrorist: Sexy Nationalism, Queer Violence," *Sexualities* 11, no. 1–2 (2008): 142–70; and Darcy Leigh and Cynthia Weber, "Gendered and Sexualized Figurations of Security," in *The Routledge Handbook of Gender and Security,* ed. Caron Gentry, Laura Shepherd, and Laura Sjoberg, 83–93 (New York: Routledge, 2019).

17. Cynthia Weber, *Queer International Relations: Sovereignty, Sexuality and the Will to Knowledge* (Oxford: Oxford University Press, 2016), 28–33.

18. Judith Butler, "Bodies and Power Revisited," in *Feminism and the Final Foucault,* ed. Diana Taylor and Karen Vintges, 183–94 (Champaign: University of Illinois Press, 2004).

19. Najeeb Jan discusses how Islam is spatialized in the service of biopower in Najeeb Jan, *The Metacolonial State: Pakistan, Critical Ontology, and the Biopolitical Horizons of Political Islam* (Hoboken, NJ: Wiley, 2019). I follow Jan, but instead of seeing Islam or Muslimness as the space, I see *ummah* as the sovereign space.

20. Muhammad Qasim Zaman, in *Modern Islamic Thought in a Radical Age* (Cambridge: Cambridge University Press, 2012) notes that according to some Deobandi scholars, suicide bombings and other violence may not target fellow Muslims or inviolable non-Muslims.

21. Lauren Berlant and Lee Edelman, *Sex, or the Unbearable* (Durham, NC: Duke University Press, 2014).

22. Muhammad Qasim Zaman, *Islam in Pakistan: A History* (Princeton, NJ: Princeton University Press, 2018), 6.

23. Rafay Mahmood as cited in Fasi Zaka, "The Resurgence of Nationalism in Popular Culture," *Dawn Herald*, February 19, 2019, https://herald.dawn.com /news/1398795.

24. Cynthia Mahmood, *Fighting for Faith and Nation: Dialogues with Sikh Militants* (Philadelphia: University of Pennsylvania Press, 2010), 272.

25. Stathis Kalyvas, *The Logic of Violence in Civil War* (Cambridge: Cambridge University Press, 2006): 218–19.

26. Katherine Brown, in her study of Daesh, argues that instead of seeing such groups as lawless and unorganized or as simply motivated to spread fear, it may be more appropriate to consider them as "proto-states," emerging centers of power that are antagonistic to local structures and seek to wrest authority from them. See Katherine Brown, "Violence and Gender Politics in the Proto-State 'Islamic State,'" in *Revisiting Gendered States,* ed. Swati Parashar, Ann Tickner, and Jacqui True, 174–90 (Oxford: Oxford University Press, 2018): 175.

27. Faisal Devji, *The Terrorist in Search of Humanity: Militant Islam and Global Politics* (London: Hurst, 2009); Talal Asad, "On Suicide Bombing," *Arab Studies Journal* 15/16, no. 2/1 (Fall 2007/Spring 2008): 123–30.

28. Asad, "On Suicide Bombing," 126.

29. Thomas Blom Hansen and Finn Stepputat, "Sovereignty Revisited," *Annual Review of Anthropology* 35 (2006): 296.

30. US Department of State, "Country Reports on Terrorism 2015," https://2009–2017.state.gov/j/ct/rls/crt/2015/257522.htm, accessed September 4, 2019.

31. For a history of this entanglement, see Saadia Toor, *The State of Islam: Culture and Cold War Politics in Pakistan* (London: Pluto Press, 2011); and Ayesha Jalal. *The Struggle for Pakistan* (Cambridge, MA: Harvard University Press, 2014).

32. Charles Hirschkind and Saba Mahmood, "Feminism, the Taliban, and Politics of Counter-Insurgency," *Anthropological Quarterly* 75 no. 2 (2002): 342.

33. Hirschkind and Mahmood, "Feminism, the Taliban, and Politics of Counter-Insurgency," 343.

34. For more see Ahmed Rashid, *Taliban: Militant Islam, Oil and Fundamentalism in Central Asia* (New Haven, CT: Yale University Press, 2010), 21.

35. Muhammad Qasim Zaman, *The Ulama in Contemporary Islam: Custodians of Change* (Princeton, NJ: Princeton University Press, 2007), 137.

36. Zaman, *The Ulama in Contemporary Islam*, 138.

37. The term *sharia* means "path to the water" and denotes divine guidance to human beings for ethical living. Through the careful study of the Quran, Prophetic tradition, and, in the case of the Shia, the tradition of the imams, qualified scholars contemplate the *sharia* to derive laws *(fiqh)*.

38. Azam Tariq, *The Life of Baitullah Masood* (Global Islamic Media Front, n.d.).

39. Tariq, *The Life of Baitullah Masood*.

40. Mona Sheikh, *Guardians of God: Inside the Religious Mind of the Pakistani Taliban* (Oxford: Oxford University Press, 2016), 24.

41. "Pakistani Civilians," *Costs of War*, https://watson.brown.edu/costsofwar/costs/human/civilians/pakistani, last modified November 2018.

42. See chapter 1 in Sheikh, *Guardians of God*, for a detailed history of the rise of the Pakistani Taliban.

43. Shura Ittehad-ul Mujahidin, "The Formation of Shura Ittehad-ul Mujahidin," pamphlet, 2009.

44. Agence France-Presse, "Faction of Pakistani Taliban Announces Breakaway," *Guardian*, May 28, 2014, https://www.theguardian.com/world/2014/may/28/breakaway-faction-splitting-pakistani-taliban.

45. As cited in Ilyas Khan, "Pakistan Violence: Mehsud Faction Walks out of Taliban," *BBC*, May 28, 2014, https://www.bbc.com/news/world-asia-27605651.

46. Bill Roggio, "Mehsud Faction Rejoins the Movement of the Taliban in Pakistan," *Long War Journal*, February 4, 2017 https://www.longwarjournal.org/archives/2017/02/mehsud-faction-rejoins-the-movement-of-the-taliban-in-pakistan.php.

47. "Statement of Leaders Regarding Restructuring," *Ihya-e-Khilafat* (English), Issue 1, October 2014, 4–5.

48. For more details, see Qandeel Siddique, *Tehrik-e-Taliban Pakistan* (Copenhagen: Danish Institute for International Studies, 2010).

49. Founded in 1999, Daesh is an Islamist group that occupied and established a proto-state in parts of Syria and Iraq.

50. Mushtaq Yusufzai, "Pakistani Taliban Fires Spokesman over ISIS Pledge of Allegiance," *NBC News,* August 27, 2014, https://www.nbcnews.com/news/world /pakistani-taliban-fires-spokesman-over-isis-pledge-allegiance-n230511.

51. TTP, "Statement on UN Report," Umar Media, July 29, 2020.

52. For more on religion and sovereignty, see David Gilmartin, Pamela Price, and Arild Ruud, eds., *South Asian Sovereignty: The Conundrum of Worldly Power* (New York: Routledge, 2020).

53. Mullah Fazllulah, who led this takeover, was for a long time an activist of Tehrik-e-Nifaz-i-Sharia Muhammadi (TNSM), an organization founded by his father-in-law, Sufi Muhammad, in 1989 with the objective of instituting *sharia* in the Swat region. In 2001, Sufi Muhammad led a group of fighters to Afghanistan to resist US and NATO bombings; in 2002, Pervez Musharraf, then the president of Pakistan, banned TNSM and arrested Sufi Muhammad. Sufi's arrest made Mullah Fazllulah the de facto leader of the now banned TNSM. The organization continued its activities, moving into the political domain and supporting right-wing religious parties. When the Tehrik-e-Taliban was formed in 2007, some analysts, such as Qandeel Siddique note that Mullah Fazllulah was declared the head of the Swat chapter of TTP; Siddique, *Tehrik-e-Taliban Pakistan.* Others, such as Hassan Abbas, note that TNSM was not formally a member but was anxious to join; Hassan Abbas, "A Profile of Tehrik-i-Taliban Pakistan," *CTC Sentinel* 1 no. 2 (2009): 1–4. There is however agreement that Mullah Fazllulah ultimately became the amir of TTP after the death of Baitullah Mehsud.

54. Siddique, *Tehrik-e-Taliban,* 62.

55. Islamabad Policy Research Institute, "Text of Swat Peace Accord," https:// peacemaker.un.org/sites/peacemaker.un.org/files/PA_090116_Swat%20Peace%20 Accord.pdf, accessed September 4, 2019.

56. Shahzad Akhtar, "Defeating TTP: An Appraisal of Pakistan's Counterinsurgency Operations," *Pakistan Politico,* December 12, 2018, http://pakistanpolitico .com/defeating-ttp-an-appraisal-of-pakistans-counterinsurgency-operations/; Ayesha Siddiqa, *Pakistan Military: Ethnic Balance in the Armed Forces and Problems of Federalism,* Manekshaw Papers, no. 39 (New Delhi: Centre for Land Warfare Studies, 2013); Amira Jadoon and Sara Mahmood, "Fixing the Cracks in the Pakistani Taliban's Foundation," *CTC Sentinel* no. 11 (2018): 21–25.

57. Tehrik-e-Taliban, "Lah-e-Amal" (Code of Conduct), Umar Media, September 2018.

58. Dilawar Wazir, "Pamphlet Warns Police to Leave S. Waziristan in Three Days," *Dawn,* April 23, 2019, https://www.dawn.com/news/1477791/pamphlet-warns-police-to-leave-s-waziristan-in-three-days.

59. Pazir Gul, "TTP Warns against Playing Music, Women Going out Alone in Miramshah," *Dawn*, August 1, 2019, https://www.dawn.com/news/1497395.

60. Gul, "TTP Warns." In the Pakistani context, DJs are often hired to play at weddings or other festive events.

61. Abdul Basit, "The Rebranded 'Pakistani Taliban' May Pose a Renewed Threat," *TRTworld*, August 22, 2020, https://www.trtworld.com/opinion/the-rebranded-pakistani-taliban-may-pose-a-renewed-threat-39082; Amira Jadoon (@amirajadoon), "As I have said before, we can't be complacent about the Pakistani Taliban," Twitter, August 14, 2020, 9:25 A.M. https://twitter.com/AmiraJadoon/status/1294294119632850947.

62. Abu Mansoor Asim, "To the Mujahidin Busy Undertaking Jihad in Pakistan," *Mujalla Tehrik-e-Taliban*, no. 8, November 2020, pp. 4–7.

63. See note 6 above.

64. Also see Inderpal Grewal, *Saving the Security State* (Durham, NC: Duke University Press, 2017); Stephen Krasner, *Sovereignty: Organized Hypocrisy* (Princeton, NJ: Princeton University Press, 1999); Sigal Ben-Porath and Rogers Smith, *Varieties of Sovereignty and Citizenship* (Philadelphia: University of Pennsylvania Press, 2012); Luke Glanville, "The Myth of 'Traditional' Sovereignty," *International Studies Quarterly* 57, no. 1 (2013): 79–90.

65. See Amit Baishya's analysis of the writings of militants from Assam in India; Amit Baishya, *Contemporary Literature from Northeast India* (London: Routledge, 2019). In addition, both Lucia Michelutti and Caroline Humphrey point to mafia networks as localized systems of sovereignties premised on the capacity for violence, control over underground economies, and administration of justice; Lucia Michelutti, *Mafia Raj: The Rule of Bosses in South Asia* (Stanford, CA: Stanford University Press, 2018); Humphrey, "Sovereignty."

66. Anushay Malik, "Public Authority and Local Resistance: Abdur Rehman and the Industrial Workers of Lahore, 1969–1974," *Modern Asian Studies* 52, no. 3 (2018): 815–48; Sanaa Alimia, "Performing the Afghanistan-Pakistan Border through Refugee ID Cards," *Geopolitics* 24, no. 2 (2019): 391–425.

67. Darryl Li, "From Exception to Empire: Sovereignty, Carceral Circulation, and the 'Global War on Terror,'" in *Ethnographies of U.S. Empire,* ed. Carole McGranahan and John Collins, 457–58 (Durham, NC: Duke University Press, 2018). Also see Saskia Sassen, *Territory, Authority, Rights: From Medieval to Global Assemblages* (Princeton, NJ: Princeton University Press, 2006).

68. Thomas Hansen and Finn Stepputat, *Sovereign Bodies: Citizens, Migrants, and States in the Postcolonial World* (Princeton, NJ: Princeton University Press, 2005), 3.

69. Weber, "Performative States," 92.

70. Giorgio Agamben, *Homo Sacer: Sovereign Power and Bare Life*, translated by Daniel Heller-Roazen (Stanford, CA: Stanford University Press, 1998).

71. Rubina Saigol, *The Pakistan Project: A Feminist Perspective on Nation and Identity* (Delhi: Women Unlimited, 2013), 14; Lala Rukh, "ImageNation: A Visual Text," in *Engendering the Nation-State,* ed. Neelam Hussain, Samiya Mumtaz, and

Rubina Saigol, 75–101 (Lahore: Simorg, 1997); Aneela Zeb Babar, "Texts of War: The Religio-Military Nexus and Construction of Gender Identity in Pakistan and India," *Gender, Technology and Development* 4 no. 3 (2000): 441–64. On this topic, also see Katherine Zien's work in the interstitial space of the Panama Canal Zone, which furnishes us with an example of how popular entertainments, patriotic pageants, opera concerts, and national theater can be sites for struggle for sovereignty; Katherine Zien, *Sovereign Acts: Performing Race, Space, and Belonging in Panama and the Canal Zone* (New Brunswick, NJ: Rutgers University Press, 2017). Also see Catherine Lutz, "A Military History of the American Suburbs, the Discipline of Economics, and All Things Ordinary," *Antipode* 43, no. 3 (2011): 901–6, in which the author emphasizes the critical role of cultural deployments in warfare.

72. Judith Butler theorizes performativity as a stylization of repeated acts that give gender an illusion of stability, as a naturally occurring formation; Judith Butler, "Performative Acts and Gender Constitution: An Essay in Phenomenology and Feminist Theory," *Theatre Journal* 40, no. 4 (1988): 519–31. Also see Mark Slater, "Places Everyone! Studying the Performativity of the Border," *Political Geography* 30, no. 2 (2011): 61–69.

73. Michael Warner, "Publics and Counterpublics," *Public Culture* 14, no. 1 (2002): 49–90; Lauren Berlant, *The Female Complaint: The Unfinished Business of Sentimentality in American Culture* (Durham, NC: Duke University Press, 2008).

74. Stoler, "Affective States," 9.

75. There are multiple ways of studying affect, and different academic disciplines have advanced their own conceptualizations of it. Brian Massumi describes affects as "pre-personal intensities" that cannot be fully realized in language and are always prior to and/or outside of consciousness. In contrast, feelings are personal and biographical sensations that an individual can compare to previous experiences and interpret accordingly; thus, people draw on their personal histories and experiences to interpret their feelings. Emotions, meanwhile, are the *social* expressions or projections of those feelings, and can be genuine or feigned as they are for the consumption of others; Brian Massumi, "Notes on the Translation and Acknowledgments," in *A Thousand Plateaus*, edited by Gilles Deleuze and Felix Guattari, xvi–xix (Minneapolis: University of Minnesota Press, 1987). Affect, feeling, and emotion, however, are linked. I draw on the work of Sara Ahmed, who uses *affect* and *emotion* interchangeably, and Sianne Ngai who views their difference as one of intensity; Sara Ahmed, *The Cultural Politics of Emotion* (Edinburgh: Edinburgh University Press, 2004), and Sianne Ngai, *Ugly Feelings* (Cambridge, MA: Harvard University Press, 2007). Ngai notes that while affects are less formed than emotions, they do not lack form or structure altogether; that is, affects are not meaningless, nor are they devoid of organization or diagnostic power. Affects acquire intensities through movements and transitions: "the passages whereby affects acquire the semantic density and narrative complexity of emotions, and emotions conversely denature into affects" (Ngai, 27). I follow this productive aspect of affects, feelings, and emotions to understand how certain figures—such as the terrorist, the sexually violated sister, or the mourning mother—are not only affectively charged, but also *produce* affective attachments

that may bind or unbind a public. Recent work on the Pakistani state has paid attention to this productive dimension of affect. Nosheen Ali in her examination of the state's management of the Kashmir conflict unpacks how the state is affectively structured and experienced on the ground, and Maria Rashid's work with the families and relatives of fallen soldiers of the Pakistani army provides yet another glimpse into the affective technologies of the state; Nosheen Ali, *Delusional States: Feeling Rule and Development in Pakistan's Northern Frontier* (Cambridge: Cambridge University Press, 2019); Maria Rashid, *Dying to Serve: Militarism, Affect, and the Politics of Sacrifice in the Pakistan Army* (Stanford, CA: Stanford University Press, 2020). For more on affect as circulating, see Sara Ahmed, "Affective Economies," *Social Text* 79, no. 22 (2004), 117, 119.

76. See Ahmed, "Communities That Feel"; Robbie Duschinsky, Monica Greco, and Judith Solomon, "Wait Up!: Attachment and Sovereign Power," *International Journal of Politics, Culture, and Society* 28, no. 3 (2015): 223–42.

77. John Bowlby, "The Nature of the Child's Tie to His Mother," *International Journal of Psychoanalysis* 39 (1958): 350–73.

78. Judith Butler, *The Psychic Life of Power* (Stanford, CA: Stanford University Press, 1997), 45.

79. Lauren Berlant, *Cruel Optimism* (Durham, NC: Duke University Press, 2011), 184.

80. Lauren Berlant, "A Properly Political Concept of Love," *Cultural Anthropology* 26, no. 4 (2011): 683–91, 687.

81. Judith Butler, *Notes toward a Performative Theory of Assembly* (Cambridge, MA: Harvard University Press, 2015), 16.

82. See Rosalind O'Hanlon, "Issues of Masculinity in North Indian History," *Indian Journal of Gender Studies* 4, no. 1 (1997): 1–19; Mrinalini Sinha, "Giving Masculinity a History," *Gender and History* 11, no. 3 (1999): 445–60; Sudipo Kaviraj, "The Myth of Praxis: The Construction of the Figure of Krishna in Krishnacharitra," *Nehru Memorial Museum and Library Occasional Papers on History and Society,* no. 50 (1987): 72–106.

83. See Brown, "Finding the Man in the State"; Parashar, Tickner, and True, *Revisiting Gendered States;* Todd Reeser, *Masculinities in Theory: An Introduction* (West Sussex: Wiley-Blackwell, 2010); R. W. Connell, and James Messerschmidt, "Hegemonic Masculinity: Rethinking the Concept," *Gender and Society* 19, no. 6 (2005): 829–59.

84. Jack Halberstam, *Female Masculinity* (Durham, NC: Duke University Press, 2019).

85. Sinha, "Giving Masculinity a History," 455.

86. See Iris Marion Young, "The Logic of Masculinist Protection: Reflections on the Current Security State," *Signs* 29, no. 1 (2003): 1–25; J. Ann Tickner, *Gender in International Relations* (New York: Columbia University Press, 1992).

87. Anuradha Kapur, "Deity to Crusader: The Changing Iconography of Ram," in *Hindus and Others: The Question of Identity in India Today,* ed. Gyanendra Pandey, 74–109 (New Delhi: Viking Publishers, 1993); Sudipo Kaviraj, "The Myth of

Praxis"; Sikata Banerjee, "Gender and Nationalism: The Masculinization of Hinduism and Female Political Participation in India," *Women's Studies International Forum* 26, no. 2 (2003): 167–79.

88. See Akbar Ahmed, *Jinnah, Pakistan and Islamic Identity: The Search for Saladin* (London: Routledge, 1997); Ayesha Jalal, *The Sole Spokesman: Jinnah, the Muslim League and the Demand for Pakistan* (Cambridge: Cambridge University Press, 1985). In addition, due to the recent turn to women's empowerment in the international development regime, greater foreign funding has become available for the study of masculinity by nonprofit organizations that trace men's attitudes and behaviors in order to address violence against women. This includes studies emerging from USAID and Aurat Foundation, as well as from the South Asian Network to Address Masculinities, a collective of NGOs, academics, and activists. For more, see USAID and Aurat Foundation, *Masculinity in Pakistan: A Formative Research Study,* Gender Equity Program, Aurat Foundation, September 2016.

89. See Maleeha Aslam, *Gender-based Explosions: The Nexus between Muslim Masculinities, Jihadist Islamism and Terrorism* (Tokyo: UNU Press, 2012); Amanullah De Sondy, *The Crisis of Islamic Masculinities* (London: Bloomsbury, 2014); Arsalan Khan, "Pious Masculinity, Ethical Reflexivity, and Moral Order in an Islamic Piety Movement in Pakistan," *Anthropological Quarterly* 91, no. 1, (2018): 53–78.

90. Bonnie Mann, *Sovereign Masculinity: Gender Lessons from the War on Terror* (Oxford: Oxford University Press, 2014).

91. For more, see SherAli Tareen, *Defending Muhammad in Modernity* (Notre Dame, IN: University of Notre Dame Press, 2020), 48–49; Azfar Moin, *The Millennial Sovereign: Sacred Kingship and Sainthood in Islam* (New York: Columbia University Press, 2010).

92. Najam-u-Din, "Pakistan—Media Landscape," *Media Landscapes,* 2019, https://medialandscapes.org/country/pakistan, accessed June 30, 2020.

93. Pakistan Telecommunication Authority, "Achievements," https://www.pta .gov.pk/en/achievements, accessed September 4, 2019.

94. There were 308 daily newspapers in 2016, compared to 437 in 2007, 72 weeklies (463 in 2007), 18 fortnightlies (92 in 2007), 137 monthlies (686 in 2007), and three quarterly publications in 2016 (71 in 2007), as cited in Najam-u-Din, "Pakistan."

95. Najam-u-Din, "Pakistan."

96. Timothy Mitchell, *Colonising Egypt,* Cambridge Middle East Library (Cambridge: Cambridge University Press, 1988).

97. Hansen and Stepputat, *Sovereignty Revisited,* 303.

98. Hansen and Stepputat, *Sovereignty Revisited,* 303.

99. Rashid, *Dying to Serve.* Rashid notes that while the Pakistan Armed Forces consist of three main branches—army, navy, and air force—the land-based force, the army, enjoys access to the most resources, political clout, and privilege.

100. For more see Rashid, *Dying to Serve.*

101. Rubina Saigol argues that the notion of divine sovereignty is often used as an instrument by military dictators and civilian rulers as a way to interpret the divine in a manner that suits their interests; Saigol, *The Pakistan Project.*

102. 92 News HD, "How ISPR works? Haroon Ur Rasheed Comments," February 1, 2020, video, 4:37, https://www.youtube.com/watch?v=_72QXbUnA5w.

103. 92 News HD, "How ISPR works?"

104. "DG ISPR Urges Media to Show Progress, Potential of Pakistan," *Geo News*, December 6, 2018, https://www.geo.tv/latest/220948-dg-ispr-urges-asks-media-to-show-progress-potential-of-pakistan.

105. "Media First Line of Defence in Hybrid War: DG ISPR," *Nation*, November 28, 2018, https://nation.com.pk/28-Nov-2018/media-first-line-of-defence-in-hybrid-war-dg-ispr; "Pak's Media First Line of Defense in Hybrid Warfare: DG ISPR," *Radio Pakistan*, November 27, 2018, http://www.radio.gov.pk/27-11-2018/pakistans-media-first-line-of-defense-in-hybrid-warfare-dg-ispr.

106. *Hilal English* was launched in 2014; *Hilal for Her* in 2018; *Hilal for Kids* (Urdu and English) was launched in November 2018.

107. "About Ourselves," *Mujahid*, October 31, 1952. The first monthly issue of *Hilal Urdu* available on the online ISPR archive is from September 2007. Archived *Hilal* magazines are available online on the ISPR website, https://www.hilal.gov.pk/archive-timeline, accessed August 2020.

108. ISPR and Hafsa Rehan, *Dam-e-Lahoo* (Islamabad: Pakistan Post Foundation, 2018); ISPR, *Junoon-e-Rukh-e-Wafa* (Rawalpindi Cantt: Hilal Publishers, 2018); ISPR, *Moonglade* (Rawalpindi Cantt: Hilal Publishers, 2018). The title *Junoon-e-Rukh-e-Wafa* draws on a poem by Faiz Ahmed Faiz.

109. Some include: Ayesha Siddiqa, *Military Inc.: Inside Pakistan's Military Economy* (Karachi: Oxford University Press, 2007); Hasan Rizvi, *Military, State and Society in Pakistan* (Lahore: Sang-e-Meel Publications, 2003).

110. Some scholars, such as Orla Lehane et al. (2018), believe that *Azan* is published by Afghan Taliban; Orla Lehane et al., "Brides, Black Widows and Baby-Makers; or Not: An Analysis of the Portrayal of Women in English Language Jihadi Magazine Image Content," *Critical Studies on Terrorism* 11, no. 3 (2018): 505–20. However, I align with Haroro Ingram (2015) who argues that it likely associated with Pakistani Taliban; Haroro Ingram, "An Analysis of the Taliban in Khurasan's *Azan* (Issues 1–5)," *Studies in Conflict and Terrorism* 38, no. 7 (2015): 560–79. The basis for this claim is the geographically specific content of the articles.

111. A range of pamphlets archived at the Danish Institute for International Studies give a sense of TTP operations. The collection is an initiative by researcher Mona Kanwal Sheikh:

(a) Unnamed Mujahidin Islam, "Khadija Abdul Qahar" (North Waziristan: North Waziristan Press Club, 2009). In this pamphlet, the authors alert the Pakistani and Canadian governments that Qahar, a Canadian reporter, will be killed shortly if their demands are not met. It asserts that she is actually not a reporter but was collecting intelligence and hence, her killing is legitimate.

(b) "Intiqam" (revenge), 2012. This pamphlet discusses an army operation conducted on January 1, 2012 in the Khyber agency in which the army killed *mujahidin* and arrested women and children. The TTP vows to take revenge and carry out attacks.

(c) Shura Ittehad-ul Mujahidin, "The Formation of Shura Ittehad-ul Mujahidin," 2009. This e-pamphlet announces the establishment of this alliance and lists the names of several faction leaders, including Baitullah Mehsud, Mullah Nazir, and Hafiz Gul Bahadur.

(d) Amir and Shura of North Waziristan, "Announcement from Shura Waziristan for All Inhabitants of Waziristan," 2010. This e-pamphlet informs residents that while the agreement with the government of Pakistan is still in place, it is possible that the Pakistan army may begin operations in Waziristan in exchange for funds from the United States. The Shura asks the government not to do so if it wishes to avoid destruction of additional homes; if the government starts an operation, the TTP will respond with *jihad*. The Shura also asks inhabitants of Waziristan to join forces with the Taliban.

(e) Shura Ittehad-ul Mujahidin, "Announcement," n.d. In this pamphlet the Shura notes that the army is violating agreements according to which it was to remove itself from Waziristan. The note calls for the army to limit military drills to certain days of the month, to leave specific areas, to cease drone strikes, and to release all prisoners. The Shura gives the army ten days to do so.

(f) Shura Mujahidin, "War Restrictions in North Waziristan," 2009. This pamphlet informs residents of North Waziristan that after the declaration of war, entrance to forts and city centers will be forbidden. Furthermore, public gatherings of five or more people are also forbidden. Those who violate these injunctions will be considered part of the government's peace committees and will be killed.

(g) Amir and Shura of Mujahidin, North Waziristan Agency, "Warning against Kidnapping," 2009. This pamphlet notes that all Muslims are brothers and it is not legitimate for a Muslim to hurt another Muslim. Specifically, it says: "We are neither cruel, nor do we align with those who are cruel. In fact, it is our responsibility to help every vulnerable Muslim. However, for the enemies of Allah we are sharper than a sword." It goes on to note that the leader of the North Waziristan TTP faction, Hafiz Gul Bahadur, has announced that anyone who has kidnapped an adult or child, or stolen a car for ransom and reasons other than espionage has five days to release them or return them to their owners. Severe action will be taken by the Shura of Mujahidin of North Waziristan against those who do not abide by this instruction.

112. Some of the TTP's statements and audio recordings are released concurrently in Pashto and Urdu. For more on Taliban's national ambitions, see Jadoon and Mahmood, "Fixing the Cracks."

113. Editors, *Sunnat-e-Khola*, no. 2, 2017, 8.

114. For instance, articles address ongoing questions that the *mujahidin* may themselves be grappling with. In the third issue of *Mujalla Tehrik-e-Taliban*, we find an article entitled "Why This Difference?," in which the author tries to dispel the *mujahidin*'s views that *jihad* in Pakistan is different or de-linked from *jihad* in Afghanistan ("Why This Difference?" *Mujalla Tehrik-e-Taliban*, no. 3, June 2017, 9). Likewise, an editorial in *Ihya-e-Khilafat* (English) explains the restructuring of the Taliban primarily for the benefit of its own rank and file ("Editorial," *Ihya-e-*

Khilafat English, no. 1, 2014). The editors chastise the *mujahidin* for their ongoing divisions and fragmentations, which they argue have resulted in their recent mission failures.

115. As a practicing Muslim, I send peace upon the Prophet and his progeny. Unfortunately, the constraints of the book do not permit me to include the salutation at each mention of his name.

116. *Azan*'s "From the Pages of History" section, for instance, features excerpts from a text by al-Ghazali, a prominent Muslim philosopher and theologian from the eleventh century.

117. *Azan,* no. 3, 52.

118. See a translation of a Pashto speech by Mullah Fazlullah in *Sunnat-e-Khola,* no. 1, 2017.

119. Donna Haraway, *Modest_Witness@Second_Millennium.FemaleMan_ Meets_OncoMouse: Feminism and Technoscience* (New York: Routledge, 1997), 23; this theorization is explained further in Weber, *Queer International Relations,* 28–33.

120. Imogen Tyler, "Class Disgust in Contemporary Britain," *Feminist Media Studies* 8, no. 1 (2008): 18.

121. For manhood and the post-9/11 United States, see Ann Ferguson, "Cowboy Masculinity, Globalization, and the US War on Terror," *Center for Global Justice,* October 1, 2017, https://www.globaljusticecenter.org/papers/cowboy-masculinity-globalization-and-us-war-terror. Also see George W. Bush's memoir, *Decision Points* (New York: Broadway Books, 2011) for how he invoked kinship feelings in the aftermath of 9/11.

122. In particular, see the work of Cynthia Weber, Bonnie Mann, and Inderpal Grewal.

123. See David Gilmartin, Price, and Ruud, *South Asian Sovereignty* for a range of case studies.

124. Amnesty International, "Death Sentences and Executions in 2015," https://www.amnesty.org/en/latest/research/2016/04/death-sentences-executions-2015/.

125. Amnesty International, "Death Sentences and Executions in 2015."

126. BBC Urdu, "Women of Waziristan," *BBC,* January 31, 2019, https://www.bbc.com/urdu/pakistan-47054881.

127. BBC Urdu, "Women of Waziristan."

128. Judith Butler, *Frames of War* (New York: Verso, 2009).

129. Malala Yousafzai and Christina Lamb, *I Am Malala: The Girl Who Stood Up for Education and Was Shot by the Taliban* (London: Little, Brown, 2013), 65.

CHAPTER 1. NARRATING THE SOVEREIGN

1. Pervez Musharraf, *In the Line of Fire: A Memoir* (New York: Free Press, 2006), 201.

2. Milinda Banerjee, *The Mortal God: Imagining the Sovereign in Colonial India* (Cambridge: Cambridge University Press, 2018), 162.

3. Najeeb Jan, *The Metacolonial State: Pakistan, Critical Ontology, and the Biopolitical Horizons of Political Islam* (Hoboken, NJ: Wiley, 2019).

4. Elleke Boehmer, *Stories of Women* (Manchester: Manchester University Press, 2005), 68.

5. For example, Musharraf's autobiography is published by Free Press, which is located in the United States, Bhutto's *Reconciliation* by HarperCollins, also headquartered in the United States, and Khan's by Bantam Press, headquartered in London. Sometimes electronic and audio versions of the books follow a year or two after publication, as in the case of Bhutto's *Reconciliation*.

6. Musharraf, *In the Line of Fire*, 168.

7. Musharraf, *In the Line of Fire*, 295.

8. For more on military masculinities, see R. W. Connell, *Masculinities* (Oakland: University of California Press, 1995); Paul Higate, *Military Masculinities: Identity and the State* (Westport, CT: Praeger, 2003).

9. Musharraf, *In the Line of Fire*, 27.

10. Musharraf, *In the Line of Fire*, 27.

11. Musharraf, *In the Line of Fire*, 32.

12. Musharraf, *In the Line of Fire*, 22.

13. Musharraf, *In the Line of Fire*, 3, 4, 23, 34, 46.

14. Musharraf, *In the Line of Fire*, 47, 121, 139, 140.

15. Musharraf, *In the Line of Fire*, 41.

16. Musharraf, *In the Line of Fire*, 41 and 43.

17. Musharraf, *In the Line of Fire*, 40 and 41.

18. Musharraf, *In the Line of Fire*, 41.

19. Musharraf, *In the Line of Fire*, 49.

20. Salih Can Aciksoz, "Sacrificial Limbs of Sovereignty: Disabled Veterans, Masculinity, and Nationalist Politics in Turkey," *Medical Anthropology Quarterly* 26, no. 1 (2012): 13.

21. Elizabeth Spellman, "Woman as Body: Ancient and Contemporary Views," *Feminist Studies* 8, no. 1 (1982): 109–31.

22. Musharraf, *In the Line of Fire*, 35.

23. Musharraf, *In the Line of Fire*, 32.

24. Musharraf, *In the Line of Fire*, 32.

25. Musharraf, *In the Line of Fire*, 32. A recent ISPR-sponsored televisual production, *Ehd-e-wafa* (Promise of loyalty, 2019–20), features these contrasting masculinities as well, with four actors representing the military, civilian bureaucracy, feudal politics, and journalism.

26. Musharraf, *In the Line of Fire*, 328.

27. Musharraf, *In the Line of Fire*, 85.

28. Musharraf, *In the Line of Fire*, 125, 135–36.

29. Musharraf, *In the Line of Fire*, 159, 175.

30. Musharraf, *In the Line of Fire*, 137, 78.

31. Musharraf, *In the Line of Fire*, 202.

32. Musharraf, *In the Line of Fire*, 203.

33. Musharraf, *In the Line of Fire*, 208, 223, 214, 232.

34. Musharraf, *In the Line of Fire*, 252.

35. Musharraf, *In the Line of Fire*, 252, 253, 234.

36. Musharraf, *In the Line of Fire*, 202–3.

37. Musharraf, *In the Line of Fire*, 332.

38. Musharraf, *In the Line of Fire*, 332.

39. Musharraf, *In the Line of Fire*, 332.

40. Yasmin Saikia, "Listening to the Enemy: The Pakistan Army, Violence and Memories of 1971," in *Beyond Crisis*, ed. Naveeda Khan, 177–209 (New Delhi: Taylor and Francis, 2010), 185.

41. Musharraf, *In the Line of Fire*, 54.

42. Musharraf, *In the Line of Fire*, 253.

43. Musharraf, *In the Line of Fire*, 157.

44. Musharraf, *In the Line of Fire*, 52.

45. Musharraf, *In the Line of Fire*, 53.

46. See Musharraf, *In the Line of Fire*, 64 for detailed account of a lashing.

47. Musharraf, *In the Line of Fire*, 67.

48. Musharraf, *In the Line of Fire*, 107.

49. Musharraf, *In the Line of Fire*, 121.

50. Musharraf, *In the Line of Fire*, 126.

51. She was dismissed both times on charges of corruption and mismanagement.

52. Salman Masood, "After 8 Years in Jail, Husband of Bhutto Is Free," *New York Times*, November 23, 2004, https://www.nytimes.com/2004/11/23/world /asia/after-8-years-in-jail-husband-of-bhutto-is-free.html; "Mr Nice Guy and Mr Ten Percent," *The Economist*, May 5, 2012, https://www.economist.com/asia /2012/05/05/mr-nice-guy-and-mr-ten-percent.

53. Stephanie Nebehay, "Swiss Close Case against Zardari; $60 M ln Unfrozen," *Reuters*, August 26, 2008, https://www.reuters.com/article/us-swiss-pakistan-zardari /swiss-close-case-against-zardari-60-mln-unfrozen-idUSLQ17107020080826.

54. Todd W. Reeser, *Masculinities in Theory: An Introduction* (West Sussex, UK: Wiley-Blackwell, 2010), 211.

55. Jack Halberstam, *Female Masculinity* (Durham, NC: Duke University Press, 2019).

56. Benazir Bhutto, *Daughter of Destiny: An Autobiography* (London: Harper Collins, 1988; repr. 2007), 160.

57. Benazir Bhutto, *Reconciliation: Islam, Democracy, and the West* (New York: HarperCollins, 2009), 1.

58. Bhutto, *Daughter of Destiny*, 158.

59. Bhutto, *Daughter of Destiny*, 159.

60. Bhutto, *Daughter of Destiny*, 342.

61. Bhutto, *Daughter of Destiny*, 342.

62. Bhutto, *Daughter of Destiny*, 342. Emphasis added.

63. Bhutto, *Daughter of Destiny*, 371.

64. Bhutto, *Daughter of Destiny,* 336.

65. Bhutto, *Daughter of Destiny,* 281.

66. Bhutto, *Daughter of Destiny,* 98.

67. Bhutto, *Daughter of Destiny,* 94.

68. Bhutto, *Daughter of Destiny,* 19, 119, 120.

69. Bhutto, *Daughter of Destiny,* 90.

70. Bhutto, *Daughter of Destiny,* 97.

71. Bhutto, *Reconciliation,* 17.

72. Bhutto, *Reconciliation,* 19–20.

73. Bhutto, *Reconciliation,* 8, 2, 7, 267.

74. Benazir Bhutto, "Pakistan's Moment of Truth," *New York Times,* August 30, 2007, https://www.nytimes.com/2007/08/30/opinion/30iht-edbhutto.1.7319142.html.

75. As quoted in Nathan Gardels, "Benazir Bhutto: Only Democracy Can Defeat Terrorism," *Huffington Post,* May 25, 2011, https://www.huffingtonpost.com/nathan-gardels/benazir-bhutto-only-democ_b_62479.html.

76. Benazir Bhutto, "When I Return to Pakistan," *Washington Post,* September 20, 2007, http://www.washingtonpost.com/wp-dyn/content/article/2007/09/19/AR2007091901705.html?noredirect = on.

77. Benazir Bhutto, "Democracy for Pakistan," *Wall Street Journal,* June 8, 2007, https://www.wsj.com/articles/SB118126480463428594.

78. Bhutto, *Reconciliation,* 191.

79. Bhutto, *Reconciliation,* 198.

80. Bhutto, *Reconciliation,* 2.

81. For more see Ali Usman Qasmi, "Making Sense of Naya Pakistan—I," *Friday Times,* September 7, 2018, https://www.thefridaytimes.com/making-sense-of-naya-pakistan-i/.

82. Pakistan Tehrik-e-Insaf (@PTIofficial), "@-ImranKhanPTI training his tigers," Twitter, October 31, 2016, 1:54 A.M., https://twitter.com/PTIofficial/status/792998083936284672.

83. Imran Khan, *Pakistan: A Personal History* (London: Bantam, 2011), 107.

84. See Sadia Abbas, "Itineraries of Conversion," in *Beyond Crisis,* ed. Naveeda Khan, 344–69 (New Delhi: Taylor and Francis, 2010).

85. Khan, *Pakistan,* 98.

86. Khan, *Pakistan,* 103.

87. This is *surah* 2, *ayah* 255; see Seyyed Hossein Nasr, ed., *The Study Quran* (New York: Harper One, 2015), 110.

88. See for instance, Bhopinder Singh, "Pakistan's Imran Khan: Who Was the Future Once!" *Deccan Chronicle,* September 24, 2019, https://www.deccanchronicle.com/opinion/op-ed/240919/pakistans-imran-khan-who-was-the-future-once.html; Mehr Tarar, "Imran Khan Carried the Burden of the Seer's Prophecy, but What Does the Future Hold?" *Gulf News,* September 29, 2019, https://gulfnews.com/world/asia/pakistan/imran-khan-carried-the-burden-of-the-seers-prophecy-but-what-does-the-future-hold-1.1569757507664.

89. Pnina Werbner, "'The Lion of Lahore': Anthropology, Cultural Performance and Imran Khan," in *Anthropology and Cultural Studies,* ed. Stephen Nugent and Cris Shore, 34–67 (London: Pluto Press, 1997), 46.

90. Khan, *Pakistan,* 145, 148.

91. Khan, *Pakistan,* 280.

92. Khan, *Pakistan,* 280.

93. Khan, *Pakistan,* 52.

94. Khan, *Pakistan,* 52.

95. Khan, *Pakistan,* 391.

96. Khan, *Pakistan,* 21.

97. Khan, *Pakistan,* 403.

98. Khan, *Pakistan,* 55, 63.

99. Bonnie Mann, *Sovereign Masculinity: Gender Lessons from the War on Terror* (Oxford: Oxford University Press, 2014), 3.

100. Sara Ahmed, *The Cultural Politics of Emotion* (Edinburgh: Edinburgh University Press, 2004), 100.

CHAPTER 2. IDENTITY, ALTERITY

1. Another term used for soldiers is *sipahi.*

2. David Palumbo-Liu, "Pre-emption, the Future, and the Imagination," in *America and the Misshaping of a New World Order,* ed. Giles Gunn and Carl Gutiérrez-Jones, 59–78, (Berkeley: University of California Press, 2010), 61.

3. Ashfaq Naqvi, "Our Jawan," *Hilal Urdu,* April 11, 1980, 14.

4. For popular culture as performative, see Stuart Hall and Paddy Whannel, *The Popular Arts* (Durham, NC: Duke University Press, 2018).

5. For more on music and politics see Lara Allen, "Music and Politics in Africa," *Social Dynamics* 30, no. 2 (2004): 1–19; Achille Mbembe, "Variations on the Beautiful in the Congolese World of Sounds," *Politique Africaine* 4, no. 100 (2005): para. 25.

6. Sara Ahmed, "Affective Economies," *Social Text* 79, no. 22 (2004): 121.

7. ISPR Official, "Bara Dushman Bana Phirta Hai: Azaan Ali: APS Peshawar 2014 (ISPR Official Video)," February 20, 2018, video, 3:47, https://www.youtube.com/watch?v=Ea4RXRwG_yI.

8. Fasi Zaka, "The Resurgence of Nationalism in Popular Culture," *Dawn Herald,* February 19, 2019, https://herald.dawn.com/news/1398795.

9. I use the official ISPR translations wherever available. In other cases, translations are mine.

10. Bonnie Mann, *Sovereign Masculinity: Gender Lessons from the War on Terror* (Oxford: Oxford University Press, 2014).

11. Captain Aijaz Mehmood, "*Sherni* (Lioness)," *Hilal Urdu,* November 26, 1971, 20.

12. ISPR Official, "Mujhe Dushman ke Bachon ko Parhana Hai: APS Peshawar 2015 (ISPR Official Video)," February 20, 2018, video, 4:30, https://www.youtube.com/watch?v=wUQeQ400_cs.

13. A more literal translation would be "I want to teach my enemy's children."

14. The terrorist is viewed as a harmful influence on his own children beyond the Pakistani context as well. A leading counterterror officer in the UK, Assistant Commissioner Mark Rowley, for instance, is noted to have said that terrorists should be treated like pedophiles and have their children taken away from them. See Martin Evans, "Terrorists Should Be Treated Like Pedophiles and Have Their Children Removed, Top Cop Suggests," *The Telegraph,* February 26, 2018, https://www.telegraph.co.uk/news/2018/02/26/terrorists-should-treated-like-paedophiles-have-children-removed/.

15. ISPR Official, "Farishtay," October 4, 2016, video, 6:51, https://www.youtube.com/watch?v=pdjcxxp2OM8.

16. This is also exemplified by the backlash against the film *Zaynab kay Qatil,* which is based on the rape and murder of a seven-year-old girl from Kasur in Pakistan.

17. ISPR Official, "Ye Banday Mitti kay Banday: One Year of Zarb e Azb (ISPR Official Video)," June 2015, video, 3:56, https://www.youtube.com/watch?v=vplıFyToXck.

18. Stuart Hall, *Policing the Crisis: Mugging, the State, and Law and Order* (London: Macmillan Press, 1978), 54.

19. For more on how this relationship is established, see Shenila Khoja-Moolji, "Reading Malala: (De)(Re)Territorialization of Muslim Collectivities," *Comparative Studies of South Asia, Africa and the Middle East* 35, no. 3 (2015): 539–56.

20. Sara Ahmed, *The Cultural Politics of Emotion* (Edinburgh: Edinburgh University Press, 2004), 85.

21. For more, see Jasbir Puar and Amit Rai, "Monster, Terrorist, Fag: The War on Terrorism and the Production of Docile Patriots," *Social Text* 20, no. 3 (Fall 2002): 117–48.

22. Cynthia Weber, *Queer International Relations: Sovereignty, Sexuality and the Will to Knowledge* (Oxford, UK: Oxford University Press, 2016), 47–71.

23. Nivi Manchanda, "Queering the Pashtun: Afghan Sexuality in the Homo-Nationalist Imaginary," *Third World Quarterly* 36, no. 1 (2015): 130–46.

24. Human Terrain Team-AF6, "Research Update and Findings: Pashtun Sexuality," https://info.publicintelligence.net/HTT-PashtunSexuality.pdf, accessed June 3, 2018.

25. Human Terrain Team-AF6, "Research Update and Findings," 1.

26. ISPR Official, "Farishtay."

27. Weber, *Queer International Relations,* 52.

28. Weber, *Queer International Relations,* 52. Emphasis mine.

29. Weber, *Queer International Relations,* 77.

30. The Frontier region also included parts of Punjab. See Sonia Qadir, "The History of Dangerous Fanatics," *The News on Sunday*, May 27, 2018, https://www.thenews.com.pk/tns/detail/565592-history-dangerous-fanatics.

31. Maira Hayat, "Empire's Accidents: Law, Lies, and Sovereignty in the 'War on Terror' in Pakistan," *Critique of Anthropology* 40, no. 1 (2020): 49–80, 53.

32. Winston Churchill, *The Story of the Malakand Field Force: An Episode of Frontier War* (London: Longmans, Green and Co., 1898; repr. 2010), 189.

33. Churchill, *The Story of the Malakand Field Force,* 280.

34. As cited in Andrew Roe, *Waging War in Waziristan: The British Struggle in the Land of Bin Laden, 1849–1947* (Lawrence: University Press of Kansas, 2010), 91.

35. As cited in Madiha Tahir, "The Ground Was Always in Play," *Public Culture* 29, no. 1 (2017): 5–16, 8.

36. Qadir, "The History of Dangerous Fanatics."

37. As cited in Qadir, "The History of Dangerous Fanatics."

38. Qadir, "The History of Dangerous Fanatics."

39. Mukulika Banerjee, *The Pathan Unarmed: Opposition and Memory in the North West Frontier* (Oxford: Oxford University Press, 2000).

40. Tahir, "The Ground Was Always in Play," 8.

41. Ammara Maqsood, "Mobility and Spatiality among Tribal Pashtuns," *Tanqeed,* no. 10, (January 2016).

42. As cited in Diaa Hadid, "Caught between the Military and the Militants, Pakistan's Pashtuns Fight for Rights," *NPR,* April 7, 2018. https://www.npr.org/sections/parallels/2018/04/07/598045758/caught-between-the-military-and-militants-pakistans-pashtuns-fight-for-rights.

43. Stereotypes of "effeminacy," as well as the elaboration of definitions of martial and nonmartial races, were discursive techniques of the colonial state through which English masculinity was constituted as superior. See Mrinalini Sinha, *Colonial Masculinity: The 'Manly Englishman' and the 'Effeminate Bengali' in the Late Nineteenth Century* (New Delhi: Kali for Women, 1997); and Kaushik Roy, "Race and Recruitment in the Indian Army: 1880–1918," *Modern Asian Studies* 47, no. 4 (2013): 1310–47.

44. Roy, "Race and Recruitment."

45. Roy, "Race and Recruitment."

46. Hassan Abbas, "Musharraf Contends with the Pashtun Element in the Pakistani Army," *Terrorism Focus* 3, no. 42 (November 2, 2006), available at https://jamestown.org/program/musharraf-contends-with-the-pashtun-element-in-the-pakistani-army/.

47. Ayesha Siddiqa, "Pakistan Military: Ethnic Balance in the Armed Forces and Problems of Federalism," Manekshaw Paper, no. 39 (New Delhi: Centre for Land Warfare Studies), 8.

48. Banerjee, *The Pathan Unarmed,* 45.

49. Giorgio Agamben, *Homo Sacer: Sovereign Power and Bare Life,* trans. Daniel Heller-Roazen (Stanford, CA: Stanford University Press, 1998), 114.

50. Mateo Taussig-Rubbo, "Sacrifice and Sovereignty," in *States of Violence: War, Capital Punishment, and Letting Die,* ed. Austin Sarat and Jennifer Culbert, 83–126 (Cambridge: Cambridge University Press, 2009), 84.

51. I draw on Sara Ahmed's argument here about hate being economic; Ahmed, "The Organization of Hate," *Law and Critique* 12 (2001): 345–65, 347.

52. Ahmed, *The Cultural Politics of Emotion,* 88–89.

53. I. Melikoff, "Ghazi," in *Encyclopedia of Islam,* 2nd ed., ed. P. Bearman, Th. Bianqghauis, C. E. Bosworth, E. van Donzel, and W. P. Heinrichs (Leiden: Brill, 2012). Another relevant cultural text, not reviewed in this section, is "PNS Ghazi (Shaheed)," a 1998 production by the ISPR. On the honorific of *ghazi* in the context of nationalist politics in Turkey, see Salih Can Ackisoz, *Sacrificial Limbs: Masculinity, Disability, and Political Violence in Turkey* (Oakland: University of California Press, 2019).

54. "What Is Shahadat," *Hilal Urdu,* December 20, 2001, 5–8.

55. The same poem by Allama Iqbal appears on the back cover of *Mujalla Tehrik-e-Taliban,* no. 7, December 2019, signaling the correspondences in how each constructs military and militant masculinity.

56. ISPR Official, "Ye Ghazi Ye Tere Pur Asrar Banday: Junaid Jamshed (ISPR Official Video)," January 22, 2018, video, 4:17, https://www.youtube.com /watch?v=uDojlfkx_Ms&list=PLcAPTl-NPAstG3FKJUvZtj_CLv_sDGCKf &index=44.

57. On Iqbal's notion of *mard-e-momin,* see Riffat Hassan, "Iqbal's Concept of *Mard-e-momin* and Rumi's Influence," *Journal of the Regional Cultural Institute* 5, no. 2–3 (1972): 61–83; and Rubina Saigol, *The Pakistan Project: A Feminist Perspective on Nation and Identity* (Delhi: Women Unlimited, 2013), 85–97.

58. ISPR Official, "Ghazi," October 5, 2016, video, 6:46, https://www.youtube .com/watch?v=5CoHKPokTWk.

59. ISPR Official, "Ghazi."

60. Major Sardar Atif Habib, "A Page From a Soldier's Diary," *Hilal English* (February 1, 2017).

61. Habib, "A Page From a Soldier's Diary."

62. See *Hilal Urdu,* April 11, 1980, p. 10; *Hilal Urdu,* November 12, 1971, p. 10.

63. For example, see Iftikhar Ahmed, "Namaz," *Hilal Urdu,* May 2, 1965, p. 20; Mullah Wahidi, "The *Hajj* Journey of Hazrat Ahmed Barelvi," *Hilal Urdu,* May 2, 1965, p. 9; Aziz Malik, "The Beginning of Fasting," *Hilal Urdu,* January 2, 1966, p. 22.

64. Kamal Farooqi, "Islam Ka Sipahi," *Hilal Urdu,* July 11, 1965, p. 13. Editors, "Mujahidin," *Hilal Urdu,* August 8, 1965, p. 1; Arif Siddiqui, "Get up Mujahid, Get up, Move on Brave-Hearted, Move On," *Hilal Urdu,* November 12, 1971, p. 11. Asim Zabahi, "Country's Soldier," *Hilal Urdu,* April 4, 1965, p. 19. See *Hilal Urdu,* February 23, 1980, p. 24.

65. "Victory of Mecca," *Hilal Urdu,* January 16, 1966, p. 7; Muhammad Afzal, "Conquest of Mecca," *Hilal Urdu,* November 12, 1971, p. 25–28; Seerat Issue, *Hilal Urdu,* January 12, 1980.

66. Editors, "Commands about War Booty," *Hilal Urdu,* April 11, 1980, p. 1.

67. Editors, "Commands about War Booty."

68. Akram Mulk, "A Letter from a *Shahid*," *Hilal*, December 31, 1971, p. 6.

69. Mulk, "A Letter from a *Shahid*."

70. Editors, "Blessings for Shahid and Ghazi," *Hilal Urdu*, February 23, 1980, p. 1.

71. Asif Ghafoor, "Preface," in *Junoon-e-Rukhe Wafa* (Rawalpindi: Hilal Publications, 2018), 6.

72. Ghafoor, "Preface," 7.

73. Hayat Ali, "Lahoo," *Hilal Urdu*, November 7, 1965, p. 18–19.

74. Muhammad Amjad Chaudhary, "Quam Kay Betay," in *Junoon-e-Rukhe Wafa* (Rawalpindi: Hilal Publications, 2018), 15.

75. Major Naeem, "Blood's Tribute," in *Junoon-e-Rukhe Wafa* (Rawalpindi: Hilal Publications, 2018).

76. Zafar Javed, "I Will Walk in the Footsteps of My Father," *Hilal Urdu*, October 10, 1965, p. 20.

77. ISPR Official, "Ye Banday Mitti kay Banday," translation mine.

78. ISPR Official, "Faseel e Jaan Se Agay: Promo: 2011 (ISPR Official Promo)," March 13, 2018, video, 0:50, https://www.youtube.com/watch?v=2ZIrN7cS_dc.

79. ISPR Official, "Faseel e Jaan Se Agay: Promo."

80. ISPR Official, "Faseel-e-Jaan Se Aagay—Eik Beti Eik Kahani," July 12, 2018, video, 56:15, https://www.youtube.com/watch?v=swOT9gvEJK4.

81. ISPR Official, "Tu Thori Dair: Farhan Saeed (ISPR Official Video)," January 24, 2018, video, 5:53, https://www.youtube.com/watch?v=ZXJRLPRe7bI.

82. On this point, also see Purnima Mankekar, *Screening Culture, Viewing Politics: An Ethnography of Television, Womanhood, and Nation in Postcolonial India* (Durham, NC: Duke University Press, 1999), 269.

83. Student Channel, "'Yeh Jung Bhi Hum Hi Jeete Gey,' ISPR Song," December 16, 2015, video, 3:24, https://vimeo.com/149160374.

84. Ali Azmat, "Yeh Jung bhi hum hi jeetey gey!," Facebook post, December 15, 2015, https://www.facebook.com/AliAzmatOfficial/videos/10153859969883223.

85. See Laleh Khalili on the figure of the "counterinsurgent woman" in the context of the United States and how it creates space for women of a particular social class and race to participate in otherwise male-dominated state apparatuses. Laleh Khalili, "Gendered Practices of Counterinsurgency," *Review of International Studies* 37, no. 4 (2010): 1471–91.

86. Michel Foucault, *The History of Sexuality*, trans. R Hurley, vol. 1, *The Will to Knowledge* (New York: Pantheon Books, 1976), 137; Michel Foucault, *Society Must Be Defended: Lecture Series at the Collège de France, 1975–76*, trans. D Macey (New York: Picador, 2003), 61.

87. On stickiness, see Ahmed, *The Cultural Politics of Emotion*, 90.

CHAPTER 3. COMPETING SOVEREIGNS

1. Jamaat-ul-Ahrar-TTP, "Bara General Bana Phirta Hai Dollar Le Ke Larta Hai," February 26, 2015, video, 15:41:24, originally posted on ihyaekhilafat.net,

available at https://archive.org/details/BaraGeneral, accessed September 13, 2019. The group splintered away from TTP Central in 2014 but rejoined in 2020.

2. The Quran is divided into thirty parts, each is called a *juz* (Arabic) or *para* (Urdu).

3. This refers to the Muslim ritual of welcoming infants to the Islamic faith through the recitation of the *azan* in their ears.

4. See Shenila Khoja-Moolji, *Forging the Ideal Educated Girl: The Production of Desirable Subjects in Muslim South Asia* (Oakland: University of California Press, 2018); David Edwards, *The Caravan of Martyrs: Sacrifice and Suicide bombing in Afghanistan* (Oakland: University of California Press, 2017).

5. Edwards, *Caravan of Martyrs,* 57.

6. For more on militant newspapers see Faizullah Jan, "Representing the Self and the Other: Discourse of Pakistan-Based Militant Organizations," PhD diss., American University, 2014.

7. The *shabnameh* are unsigned letters distributed clandestinely overnight and are a traditional means of communication in the tribal areas; see Mona Sheikh, *Guardians of God: Inside the Religious Mind of the Pakistani Taliban* (Oxford: Oxford University Press, 2016), 125.

8. Thomas Johnson in his study of Afghan Taliban cultural texts argues that whereas texts aimed at local populations are often in the Pashto and Dari languages, those targeting neighboring countries and international audiences are in Urdu and English. See Thomas Johnson, *Taliban Narratives: The Use and Power of Stories in the Afghanistan Conflict* (Oxford: Oxford University Press, 2018).

9. See *Azan,* no. 1, 2013.

10. Haroro Ingram, "An Analysis of the Taliban in Khurasan's *Azan* (Issues 1–5)," *Studies in Conflict and Terrorism* 38, no. 7 (2015): 560–79.

11. Tariq Rahman, *Interpretations of Jihad in South Asia: An Intellectual History* (Berlin: De Gruyter, 2018), 231.

12. As noted by Jaffer Hussain in "The Drone Chain," *Azan,* no. 1, 2013, 18: "this is all North West Pakistan, adjacent to Afghanistan which together forms the area of Khorasaan that was given special mention in the Ahadith of Prophet Muhammad."

13. "Editorial," *Azan,* no. 1, 2013. Emphasis added.

14. "Editorial," *Azan,* no. 1, 2013.

15. This name is spelled "Khaula" elsewhere in the magazine.

16. "Editorial," *Sunnat-e-Khola,* no. 1, 2017.

17. "Editorial," *Sunnat-e-Khola,* no. 1, 2017.

18. *Ihya-e-Khilafat English,* no. 1, December 2014, p. 2.

19. *Ihya-e-Khilafat English,* no. 1, December 2014, p. 2.

20. "Editorial," *Mujalla Tehrik-e-Taliban,* November 2016, p. 3.

21. According to Qandeel Siddique, the number of TTP fighters in Pakistan ranges from five thousand to thirty thousand; Qandeel Siddique, *Tehrik-e-Taliban Pakistan* (Copenhagen: Danish Institute for International Studies, 2010), 11.

22. As cited in Sheikh, *Guardians of God,* 126–27.

23. Jean Laplanche and Jean-Bertrand Pontalis, *Language of Psychoanalysis* (London: Abingdon, 1988), 26.

24. Sigmund Freud, *Beyond the Pleasure Principle,* trans. by C.J.M. Hubback (London: The International Psycho-analytic Press, 1922).

25. Qazi Muhammad Saqib, *Ihya-e-Khilafat Urdu,* no. 3, March 2012, p. 75.

26. Abu Saif Saheb, "Quaid-e-Azam's Pakistan or Taliban's Pakistan," *Ihya-e-Khilafat Urdu,* no. 5, January 2013, p. 33.

27. Saheb, "Quaid-e-Azam's Pakistan or Taliban's Pakistan," 33.

28. Editors, "Editorial," *Mujalla Tehrik-e-Taliban,* no. 7, December 7, 2019, p. 4.

29. Mowlana Zakir, "A Message to Ordinary Muslims from a Mujahid of Tehrik-e-Taliban Ahrar," *Ihya-e-Khilafat Urdu,* no. 11, March 2016, p. 22. Emphasis added.

30. Zakir, "A Message to Ordinary Muslims," 22.

31. Sadiq Yarmomand, "We Are Pakistan and Pakistan Is Ours," *Ihya-e-Khilafat Urdu,* no. 13, November 2016, p. 43.

32. Yarmomand, "We Are Pakistan," 43. Emphasis added.

33. Yarmomand, "We Are Pakistan," 43.

34. As cited in Sheikh, *Guardians of God,* 136. While the term *kufr* means disbelief and ingratitude, in this context it is used to denote corruption and willful refusal of God's commandments by the Pakistani government.

35. TTP, *Bloodshed and Revenge,* July 2009, video, 40:12, Umar Studio, available at https://archive.org/details/Tehreek-e-talibanPakistan_umarStudiojuly2009, accessed April 6, 2020.

36. TTP, *Bloodshed and Revenge.*

37. *Sunnat-e-Khola,* no. 1, 2017.

38. Brannon Wheeler, "Ummah," in *Encyclopedia of Religion,* ed. Lindsay Jones, 9446–48, vol. 14 (New York: Macmillan Reference USA, 2005).

39. Michel Foucault, *Power/Knowledge: Selected Interviews and Other Writings, 1972–1977,* ed. Colin Gordon (New York: Pantheon Books, 1980), 68.

40. Ibn Taymiyah (1263–1328) emphasized the need for territory where the *ummah* could fulfill its obligations to God, with the *khalifa* or even a jurist facilitating this. These obligations are often delineated by the different schools of Islamic law and operate at two levels: between the individual and God *('ibadat),* and between the individual and society *(mu'amalat).*

41. Darryl Li, "Jihad in a World of Sovereigns: Law, Violence, and Islam in the Bosnia Crisis," *Law and Social Inquiry* 41 no. 2 (2016): 371–401.

42. "Full Text: BBC Interview with Taliban's Mehsud," *BBC,* October 9, 2013, https://www.bbc.com/news/world-asia-24466791.

43. Muhammad Qasim, "Destroying the Country Idol: Part 1," *Azan,* no. 3, 2013, p. 25.

44. Qasim, "Destroying the Country Idol," 26.

45. Qasim, "Destroying the Country Idol," 26

46. Qasim, "Destroying the Country Idol," 30.

47. Editors, "Editorial," *Mujalla Tehrik-e-Taliban,* no. 6, September 9, 2019, p. 2.

48. Maulana Abdullah Muhammadi, "Nationalism and Islam," *Azan*, no. 1, 2013, p. 69.

49. Muhammad Qasim, "Destroying the Country Idol: Part 3," *Azan*, no. 5, 2014, p. 15.

50. Muhammad Qasim Zaman, *Islam in Pakistan: A History* (Princeton, NJ: Princeton University Press, 2018), 137.

51. Zaman, *Islam in Pakistan*, 137.

52. SherAli Tareen, "Contesting Friendship in Colonial Muslim India," *South Asia: Journal of South Asian Studies* 38, no. 3 (2015): 419–34.

53. See Tareen, "Contesting Friendship" for Abdul Kalam Azad and Ahmad Raza Khan's views.

54. Zaman, *Islam in Pakistan*, 145.

55. As cited in Zaman, *Islam in Pakistan*, 140.

56. For more on the transmutation of sovereignty and particularly the place of messianism as an avenue to sovereignty in South Asia, see Azfar Moin, "Messianism and the Constitution of Pakistan," in *South Asian Sovereignty: The Conundrum of Worldly Power,* ed. David Gilmartin, Pamela Price, and Arild Ruud, 175–95 (New York: Routledge, 2020).

57. Abu Rumaysah, "In Pursuit of Territory: The Benefits of Living under Khilafah," *Ihya-e-Khilafat English,* no. 1, 2014, p. 26.

58. Rumaysah, "In Pursuit of Territory," 30.

59. Rumaysah, "In Pursuit of Territory," 30.

60. Rumaysah, "In Pursuit of Territory," 30.

61. Umar Abdul-Hakim, "Glorious Past," *Mujalla Tehrik-e-Taliban*, no. 7, December 7, 2019, pp. 18–23.

62. Ovamir Anjum explains the evolution of the institution of *khilafat* through four models: that of the first four *rashidun* (rightly guided caliphs) who to a certain extent embodied both political and religious authority; this model gave way to the *imperial khilafat* of the Umayyad and Abbasid eras, when the *khalifa* (caliph) was primarily a political leader and religious authority was shared with the *ulama;* this was followed by a third model in which the *khalifa* was primarily a symbolic and spiritual authority, with rule exercised by governors; the fourth model, which is linked to the Ottomans, was a combination of the second and third ones, in which the *khalifa* did exercise authority but his powers were mediated by the scholars who interpreted the *sharia*. For more see, Ovamir Anjum, "Who Wants the Caliphate?" Yaqeen Institute for Islamic Research, October 31, 2019, https://yaqeeninstitute. org/ovamiranjum/who-wants-the-caliphate.

63. Tareen, "Contesting Friendship," 422.

64. Salman Sayyid, *Recalling the Caliphate: Decolonisation and the World Order* (Oxford: Oxford University Press, 2014), 118.

65. Svetlana Boym, *The Future of Nostalgia* (New York: Basic Books, 2001), 8.

66. For more on the Deobandi orientation, see SherAli Tareen, *Defending Muhammad in Modernity* (Notre Dame, IN: University of Notre Dame Press, 2020).

67. Sheikh, *Guardians of God,* 45.

68. Zaman, *Islam in Pakistan,* 138.

69. Also see Faisal Devji, *The Terrorist in Search of Humanity: Militant Islam and Global Politics* (London: Hurst Publishers, 2009) on the role of Caliphate and *ummah* in Islamist discourse.

70. Roxanne Euben, "Jihad and Political Violence," *Current History* 101, no. 658 (2002): 365–76, 368.

71. Tariq Rahman highlights the hermeneutics that were used by various groups in South Asia to arrive at militant meanings of Quranic verses on *jihad*. See Rahman, *Interpretations of Jihad in South Asia,* 12.

72. Omar Khalid Khurasani, "Our Right to Spread Terror," *Ihya-e-Khilafat English,* no. 2, October 2014, pp. 8–11.

73. TTP, *Bloodshed and Revenge.*

74. Ikrimah Anwar and Muawiya Hussaini, "Let's Understand 'Suicide Bombing,'" *Azan,* no. 2, April/May 2013, pp. 21–28. Emphasis added.

75. Olivier Roy, *Jihad and Death: The Global Appeal of Islamic State* (New York: Oxford University Press, 2017), 2.

76. Roy, *Jihad and Death,* 4.

77. Edwards, *Caravan of Martyrs.*

78. Edwards, *Caravan of Martyrs,* 42.

79. Mullah Wahdi, "Jihad and Quran," *Hilal Urdu,* June 1965, p. 4; Mullah Wahdi, "A Look at *jihad,*" *Hilal Urdu,* August 1965, pp. 7–9.

80. Aziz Mulk, "Benefits of Jihad," *Hilal Urdu,* September 1965, p. 7.

81. "The Status of Mujahidin," *Hilal Urdu,* January 12, 1979, back cover.

82. See Iqbal Ahmed, "The Jihad of the Faithful," *Hilal Urdu,* December 1971, p. 28.

83. *Hilal Urdu,* November 26, 1971, pp. 8, 15, 11, 4.

84. *Hilal Urdu,* December 10, 1971, pp. 25–26. *Hilal Urdu,* December 31, 1971, p. 6.

85. Murid Hussein, "Love of Death," *Hilal Urdu,* November 26, 1971, p. 21.

86. Hussein, "Love of Death," 21.

87. Hussein, "Love of Death," 21.

88. Hussein, "Love of Death," 21.

89. Muhammad Azam Khan, "Question of Life—Death," *Hilal Urdu,* December 10, 1971.

90. *Azan,* no. 2, pp. 23–24.

91. Irfan Ahmed's study of Jamaat-e-Islami in India shows how Prophet Muhammad was transformed into a warrior-like figure in order to counter Hindu nationalists' imagination of Ram as combative and warrior-like; Irfan Ahmed, *Islamism and Democracy in India* (Princeton, NJ: Princeton University Press, 2009), 233.

92. Moin, "Messianism," 180.

93. Milinda Banerjee, *The Mortal God: Imagining the Sovereign in Colonial India* (Cambridge: Cambridge University Press, 2018), 173.

94. Banerjee, *The Mortal God,* 173.

95. Moin, "Messianism."

96. As noted in *Ihya-e-Khilafat Urdu,* no. 11, March 2016, p. 28.

97. *Ihya-e-Khilafat Urdu,* no. 11, March 2016, p. 28.

98. Bilal Momin, "Background on Operation Zarb-e-Azb," *Ihya-e-Khilafat,* no. 3, November 2016, pp. 15–17.

99. Hussain, "The Drone Chain," 18–23.

100. Hussain, "The Drone Chain," 18, 20.

101. Hussain, "The Drone Chain," 19.

102. For example, Mowlana Abu Umar Saheb, "Who Is the Terrorist?" *Ihya-e-Khilafat,* no. 9, November 2014, p. 28.

103. TTP, *Bloodshed and Revenge.*

104. Ibn Hassan Khurasani, "Roshan Khayal Taliban, Moderate Taliban," *Mujalla Tehrik-e-Taliban,* no. 3, June 2017, p. 11.

105. Cabeiri deBergh Robinson's study of Kashmiri *mujahidin,* likewise, delineates the importance of personal spirituality and piety that accords a *mujahid* a morally high status. See Robinson, *Body of Victim, Body of Warrior: Refugee Families and the Making of Kashmiri Jihadists* (Oakland: University of California Press, 2013), 207.

106. Jacques Rancière, *The Future of Image* (London: Verso, 2007), 3.

107. See also the cover image of the fifth issue of *Azan,* 2014.

108. Rashid Ahmed Ludhianvi, "Engage in Extensive Remembrance of Allah," *Mujalla Tehrik-e-Taliban,* no. 6, September 9, 2019, p. 5.

109. Editors, "Growing a Beard Is *Wajib,*" *Azan,* no. 6, 2014, p. 42.

110. Editors, "Growing a Beard Is *Wajib,*" 42.

111. Muhammad Qasim, "Dajjal and World Today," *Azan,* no. 6, 2014, p. 22.

112. Anonymous, "An Exclusive Interview with the German Mujahid, Brother Abu Adam," *Azan,* no. 3, 2013, p. 64.

113. For instance, when Adnan Rasheed, a Taliban *mujahid,* was arrested and asked to shave his beard and cut his hair, he vehemently opposed doing so as a matter of principle; "Prison Break," *Azan,* no. 1, 2013, p. 45.

114. See Arsalan Khan's work on the Tablighi Jamaat in Pakistan; Arsalan Khan, "Islam and Pious Sociality," *Social Analysis* 60, no. 4 (2016): 96–113.

115. As cited in Sheikh, *Guardians of God,* 155.

116. On this idea, also see Roy, *Jihad and Death,* 49.

117. Muhammad Qasim, "Destroying the Country Idol: Part 3," *Azan,* no. 5, 2014, p. 15.

118. Ikrimah Anwar, "On U-Turns and the Pakistan Army Doctrine," *Azan,* no. 1, 2013, pp. 30–36.

119. Anwar, "On U-Turns," 32.

120. Qazi Muhammad Saqib, *Ihya-e-Khilafat Urdu,* no. 3, March 2012.

121. Hussain, "The Drone Chain," 20.

122. Hussain, "The Drone Chain," 20.

123. Adnan Rasheed, "The Mir Ali Massacre: The True Face of the Pakistan Army," *Azan,* no. 5, 2014, pp. 26–27. See also the work of numerous other writers,

such as Asadullah Khorasani, "Operation Zarb-e-Azb, The way Pakistan Army Makes Money," *Ihya-e-Khilafat English,* no. 1, December 2014, p. 13.

124. Adnan Rasheed, "The Mir Ali Massacre."

125. Adnan Rasheed, "The Mir Ali Massacre."

126. Adnan Rasheed, "The Mir Ali Massacre."

127. "Letter from Karachi Jail for Mujahidin-e-Islam," *Ihya-e-Khilafat Urdu,* no. 5, January 2013, p. 53.

128. "Letter from Karachi Jail," 53.

129. See also "Escapee from Pakistani Army's Bloody Prison," *Ihya-e-Khilafat,* no. 9, November 2014, pp. 42–44.

130. J. David Velleman, "The Genesis of Shame," *Philosophy and Public Affairs* 30, no. 1 (2005): 27–52, 39.

131. Anwar, "On U-Turns," 32.

132. Hussain, "The Drone Chain," 21.

133. Umm Vla, "O Martyr," *Ihya-e-Khilafat English,* no. 1, October 2014, p. 31.

134. "Editorial," *Ihya-e-Khilafat English,* no. 1, December 2014, p. 2.

135. Khalid Haqqani, "Army *Jawan,* Listen Carefully!!!", *Mujalla Tehrik-e-Taliban,* no. 1, November 2016, pp. 33–34.

136. Haqqani, "Army *Jawan,*" 35.

137. Haqqani, "Army *Jawan,*" 34.

138. Major Shamshad Hassan, "For Pakistan's Army," *Ihya-e-Khilafat,* no. 4, July 2012, p. 23.

139. Tariq Ali, "Former Army Officer Captain Dr. Tariq Ali's Address on Being Part of Terik-e-Taliban Ihrar," *Ihya-e-Khilafat Urdu,* no. 9, November 2014, pp. 40–41.

140. Hassan, "For Pakistan's Army," 26.

141. Omar Khalid Khurasani, "Address," *Ihya-e-Khilafat Urdu,* no. 11, March 2016, p. 2.

142. "Interview with Founder of Tehrik-e-Taliban Baitullah Meshud," *Ihya-e-Khilafat,* no. 5, January 2013, p. 28.

143. "Letter from Karachi Jail," 53.

144. Robert Asen, "Seeking the 'Counter' in Counterpublics," *Communication Theory* 10, no. 4 (2000): 424–46, 427.

145. See images in *Azan,* no. 1, 2013, p. 15; *Azan,* no. 2, 2013, p. 48.

146. Seyla Benhabib, "Toward a Deliberative Model of Democratic Legitimacy," in *Democracy and Difference: Contesting the Boundaries of the Political,* ed. S. Benhabib, 67–94 (Princeton, NJ: Princeton University Press), 1996.

CHAPTER 4. SUBORDINATED FEMININITIES

1. Editors, "Rise! Oh Daughters of Hazrat Hawwa Time of Martyrdom Has Come," *Sunnat-e-Khola,* no. 1, 2017, pp. 40–44.

2. For the chapter, I have analyzed *Hilal for Her* issues published from October 2018 to July 2020.

3. "Message of the Patron-in-Chief," *Hilal for Her,* October 2018, https://www.hilal.gov.pk/her-author/message-of-the-patron-in-chief/NTQ4.html.

4. Ramsha Anis, "Soins aux Femme: Summer Time Makeup Tips," *Hilal for Her,* April 15, 2019; Khadija Shakeel, "Lose Those Extra Pounds, Naturally!" *Hilal for Her,* August 16, 2019; Ayesha Khawaja, "Pump Up Pink Power," *Hilal for Her,* May 14, 2020; Ramsha Anis, "Soins aux Femme: The New Eyebrow Trend," *Hilal for Her,* July, 13, 2020; Ramsha Anis, "Soins aux Femme: Hair Extensions," *Hilal for Her,* August, 16, 2019; Ramsha Anis, "Soins aux Femme: Hair Color," *Hilal for Her,* March, 12, 2019.

5. Khaula Bint Abdul Aziz, "My Journey from Ignorance to Guidance," *Sunnat-e-Khola,* no. 1, 2017. This article was first featured in *Mujalla Tehrik-e-Taliban* and then later reproduced in English in *Sunnat-e-Khola.*

6. Aziz, "My Journey," 13.

7. Aziz, "My Journey," 13.

8. Aziz, "My Journey," 15, 14. Emphasis added.

9. Aziz, "My Journey," 16.

10. Aziz, "My Journey," 22.

11. Ummay Bilal, "Why Did I Join Mujahidin," *Sunnat-e-Khola,* no. 2, 2017, p. 16.

12. Bilal, "Why Did I Join Mujahidin," 17.

13. Bilal, "Why Did I Join Mujahidin," 17, 20.

14. Bilal, "Why Did I Join Mujahidin," 15.

15. Editorial, "Eid ul Adha with Sunnat-e-Khaula," *Sunnat-e-Khola,* no. 2, 2017, p. 8.

16. Editorial, "Eid ul Adha," 8.

17. Editorial, "Eid ul Adha," 8.

18. Olivier Roy, *Jihad and Death: The Global Appeal of Islamic State* (New York: Oxford University Press, 2017), 9.

19. Editorial, "Rise! Oh Daughters."

20. See "Come Lets Do Jihad with Little Mujahid Omar," *Sunnat-e-Khola,* no. 1, 2017, pp. 31–34; Hajar Mujahida, "Educating Imam Mehdi's army," *Sunnat-e-Khola,* no. 2, 2017, pp. 23–24.

21. Aziz, "My Journey," 2017.

22. Shaykh Yusuf Uyyari, "The Role of Women in Ummah's Victory," *Azan,* no. 2, 2013, p. 96.

23. Uyyari, "The Role of Women," 96.

24. Abu-Nauman Salama, "Women Who Are Patient in Hardship and during Preparation for Jihad: Part 2," *Ihya-e-Khilafat Urdu,* no. 13, November 2016, pp. 38–39.

25. Salama, "Women Who Are Patient: Part 2," 38.

26. Abu-Nauman Salama, "Women Who Are Patient in Hardship and during Preparation for Jihad: Part 1," *Ihya-e-Khilafat Urdu,* no. 12, July 2016, p. 22.

27. Ummay Bilal, "Why Did I Join Mujahidin," 20.

28. See Katherine Brown, "Violence and Gender Politics in the Proto-State 'Islamic State,'" in *Revisiting Gendered States,* ed. Swati Parashar, Ann Tickner, and Jacqui True, 174–90 (Oxford: Oxford University Press, 2018).

29. Mullah Fazlulla, "Believing Women," *Sunnat-e-Khola,* no. 1, 2017, p. 7.

30. Salama, "Women Who Are Patient: Part 2," 38.

31. Umar Shaheen Haqqani, "Muslim Women's High Achievements," *Ihya-e-Khilafat Urdu,* no. 1, March 2011, p. 10.

32. Haqqani, "Muslim Women's High Achievements," 10.

33. In other Taliban magazines too, we find images of women holding guns; see Uyyari, "The Role of Women."

34. Farhat Haq, "Militarism and Motherhood," *Signs* 32, no. 4 (2007): 1023–46, 1027.

35. Haq, "Militarism and Motherhood," 1028.

36. Haq, "Militarism and Motherhood," 1028.

37. Orla Lehane et al., "Brides, Black Widows and Baby-Makers; or Not: An Analysis of the Portrayal of Women in English-Language Jihadi Magazine Image Content," *Critical Studies on Terrorism* 11, no. 3 (2018): 505–20.

38. Extended quote: "The Lord of Medina is saying: 'My great daughters, daughters bathed in the longing for martyrdom, daughters waiting for martyrdom: I do not see anyone rising up. No one is seen rising up for the dignity of mosques and the Quran. Thus you [must] stand up for jihad.' O Prophet of Allah, we are weak. We are the weaker sex, we do not have the strength—how do we wage jihad? Then suddenly you [the Prophet Muhammad], peace be upon you, visit a girl in her dream and offer one girl a shining sword, and say: 'Daughters, rise, wage jihad. Allah will help you.'" Hamna Abdullah and Umm Hassan, "Who Are the Women in the Islamabad Standoff? A Look Inside the Jamia Hafsa Madarsa," *The Middle East Media Research Institute,* July 11, 2007, https://www.memri.org/reports/who-are-women-islamabad-standoff-look-inside-jamia-hafsa-madarsa.

39. See Salih Aciksoz, *Sacrificial Limbs: Masculinity, Disability, and Political Violence in Turkey* (Oakland: University of California Press, 2019), 116.

40. SherAli Tareen, "Sayyid Abu'l-A'la Mawdudi," in *Oxford Bibliographies Online,* 2017, https://www.oxfordbibliographies.com/view/document/obo-9780195390155/obo-9780195390155-0129.xml.

41. Abul ala Mawdudi, *Purdah and the Status of Women,* trans. Al-Ashari (1938; Lahore: Islamic Publications, 1972 reprint), 78.

42. Mawdudi, *Purdah and the Status of Women,* 78.

43. Amina Jamal, "Feminism and 'Fundamentalism' in Pakistan," in *Dispatches from Pakistan,* ed. Madiha R. Tahir, Qalandar Bux Memon, and Vijay Prashad, 104–20 (Minneapolis: University of Minnesota Press, 2014).

44. Ellen Anne McLarney, *Soft Force: Women in Egypt's Islamic Awakening* (Princeton, NJ: Princeton University Press, 2015).

45. McLarney, *Soft Force,* 9.

46. Nikki Keddie, "The New Religious Politics and Women Worldwide: A Comparative Study," *Journal of Women's History* 10, no. 4 (Winter 1999): 13.

47. Shenila Khoja-Moolji, *Forging the Ideal Educated Girl: The Production of Desirable Subjects in Muslim South Asia* (Oakland: University of California Press, 2018).

48. Maleeha Zia, "Struggle Is Triumph: Major General Nigar Johar Khan," *Hilal for Her,* December 13, 2018.

49. Commander Farah Sadia, "From Fragility to Immaculate Whites," *Hilal for Her,* October 12, 2018.

50. Sadia, "From Fragility to Immaculate Whites."

51. Captain Ayesha Khalique, "Picking Up the Pieces: Walking in the Footsteps of Major Ishaq Shahid," *Hilal for Her,* December 11, 2018.

52. Khalique, "Picking Up the Pieces."

53. Khalique, "Picking Up the Pieces."

54. Khalique, "Picking Up the Pieces."

55. Major Saba Imran, "Soldiers of Peace," *Hilal for Her,* October 12, 2018.

56. Imran, "Soldiers of Peace."

57. Captain Sana Nasri, "My Days at Pakistan Military Academy: An Experience Like No Other," *Hilal for Her,* April 15, 2019.

58. Humairah Shahbaz, "War and Women—Poetic Thoughts of Allama Iqbal," *Hilal for Her,* March 12, 2019.

59. Sadia N. Qazi, "The Strength behind the Force," *Hilal for Her,* October 12, 2018.

60. Qazi, "The Strength behind the Force."

61. Qazi, "The Strength behind the Force."

62. Qazi, "The Strength behind the Force."

63. José Muñoz, "Feeling Brown: Ethnicity and Affect in Ricardo Bracho's *The Sweetest Hangover (and Other STDs)*," *Theatre Journal* 52, no. 1 (2000): 67–79, 70.

64. Hira Sagheer, "27 Things I Didn't Know About Being an Army Wife," *Hilal for Her,* December 13, 2018.

65. The army provides housing facilitates for families of officers, however, the wives of soldiers often remain in their original homes.

66. Maj Wajiha Arshad, "An Account of a Valiant Woman," *Hilal for Her,* October 12, 2018.

67. Arshad, "An Account of a Valiant Woman."

68. Mehreen Rani, "My Brother, My Pride," in *Junoon-e-Rukhe Wafa,* ISPR, 73–76 (Pakistan: Hilal Publications, 2018).

69. Zaib Rani, "I Will Follow the Footsteps of My Father," *Hilal Urdu,* October 10, 1965, 20.

70. Rani, "I Will Follow."

71. Shruti Devgan, "Making the Disappeared Appear," *Sikh Research Journal* 5, no. 1 (2020): 73–81.

72. Zaftaan Bibi, "From Mother's Milk Are Born Lion-Hearted Soldiers," *Hilal Urdu,* October 10, 1965, 21.

73. These findings also resonate with studies of military women conducted in other contexts. See Victoria Basham and Sergio Catignani, "War Is Where the Hearth Is: Gendered Labour and the Everyday Reproduction of the Geopolitical in the Army Reserves," *International Feminist Journal of Politics* 20, no. 2 (2018): 153–71; and Laurie Weinstein and Christie White, *Wives and Warriors: Women*

and the Military in the United States and Canada (Westport, CT: Bergin and Garvey, 1997).

74. ISPR Official, "Faseel-e-Jaan Se Aagay: Mehrunnisa Ka Lashkar," July 23, 2018, video, 57:21, https://www.youtube.com/watch?v=b94j__TkuJM.

75. Note the influence of the martial race theory here, whereby Pashtuns are imagined as being skilled only in martial trades such as weaponsmithing.

76. Purnima Mankekar, *Screening Culture, Viewing Politics: An Ethnography of Television, Womanhood, and Nation in Postcolonial India* (Durham, NC: Duke University Press, 1999).

77. Durdana Najam, "Support Women Entrepreneurship!" *Hilal for Her,* May 15, 2019; Anam Sarah, "Work-Life Balance: Advice For Mothers," *Hilal for Her,* May 14, 2020; Rija Tayyab, "Being a Woman in the Workplace," *Hilal for Her,* n.d.; Noor Irshad, "Women Build Nations," *Hilal for Her,* August 16, 2019; Sabawat Gull, "How to Shift Offline Business to Online," *Hilal for Her,* July 13, 2020; Aiza Nasir, "Miami: The Magic City," *Hilal for Her,* June 10, 2019; Aiza Nasir, "Notes from Greece," *Hilal for Her,* March 12, 2019; Aiza Nasir, "Wandering the Streets of London," *Hilal for Her,* January 14, 2019; Aiza Nasir, "Travelling through History in Egypt," *Hilal for Her,* April 15, 2019.

78. Maria Rashid, for instance, documents one such unraveling of soldiers' female relations; Maria Rashid, *Dying to Serve: Militarism, Affect, and the Politics of Sacrifice in the Pakistan Army* (Stanford, CA: Stanford University Press, 2020). Also see Sue Jervis, *Relocation, Gender, and Emotion: A Psycho-Social Perspective on the Experiences of Military Wives* (London: Karnac Books, 2011); and Alexandra Hyde, "The Civilian Wives of Military Personnel: Mobile Subjects or Agents of Militarisation?" in *The Palgrave International Handbook of Gender and the Military,* ed. Rachel Woodward and Claire Duncanson, 195–210 (London: Palgrave, 2017).

CHAPTER 5. KINSHIP METAPHORS

1. "Lahore Raid: Arrested Woman Terror Suspect Linked to ISIS," *The Hindu,* April 16, 2017, www.thehindu.com/news/international/lahore-raid-arrested-woman-terror-suspect-linked-to-isis/article18071417.ece.

2. Bina Shah, "Naureen Laghari, Pakistan's Very Own IS Bride," *Express Tribune Blogs,* April 18, 2017, https://blogs.tribune.com.pk/story/48864/naureen-laghari-pakistans-very-own-is-bride.

3. Per the Counterterrorism Department, as noted in Imran Gabol, "Wife of 'Terrorist' Killed in Lahore Encounter 'Joined IS': CTD Sources," *Dawn,* April 16, 2017, https://www.dawn.com/news/1327352.

4. Scholars have written extensively about the use of kinship language and the iconography of familial space in the making of the nation. See Michael Schatzberg, *The Dialects of Oppression in Zaire* (Bloomington: Indiana University Press, 1991); Ann McClintock, "Family Feuds: Gender, Nationalism and the Family," *Feminist*

Review 44 (1993): 61–81"; Rubina Saigol, *The Pakistan Project: A Feminist Perspective on Nation and Identity* (Delhi: Women Unlimited, 2013).

5. Judith Butler, *Notes toward a Performative Theory of Assembly* (Cambridge, MA: Harvard University Press, 2015), 16; Aslı Zengin's examination of the funeral and burial practices of transgender people in Turkey points to performances of sovereignty that operate through assertions of kinship, care and intimacy. Zengin notes how transgender communities stake a claim on their members upon their death in order to provide them the kind of funeral services that they would have desired. In staking such a claim they forge an alliance against the state and the biological family. See Aslı Zengin, "The Afterlife of Gender: Sovereignty, Intimacy and Muslim Funerals of Transgender People in Turkey," *Cultural Anthropology* 34, no. 1 (2019): 78–102.

6. See Saadia Toor, "Moral Regulation in a Postcolonial Nation-State," *Interventions* 9, no. 2 (2007): 255–75; Amina Jamal, "Gender, Citizenship, and the Nation-State in Pakistan: Willful Daughters or Free Citizens?" *Signs* 31, no. 2 (2006): 283–304; Moon Charania, *Will the Real Pakistani Woman Please Stand Up?* (New York: McFarland, 2015); Shahnaz Rouse, "The Outsider(s) Within: Sovereignty and Citizenship in Pakistan," in *Appropriating Gender: Women's Activism and Politicized Religion in South Asia,* ed. Patricia Jeffrey and Amrita Basu, 52–70, Zones of Religion (New York: Routledge, 1998).

7. ARY News, "11th Hour 17th April 2017: Why Educated People Are Turning towards Extremism?" April 17, 2017, video, 37:42, https://www.youtube.com/watch?v=DOTpZCFhWzY.

8. Power TV Talk Shows, "DG ISPR Media Briefing about Noreen Laghari Case 17 April 2017," April 17, 2017, video, 45:55, https://www.youtube.com/watch?v=OSkWF2-T32w.

9. Power TV Talk Shows, "DG ISPR Media Briefing."

10. SAMAA TV, "DG ISPR Full Press Conference: Live: SAMAA TV: 10 May 2017," May 10, 2017, video, 19:31, https://www.youtube.com/watch?v = WHiy Em9njxE.

11. SAMAA TV, "DG ISPR Full Press Conference."

12. SAMAA TV, "DG ISPR Full Press Conference."

13. SAMAA TV, "DG ISPR Full Press Conference."

14. For more see Lisa Smyth, "Narratives of Irishness and the Problem of Abortion: The X Case of 1992," *Feminist Review* 60, no. 1 (1998): 61–83; Robbie Duschinsky, "Sexualization: A State of Injury," *Theory and Psychology* 23, no. 3 (2013): 351–70. For the South Asian context, see Khoja-Moolji, *Forging the Ideal Educated Girl;* Ruby Lal, *Coming of Age in Nineteenth-Century India: The Girl-Child and the Art of Playfulness* (Cambridge: Cambridge University Press, 2012).

15. Neo TV Network, "More Revelations about the Noreen Laghari, Arrested in Lahore!" April 17, 2017, video, 1:47, https://www.youtube.com/watch?v= zo8L1dvfsrY.

16. Neo TV Network, "More Revelations."

17. Neo TV Network, "More Revelations."

18. Neo TV Network, "More Revelations."

19. SAMAA TV, "DG ISPR Full Press Conference."

20. For example, 92 News HD, "Exclusive Interview with Noreen Laghari," May 8, 2017, video, 31:34, https://www.youtube.com/watch?v=dAxDHmjyt6U.

21. Ayesha Jalal, "The Convenience of Subservience: Women and the State of Pakistan," In *Women, Islam, and the State,* ed. Deniz Kandiyoti, 77–114 (London: Palgrave Macmillan, 1991), 85.

22. Khoja-Moolji, *Forging the Ideal Educated Girl.*

23. Jamal, "Gender, Citizenship, and the Nation-State."

24. "Hafiz Abdul Waheed (petitioner) versus Miss Asma Jehangir and Another (Respondents), Criminal Miscellaneous, no. 425-H of 1996, Decided on March 10, 1997," in *The All Pakistan Legal Decisions,* 301–84 (Lahore: PLD Publishers, 1997); Beena Sarwar, "Saima Wins Case; But Judgement Threatens Women's Rights," *IPS,* March 1997, http://www.ipsnews.net/1997/03/pakistan-saima-wins-case-but-judgement-threatens-womens-rights/.

25. Pakistan Legal Decisions, "Hafiz Abdul Waheed," 312–52.

26. See Asifa Quraishi and Frank Vogel, *The Islamic Marriage Contract* (Cambridge, MA: Harvard University Press, 2009).

27. Pakistan Legal Decisions, "Hafiz Abdul Waheed," 326, 351.

28. Pakistan Legal Decisions, "Hafiz Abdul Waheed," 351.

29. Pakistan Legal Decisions, "Hafiz Abdul Waheed," 343.

30. Pakistan Legal Decisions, "Hafiz Abdul Waheed," 382, 383.

31. Pakistan Legal Decisions, "Hafiz Abdul Waheed," 383.

32. Pakistan Legal Decisions, "Hafiz Abdul Waheed," 383.

33. Pakistan Legal Decisions, "Hafiz Abdul Waheed," 369.

34. Pakistan Legal Decisions, "Hafiz Abdul Waheed," 379

35. This logic is not new; it is simply a reiteration of earlier arguments about women's seclusion in which the middle-class home is imagined as the bastion of purity and crossing its boundaries signifies a woman's transformation from a good anonymous woman to a transgressive woman or an agent of *fitna* [social and moral chaos], as Amina Jamal observes; Jamal, "Gender, Citizenship, and the Nation-State."

36. 92 News HD, "Exclusive Interview with Noreen Laghari."

37. USAID, "Department of State and USAID Joint Strategy on Countering Violent Extremism," May 2016, https://2009–2017.state.gov/documents/organization /257913.pdf, 10.

38. USAID, "Pakistan," last modified March 27, 2019, https://www.usaid.gov /political-transition-initiatives/pakistan (site discontinued). On October 1, 2020 the program was closed; the archived website is available at https://www.usaid.gov /stabilization-and-transitions/closed-programs/pakistan, accessed February 2021.

39. SAMAA TV, "DG ISPR Full Press Conference."

40. "Gang-Rape Victim Narrates Ordeal," *Dawn,* July 6, 2002, https://www .dawn.com/news/46418/gang-rape-victim-narrates-ordeal.

41. Nicholas Kristof, "Sentenced to Be Raped," *New York Times,* September 29, 2004, https://www.nytimes.com/2004/09/29/opinion/sentenced-to-be-raped

.html (accessed July 5, 2020); Nicholas Kristof, "The Rosa Parks for the 21st Century," *New York Times,* Nov 8, 2005, https://www.nytimes.com/2005/11/08 /opinion/the-rosa-parks-for-the-21st-century.html.

42. Chiade O'Shea, "School Hope for Rape Victim," *BBC News,* December 7, 2004, http://news.bbc.co.uk/2/hi/south_asia/4042941.stm; Declan Walsh, "Pakistani Rape Victim Is Glamour's Woman of Year," *The Guardian,* November 2, 2005, https:// www.theguardian.com/media/2005/nov/02/pressandpublishing.pakistan.

43. For a critique of Western media practices, see Shenila Khoja-Moolji, "The Making of Humans and Their Others in and through Transnational Human Rights Advocacy: Exploring the Cases of Mukhtar Mai and Malala Yousafzai," *Signs: Journal of Women in Culture and Society* 42, no. 2 (2017): 377–402.

44. As cited in "Rape Victim Can Travel, Musharraf Says," *New York Times,* June 30, 2005, https://www.nytimes.com/2005/06/30/world/asia/rape-victim-can-travel-musharraf-says.html.

45. "Pakistan Rape Victim 'Can Travel,'" *BBC News,* June 29, 2005, http://news .bbc.co.uk/2/hi/south_asia/4635017.stm.

46. Glenn Kessler, "Musharraf Denies Rape Comments," *Washington Post,* September 19, 2005, http://www.washingtonpost.com/wp-dyn/content/article/2005 /09/18/AR2005091800554.html?noredirect = on.

47. For more on how paternal publics police women outside the intimate spaces of the home, see the discussion of Qandeel Baloch's murder in Shenila Khoja-Moolji, "The Politics of Legislating 'Honor Crime' in Contemporary Pakistan," in *Gender-Based Violence,* ed. Lila Abu-Lughod, forthcoming; and Shenila Khoja-Moolji, "Patriarchal Assemblages," *South Asia: Journal of South Asian Studies,* forthcoming 2021.

48. See Ritu Menon and Kamla Bhasin, *Borders and Boundaries: Women in India's Partition* (New Brunswick, NJ: Rutgers University Press, 1998); Urvashi Bhutalia, *The Other Side of Silence* (Durham, NC: Duke University Press, 2000); Deepti Misri, "The Violence of Memory: Renarrating Partition Violence in Shauna Singh Badwin's *What the Body Remembers,*" *Meridians* 11, no. 1 (2011): 1–25.

49. Khattab Ismail and Aafia Siddiqui, "Prisoner 650: Afia Siddiqui—The Daughter of the Ummah," *Azan,* no. 5, 2014, p. 30.

50. Ismail and Siddiqui, "Prisoner 650," 31.

51. Aasim Umer, "The Daughters of Shaam (Syria)," *Ihya-e-Khilafat Urdu,* no. 6, May 2013, p. 13.

52. *Mujalla-Tehrik-e-Taliban,* no. 4, October 2017.

53. Zahid Hussain, "The Legacy of Lal Masjid," *Dawn News,* July 9, 2017, https://www.dawn.com/news/1344098.

54. Hussain, "The Legacy of Lal Masjid."

55. Munir Ahmad, "Pakistani Woman Freed in Brothel Case," *Washington Post,* March 29, 2007, http://www.washingtonpost.com/wp-dyn/content/article/2007/03 /29/AR2007032900339.html?noredirect=on.

56. Hussain, "Legacy of Lal Masjid." See also Faisal Devji, "Red Mosque," in *Under the Drones: Modern Lives in the Afghanistan-Pakistan Borderlands,* ed.

Shahzad Bashir and Robert Crews, 153–61 (Cambridge, MA: Harvard University Press, 2012).

57. Muhammad Qasim, "Malala, Education and an Unruly Media," *Azan,* no. 1, 2013, p. 28.

58. Ikrimah Anwar, "On U-Turns and the Pakistan Army Doctrine," *Azan,* no. 1, 2013, pp. 30–37.

59. Mufti Umar Zaman, "Why Jihad in Pakistan? Part 1 of 3," *Ihya-e-Khilafat Urdu,* no. 1, March 2011, p. 35.

60. Zaman, "Why Jihad in Pakistan?"

61. Tariq Mahenna, *Azan,* no. 1, March 2013, p. 22.

62. Mahenna, *Azan,* no. 1, March 2013, p. 22.

63. Anwar, "On U-Turns," 30–37.

64. For more see "Pakistan Taliban Flaunt Attacks on Local Forces," *BBC Monitoring South Asia,* December 22, 2020.

65. M. Umar, "The Pain of Syria," *Azan,* no. 2, 2013, p. 51.

66. Umer, "The Daughters of Shaam."

67. Shaykh Khalid Husainain, "A Quiet Talk with Obama," *Azan,* no. 1, 2013, p. 29.

68. Umm Khurasan, "A Letter from a *Mujahida* in Khurasan to a *Mujahida* Sister in Syria," *Mujalla Tehrik-e-Taliban,* no. 2, March 2017, p. 42.

69. Khurasan, "A Letter from a *Mujahida.*"

70. Roxanne Euben, "Humiliation and the Political Mobilization of Masculinity," *Political Theory* 43, no. 4 (2015): 500–32, 514.

71. A. Jawzi, "Where Are the Men?" *Azan,* no. 2, 2013, p. 56.

72. Jawzi, "Where Are the Men?"

73. Jawzi, "Where Are the Men?"

74. Jawzi, "Where Are the Men?"

75. Jawzi, "Where Are the Men?"

76. Umer, "The Daughters of Shaam."

77. Osama bin Laden, *Azan* 6, 2014, back cover.

78. These findings resonate with Cabeiri Robinson's study of *mujahidin* in Kashmir. In that context too the figure of the *mujahid* emerges as a defender of victimized Kashmiri women, transforming women into the terrain of the Kashmiri struggle. See Cabeiri deBergh Robinson, *Body of Victim, Body of Warrior: Refugee Families and the Making of Kashmiri Jihadists* (Oakland: University of California Press, 2013).

79. Malala Yousafzai, "Diary of a Pakistani Schoolgirl," *BBC News,* January 19, 2009, http://news.bbc.co.uk/2/hi/south_asia/7834402.stm.

80. For more see Shenila Khoja-Moolji, "Reading Malala: (De)(Re)Territorialization of Muslim Collectivities," *Comparative Studies of South Asia, Africa and the Middle East* 35, no. 3 (2015): 539–56.

81. Qasim, "Malala, Education and an Unruly Media," 24.

82. Qasim, "Malala, Education and an Unruly Media," 25.

83. Adnan Rasheed, "An Open Letter to Malala from Adnan Rasheed," *Azan,* no. 3, June/July 2013, 48–52.

84. Rasheed, "An Open Letter to Malala," 50.

85. Hafsa Khurasaani, "Malala," *Sunnat-e-Khola,* no. 3, p. 25.

86. Dr. Khaula bint-e-Abdul Aziz, "Muslim Woman a Political Tool," *Sunnat-e-Khola,* no. 2, 2017, pp. 11–13.

87. Aziz, "Muslim Woman a Political Tool," 12.

88. Mukaram Khurasani, "My Body, My Choice," *Mujalla Tehrik-e-Taliban,* no. 7, December, 2019, pp. 58–59.

89. Khurasani, "My Body, My Choice," 58.

90. Khurasani, "My Body, My Choice," 59.

91. The chairman of PTI, Imran Khan, had been a vocal supporter of Siddiqui. When he became prime minister, she even wrote him a letter seeking his help.

92. The poster can be seen here: "Pakistan Tehrik-e-Insaaf (PTI) activists," photo by Arif Ali/AFP via Getty Images, https://www.gettyimages.com/detail /news-photo/pakistan-tehrik-e-insaaf-activists-demand-he-release-of-us-news-photo/95936412. The second poster reads: "Who is the biggest terrorist? America."

93. Another protest held by the Human Rights Network in Karachi on September 22, 2010 reiterated this notion of Pakistan's enslavement by the United States. Here, demonstrators' posters rejected American interventions and equated Siddiqui's release with achieving freedom for the nation: "We don't want enslavement by the US . . . we want Aafia's freedom." The poster can be seen here: "Pakistani political parties and human rights," photo by Asif Hassan/AFP via Getty Images, https:// www.gettyimages.com/detail/news-photo/pakistani-political-parties-and-human-rights-activists-news-photo/104353167.

94. Eve Kosofsky Sedgwick, *Touching Feeling: Affect, Pedagogy, Performativity* (Durham, NC: Duke University Press, 2003), 37.

95. The poster can be seen in "'Aafia United: Imran Khan calls up Altaf Hussain," LUBP, March 20, 2011, https://lubpak.com/archives/43182.

96. Amahl Bishara, "Sovereignty and Popular Sovereignty for Palestinians and Beyond." *Cultural Anthropology* 32, no. 3 (2017): 350.

97. Deborah Gould, "Affect and Protest," in *Political Emotions,* ed. Janet Staiger, Ann Cvetkovich, and Ann Reynolds (New York: Routledge, 2010), 25.

98. Gould, "Affect and Protest," 25.

99. Declan Walsh, "Pakistan Erupts after US Jailing of 'Daughter of Nation' Aafia Siddiqui," *The Guardian,* September 24, 2010, https://www.theguardian .com/world/2010/sep/24/pakistan-aafia-siddiqui-jailed-protests.

100. Robert Fisk, "The Mysterious Case of the Grey Lady of Bagram," *Independent,* March 19, 2010, https://www.independent.co.uk/voices/commentators/fisk /robert-fisk-the-mysterious-case-of-the-grey-lady-of-bagram-1923808.html.

101. "Imran Announces to Bring Back Aafia, Others Languishing in Foreign Jails," *Dunya News,* July 9, 2018, https://dunyanews.tv/en/Pakistan/447247-Imran-Khan-Aafia-Siddiqui-PTI-election-manifesto-jail-repatriation.

102. "Title of 'Daughter of Pakistan' Demanded for Dr Aafia," *ARY News,* March 18, 2019, https://arynews.tv/en/title-daughter-of-pakistan-for-dr-aafia/.

103. For a genealogy of how women have been tied to state projects and mascu-line honor, see Khoja-Moolji, *Forging the Ideal Educated Girl;* for this figuration's appearance in nationalist poetry, see Saigol, *The Pakistan Project,* 76–100; for women's bodies as the terrain of militarism, see Rubina Saigol, "Militarization, Nation and Gender: Women's Bodies as Arenas of Violent Conflict," in *Deconstruct-ing Sexuality in the Middle East: Challenges and Discourses,* ed. Pinar Ilkkaracan, 165–75 (Burlington, VT: Ashgate Publishing, 2008).

104. Misri, "The Violence of Memory," 11.

CHAPTER 6. MANAGING AFFECT

1. Pakistani Heroes, "ISPR Releases New Song Mitti Ki Maaye," 2015, video, 4:25, https://www.dailymotion.com/video/x377yya, accessed July 5, 2020.

2. See Sara Ruddick, *Maternal Thinking: Toward a Politics of Peace* (Boston: Beacon, 1989); Cynthia Enloe, *Maneuvers: The Militarization of Women's Lives* (Berkeley: University of California Press, 2000); Laleh Khalili, *Heroes and Martyrs of Palestine: The Politics of National Commemoration* (Cambridge: Cambridge University Press, 2009).

3. See Enloe, *Maneuvers;* Susan Zeiger, "She Didn't Raise Her Boy to Be a Slacker: Motherhood, Conscription, and the Culture of the First World War," *Feminist Studies* 22, no. 1 (1996): 7–39; Lorraine Bayard de Volo, "Mobilizing Moth-ers for War: Cross-National Framing Strategies in Nicaragua's Contra War," *Gender and Society* 18, no. 6 (2004): 715–34.

4. Swati Parashar, "The Postcolonial/Emotional State," in *Revisiting Gendered States,* ed. Swati Parashar, Ann Tickner, and Jacqui True, 157–73 (Oxford: Oxford University Press, 2018).

5. Sigmund Freud, "Mourning and Melancholia," in *A General Selection from the Works of Sigmund Freud,* ed. John Richman, 36–53 (New York: Anchor Books, 1989). Freud later rescinded this stark distinction, arguing that melancholia may be an integral component of mourning.

6. Freud, "Mourning and Melancholia," 253.

7. See David Eng and David Kazanjian, eds., *Loss: The Politics of Mourning* (Berkeley: University of California Press, 2003).

8. See Sara Ahmed, "Happy Objects," in *The Affect Theory Reader,* ed. Melissa Gregg and Gregory Seigworth, 29–51 (Durham, NC: Duke University Press, 2010), 39.

9. *Nawa-i-Waqt,* December 17, 2014.

10. Personal communication with the artist.

11. Marta Zarzycka, "The World Press Photo Contest and Visual Tropes," *Pho-tographies* 6, no. 1 (2013): 177–84, 179.

12. Diana Taylor, *Disappearing Acts: Spectacles of Gender and Nationalism in Argentina's "Dirty War,"* (Durham, NC: Duke University Press, 1997).

13. Barbie Zelizer, *About to Die: How News Images Move the Public* (New York: Oxford University Press, 2010).

14. Arlie Hochschild, *The Managed Heart* (Berkeley: University of California Press, 2012), 20.

15. Salih Aciksoz, "Sacrificial Limbs of Sovereignty: Disabled Veterans, Masculinity, and Nationalist Politics in Turkey," *Medical Anthropology Quarterly* 26, no. 1 (2012): 4–25, 13.

16. Ali Moen Nawazish, "Maa(n), mujhay maaf kar daina," *Jang Urdu,* December 18, 2014, https://jang.com.pk/news/17853.

17. Nawazish, "Maa(n)."

18. Nawazish, "Maa(n)."

19. Nawazish, "Maa(n)."

20. Rafia Zakaria, "Woman of the Year: The Pakistani Mother," *Dawn,* December 29, 2014, https://www.dawn.com/news/1153845.

21. Faiza Iqbal, "14 Pakistani Women Who Help Us Hold Our Heads Up High," *Express Tribune Blogs,* March 8, 2015, https://blogs.tribune.com.pk/story/26507/14-pakistani-women-who-help-us-hold-our-heads-up-high/.

22. Iqbal, "14 Pakistani Women."

23. Funny Compilations, "Rahim Shah Brand-New Song Maa Kisko Jhulao 2015," June 16, 2015, video, 4:15, https://www.youtube.com/watch?v=0Z2WLvJvFns.

24. Sheema Mehkar, "O' Mother, Cry Not," *Express Tribune Blogs,* December 16, 2015, https://blogs.tribune.com.pk/story/30854/o-mother-cry-not/.

25. Mehkar, "O' Mother."

26. Amir Zia, "Beyond the Day of APS Tragedy," *Hilal English,* November 30, 2015.

27. Enloe, *Maneuvers,* 237.

28. Enloe, *Maneuvers,* 237.

29. ISPR Official, "Chadar hai Maa ki: Najam Sheraz (ISPR Official Video)," January 11, 2018, https://www.youtube.com/watch?v=Zg5foKxeUmI. This video was posted to YouTube in January 2018 and boasts over half a million views as of January 2021.

30. Readers familiar with the Urdu language will note that the ISPR's translation is not precise. It simply seeks to convey the crux of their message.

31. Muhammad Usman Ghani, "Khak Jo Khoon Main Milai Hai: *ISPR New Pakistan Army Song:* Rahat Fateh Ali Khan," September 9, 2016, video, 4:44, https://www.dailymotion.com/video/x4spurw. This video has not been posted officially by the ISPR, but this unofficial posting boasts more than 29,000 views as of January 2021.

32. Maleeha Zia, "Mother of a Martyr: A Hero in Her Own Right," *Hilal for Her,* 2019.

33. Zia, "Mother of a Martyr."

34. Zia, "Mother of a Martyr."

35. ISPR Official, "Yaaro mera yaar na raha: Sahir Ali Bagga: Defence and Martyrs Day 2015 (ISPR Official Song)," January 4, 2018, video, 4:48, https://www.youtube.com/watch?v=meNnWScf6ss. As of January 2021, it has over two and a half million views.

36. Andaleeb, the mother of APS student Hazefa Abtab, embodies this figural mourning mother. In an interview with her, published in *Hilal Urdu,* she explains: "On this occasion I would give this message to my son, 'Son, your martyrdom is the result of my prayers where I used to ask for a life full of happiness and high status for you.' The status that our son Hazefa Abtab *shahid* has obtained for us [alluding to her status as the mother of *shahid*], no child can obtain a higher honor for his parents. For this we will remain forever grateful to Hazefa Abtab *shahid*"; as cited in Rabia Rahem Ruhi, "Even Today I Smell Your Fragrance," *Hilal Urdu,* December 2015.

37. Ben Anderson, "Affective Atmospheres," *Emotion, Space and Society* 2, no. 2 (December 2009): 77–81, 79.

38. Images from the Muttahida Quami Movement rally in Karachi on December 19, 2014 can be found here: "Document Date: December 19, 2014," photo by Reuters/Athar Hussain, https://pictures.reuters.com/CS.aspx?VP3=SearchResult &VBID=2CoFCI1PW9oM5&SMLS=1&RW=1280&RH=648&POPUPPN=10 &POPUPIID=2Co408WUX4AG1.

39. Images from the Pakistan Tehreek Insaf women's wing rally in Lahore on December 18, 2014 can be found here: "Pakistani Workers of Political Party Pakistan Tehreek Insaf," photo by Rana Sajid Hussain/Pacific Press/LightRocket, https://www.gettyimages.dk/detail/news-photo/pakistani-workers-of-political-party-pakistan-tehreek-insaf-news-photo/460740322?adppopup = true.

40. Ghareeda Farooqi, "They Are Not from Us," *Hilal Urdu,* February 2015.

41. Maryam Irshad, "Martyr Brother of Two Sisters," *Hilal Urdu,* December 2015.

42. As cited in Mohammad Ashfaq, "Emotional Scenes as Parents of APS Students Gather," *Dawn,* July 15, 2015, https://www.dawn.com/news/1194583.

43. Amir Zia, "Beyond the Day of APS Tragedy," *Hilal English,* November 30, 2015; article titles in the February 2015 issue of *Hilal Urdu* include "Ending Terrorism Is a National Responsibility," "These Steps Will Not Stop," "Ending Terrorism," and "They Are Not from Us."

44. de Volo, "Mobilizing Mothers for War," 730.

45. Lorraine de Volo, "Drafting Motherhood: Maternal Imagery and Organizations in the United States and Nicaragua," in *The Women and War Reader,* ed. Lois Ann Lorentzen and Jennifer Turpin, 240–53 (New York: New York University Press, 1998), 242.

46. See for instance: "Pakistan Taliban: Peshawar School Attack Leaves 141 Dead," *BBC,* December 16, 2014, https://www.bbc.com/news/world-asia-30491435; Peter Popham, "Peshawar School Attack: 'I Will Never Forget the Black Boots . . . It Was Like Death Approaching Me,'" *Independent,* December 16, 2014, https://www.independent.co.uk/news/world/asia/peshawar-school-attack-i-will-never-forget-the-black-bootsit-was-like-death-approaching-me-9929563.html; "Taliban Storms Pakistan School," *CBS News,* https://www.cbsnews.com/pictures/taliban-storm-pakistan-school/5/; Ismail Khan, "Taliban Massacre 131 Schoolchildren: Principal among 141 Dead in Attack on Army Public School, Peshawar," *Dawn,* December 17, 2014, https://www.dawn.com/news/1151361; Declan Walsh, "Taliban Besiege Pakistan School, Leaving 145 Dead," *New York Times,* December 16, 2014,

https://www.nytimes.com/2014/12/17/world/asia/taliban-attack-pakistani-school.html.

47. Qasim Nauman, Safdar Dawar, and Saeed Shah, "Taliban Militants Attack Pakistan school," *Wall Street Journal*, December 17, 2014, https://www.wsj.com/articles/taliban-militants-attack-pakistan-school-1418716418.

48. Roland Barthes, *Camera Lucida: Reflections on Photography*, trans. Richard Howard (New York: Hill and Wang, 1981), 82, 77.

49. Sara Ahmed, "Killing Joy: Feminism and the History of Happiness," *Signs* 35, no. 3 (2010): 571–94, 582.

50. Eng and Kazanjian, *Loss*, 2.

51. Jonathan Flatley, *Affective Mapping* (Cambridge, MA: Harvard University Press, 2008).

52. Catriona Mortimer-Sandilands, "Melancholy Natures, Queer Ecologies," in *Queer Ecologies: Sex, Nature, Politics, Desire*, ed. Catriona Mortimer-Sandilands and Bruce Erickson, 331–58 (Bloomington: Indiana University Press: 2010), 333.

53. Ahmed, "Happy Objects," 39.

54. Pakistan Media Today, "Pakistani Media Hided [*sic*] This Video || APS Mothers Protesting Oustide [*sic*] Charsadda Hospital," January 26, 2016, video, https://www.youtube.com/watch?v=9sDPWg-DmW8, accessed September 9, 2019, listed as "private" as of February 2021.

55. Pakistan Media Today, "Pakistani Media Hided." Translation mine.

56. Pakistan Media Today, "Pakistani Media Hided."

57. The family of slain student Hassan Zeb created a rooftop shrine covered with pictures of the students and staff killed in the APS attack. It has become a central gathering place for all the APS families.

58. As cited in Atika Rehman, "One Year Later: Together in Grief," *Dawn*, December 16, 2015, https://www.dawn.com/news/1226718.

59. "Imran Khan Faces Wrath of Protesting Parents as He Arrives at APS," *Express Tribune*, January 14, 2015, https://tribune.com.pk/story/821671/imran-khan-faces-wrath-of-protesting-parents-as-he-arrives-at-aps/.

60. Amel Ghani, "Peace Conference: Mothers of APS Victims Demand Justice," *Express Tribune*, May 28, 2015, https://tribune.com.pk/story/893477/peace-conference-mothers-of-aps-victims-demand-justice/.

61. "They Named a Road after My Martyred Child. What Good Is That?" *Geo TV*, 2017, https://www.geo.tv/latest/172447, accessed July 6, 2020.

62. The Pakistani, "Very Emotional Speech of Mother of an APS Martyr," October 9, 2016, video, 1:22, https://www.youtube.com/watch?v=L9sYCOIbrJ4.

63. "No One Wants Us to Speak," *Geo TV*, 2017, https://www.geo.tv/latest/172485, accessed July 6, 2020.

64. Haq Media Group, "APS Peshawar Mother," January 31, 2016, video, 2:50, https://www.youtube.com/watch?v=WcmIqzb73MM.

65. Haq Media Group, "APS Peshawar Mother."

66. Salih Aciksoz, *Sacrificial Limbs: Masculinity, Disability, and Political Violence in Turkey* (Oakland: University of California Press, 2019), 2.

67. Haq Media Group, "APS Peshawar Mother."

68. Haq Media Group, "APS Peshawar Mother."

69. Judith Butler, *Notes Toward a Performative Theory of Assembly* (Cambridge, MA: Harvard University Press, 2015), 94.

70. PlayMax, "Shaheed Aimal Khan: Parents Vedio [*sic*]: Aimal Khan Parents at ARY Studio: Programme Good Morning Pakistan," March 6, 2015, video, 20:02, https://www.dailymotion.com/video/x2ito4c.

71. Mortimer-Sandilands, "Melancholy Natures," 333; also see Ann Cvetkovich on the creative potential of melancholy in *An Archive of Feelings: Trauma, Sexuality, and Lesbian Public Cultures* (Durham, NC: Duke University Press, 2003).

72. "They Named a Road after My Martyred Child."

73. Abu Salamah al-Muhajir, "Oh my Mother!" *Azan*, no. 4, 2013, p. 35.

74. Editors, "Rise! Oh Daughters of Hazrat Hawwa Time of Martyrdom Has Come," *Sunnat-e-Khola*, no. 1, 2017, pp. 40–44.

75. Abu Salamah Al Muhajir, "To the Jihadis in the West," *Azan*, no. 4, 2013, pp. 25–34.

76. Muhajir, "To the Jihadis in the West," 28.

77. Maulana Asim Umar, "The Pain of Syria," *Azan*, no. 2, 2013, p. 52.

78. Maulana Asim Umar, "To the Muslims of India," *Azan*, no. 3, 2013, p. 46.

79. Editors, "Eid ul adha with Sunnat e Khaula," *Sunnat-e-Khola*, no. 2, 2017, p. 5. Editors, "Pak-India Decisive War," *Sunnat-e-Khola*, no. 1, 2017, p. 5.

CONCLUSION

1. Lauren Berlant has made this observation about family life in the context of the United States. Lauren Berlant, *Cruel Optimism* (Durham, NC: Duke University Press, 2011); and Lauren Berlant, *The Anatomy of National Fantasy* (Chicago: University of Chicago Press, 1991).

2. Ann Stoler draws attention to graded variations and degrees of sovereignty in Stoler, "On Degrees of Imperial Sovereignty," *Public Culture* 18, no. 1 (2006): 125–46.

3. ISPR Official, "Ye Banday Mitti kay Banday: One Year of Zarb e Azb (ISPR Official Video)," June 2015, video, 3:56, https://www.youtube.com/watch?v=vpl1FyToXck..

4. Muhammad Ali Jinnah, "Address to Muslims of Gaya" (1938), *Jinnah: Speeches and Statements 1947–1948* (Karachi: Oxford University Press, 2000).

5. Pervez Hoodbhoy, "Jinnah and the Islamic State: Setting the Record Straight," *Economic and Political Weekly* 42, no. 32 (Aug. 11–17, 2007): 3,300–3.

6. Salih Aciksoz, *Sacrificial Limbs: Masculinity, Disability, and Political Violence in Turkey* (Oakland: University of California Press, 2019), 133.

7. Nira Yuval-Davis, *Gender and Nation* (London: SAGE Publications, 1997); Anne McClintock, "Family Feuds: Gender, Nationalism and the Family," *Feminist Review* 44 (1993): 61–81; Tamar Mayer, ed., *Gender Ironies of Nationalism: Sexing*

the Nation (New York: Routledge, 2000); Veena Das, "Violence, Gender, and Subjectivity," *Annual Review of Anthropology* 37 (2008): 283–99.

8. In doing so, I join emergent scholarship that focuses on the role of masculinities in the process of nation-building, particularly Pablo Anderson and Simon Wendt, *Masculinities and the Nation in the Modern World* (New York: Palgrave, 2015); Joanne Nagel, "Masculinity and Nationalism: Gender and Sexuality in the Making of Nations," *Ethnic and Racial Studies* 21, no. 2 (1998): 242–69; and Sikata Banerjee, *Make Me a Man! Masculinity, Hinduism, and Nationalism in India* (New York: SUNY Press, 2005).

9. See Shireen Burki, "The Politics of Misogyny: General Zia-ul-Haq's Islamization of Pakistan's Legal System," *Contemporary Justice Review* 19 no. 1 (2016): 103–19; Sara Brightman, "Rights, Women, and the State of Pakistan," *Contemporary Justice Review* 18, no. 3 (2015): 334–51.

10. For more, see Shenila Khoja-Moolji, "The Politics of Legislating 'Honor Crime' in Contemporary Pakistan," in *Gender-Based Violence,* edited by Lila Abu-Lughod, forthcoming.

11. Victoria Bernal, "Diaspora and the Afterlife of Violence: Eritrean National Narratives and What Goes without Saying," *American Anthropologist* 119, no. 1 (2017), 23–34, 23.

12. Also see Lorraine Dowler, "Gender, Militarization and Sovereignty," *Geography Compass* 6, no. 8 (2012): 490–99.

13. Nazish Brohi and Saba Gul Khattak, *Exploring Women's Voices: Women in Conflict Zones: The Pakistan Study: Community Conversations in Balochistan and Swat* (Pakistan: Women's Regional Network, 2014), 39. For Pakistani feminists' critique of militarization, see essays in Neelam Hussain, Samlya Mumtaz, and Rubina Saigol, eds., *Engendering the Nation-State* (Lahore: Simorgh, 1997).

14. Achille Mbembe, *Necropolitics* (Durham, NC: Duke University Press, 2019), 36–38.

BIBLIOGRAPHY

Abbas, Hassan. "Musharraf Contends with the Pashtun Element in the Pakistani Army." *Terrorism Focus* 3, no. 42 (November 2006), https://jamestown.org/program/musharraf-contends-with-the-pashtun-element-in-the-pakistani-army/.

———. "A Profile of Tehrik-i-Taliban Pakistan." *CTC Sentinel* 1, no. 2 (2009): 1–4.

Abbas, Sadia. "Itineraries of Conversion." In *Beyond Crisis: Re-Evaluating Pakistan,* edited by Naveeda Khan, 344–69. New Delhi: Taylor and Francis Group, 2010.

Abdullah, Hamna, and Umm Hassan. "Who Are the Women in the Islamabad Standoff? A Look Inside the Jamia Hafsa Madarsa," *The Middle East Media Research Institute,* July 11, 2007, https://www.memri.org/reports/who-are-women-islamabad-standoff-look-inside-jamia-hafsa-madarsa.

Abu-Lughod, Lila. *Remaking Women: Feminism and Modernity in the Middle East.* Princeton, NJ: Princeton University Press, 1998.

Aciksoz, Salih. "Sacrificial Limbs of Sovereignty: Disabled Veterans, Masculinity, and Nationalist Politics in Turkey." *Medical Anthropology Quarterly* 26, no. 1 (2012): 4–25.

———. *Sacrificial Limbs: Masculinity, Disability, and Political Violence in Turkey.* Oakland: University of California Press, 2019.

Agamben, Giorgio. *Homo Sacer: Sovereign Power and Bare Life.* Translated by Daniel Heller-Roazen. Stanford, CA: Stanford University Press, 1998.

Ahmed, Akbar. *Jinnah, Pakistan and Islamic Identity: The Search for Saladin.* London: Routledge, 1997.

Ahmed, Irfan. *Islamism and Democracy in India.* Princeton, NJ: Princeton University Press, 2009.

Ahmed, Sara. "Affective Economies." *Social Text* 79, no. 22 (2004): 117–39.

———. "Communities That Feel: Intensity, Difference and Attachment." In *Affective Encounters,* edited by Anu Koivunen and Susanna Paasonen, 10–24. Turku: University of Turku, 2001.

———. *The Cultural Politics of Emotion.* Edinburgh: Edinburgh University Press, 2004.

———. "Happy Objects." In *The Affect Theory Reader,* edited by Melissa Gregg and Gregory Seigworth, 29–51. Durham, NC: Duke University Press, 2010.

———. "Killing Joy: Feminism and the History of Happiness." *Signs* 35, no. 3 (2010): 571–94.

———. "The Organization of Hate," *Law and Critique* 12 (2001): 345–65.

Ali, Nosheen. *Delusional States: Feeling Rule and Development in Pakistan's Northern Frontier.* Cambridge: Cambridge University Press, 2019.

Alimia, Sanaa. "Performing the Afghanistan-Pakistan Border through Refugee ID cards." *Geopolitics* 24, no. 2 (2019): 391–425.

Allen, Lara. "Music and Politics in Africa." *Social Dynamics* 30, no. 2 (2004): 1–19.

Amnesty International. "Death Sentences and Executions in 2015." https://www.amnesty.org/en/latest/research/2016/04/death-sentences-executions-2015/. Accessed September 9, 2019.

Anderson, Ben. "Affective Atmospheres." *Emotion, Space and Society* 2, no. 2 (2009): 77–81.

Anderson, Pablo, and Simon Wendt. *Masculinities and the Nation in the Modern World.* New York: Palgrave, 2015.

Anjum, Ovamir. "Who Wants the Caliphate?" Yaqeen Institute for Islamic Research, October 31, 2019. https://yaqeeninstitute.org/ovamiranjum/who-wants-the-caliphate.

Asad, Talal. "On Suicide Bombing." *The Arab Studies Journal* 15/16, nos. 2/1 (Fall 2007/Spring 2008): 123–30.

———. *Secular Translations.* New York: Columbia University Press, 2018.

Asen, Robert. "Seeking the 'Counter' in Counterpublics," *Communication Theory* 10, no. 4 (2000): 424–46.

Aslam, Maleeha. *Gender Based Explosions: The Nexus between Muslim Masculinities, Jihadist Islamism and Terrorism.* Tokyo: UNU Press, 2012.

———. "Islamism and Masculinity: Case Study Pakistan." *Historical Social Research* 39, no. 3 (2014): 135–49.

Babar, Aneela Zeb. "Texts of War: The Religio-Military Nexus and Construction of Gender Identity in Pakistan and India." *Gender, Technology and Development* 4, no. 3 (2000): 441–64.

Baishya, Amit. *Contemporary Literature from Northeast India.* London: Routledge, 2019.

Banerjee, Milinda. *The Mortal God: Imagining the Sovereign in Colonial India.* Cambridge: Cambridge University Press, 2018.

Banerjee, Mukulika. *The Pathan Unarmed: Opposition and Memory in the North West Frontier.* Oxford: Oxford University Press, 2000.

Banerjee, Sikata. "Gender and Nationalism: The Masculinization of Hinduism and Female Political Participation in India." *Women's Studies International Forum* 26, no. 2 (2003): 167–79.

———. *Make Me a Man! Masculinity, Hinduism, and Nationalism in India.* New York: SUNY Press, 2005.

Barthes, Roland. *Camera Lucida: Reflections on Photography.* Translated by Richard Howard. New York: Hill and Wang, 1981.

Basham, Victoria, and Sergio Catignani. "War Is Where the Hearth Is: Gendered Labour and the Everyday Reproduction of the Geopolitical in the Army Reserves." *International Feminist Journal of Politics* 20, no. 2 (2018): 153–71.

Benhabib, Seyla. "Toward a Deliberative Model of Democratic Legitimacy." In *Democracy and Difference: Contesting the Boundaries of the Political,* edited by S. Benhabib, 67–94. Princeton, NJ: Princeton University Press, 1996.

Ben-Porath, Sigal, and Rogers Smith, *Varieties of Sovereignty and Citizenship.* Philadelphia: University of Pennsylvania Press, 2012.

Berlant, Lauren. *The Anatomy of National Fantasy.* Chicago: University of Chicago Press, 1991.

———. *Cruel Optimism.* Durham, NC: Duke University Press, 2011.

———. *The Female Complaint: The Unfinished Business of Sentimentality in American Culture.* Durham, NC: Duke University Press, 2008.

———. "A Properly Political Concept of Love." *Cultural Anthropology* 26, no. 4 (2011): 683–91.

Berlant, Lauren, and Lee Edelman. *Sex, or the Unbearable.* Durham, NC: Duke University Press, 2014.

Bernal, Victoria. "Diaspora and the Afterlife of Violence: Eritrean National Narratives and What Goes without Saying." *American Anthropologist* 119, no. 1 (2017): 23–34.

Bhutalia, Urvashi. *The Other Side of Silence.* Durham, NC: Duke University Press, 2000.

Bhutto, Benazir. *Daughter of Destiny: An Autobiography.* London: HarperCollins, 1988 (repr. 2007).

———. *Reconciliation: Islam, Democracy, and the West.* New York: HarperCollins, 2009.

Bishara, Amahl. "Sovereignty and Popular Sovereignty for Palestinians and Beyond." *Cultural Anthropology* 32, no. 3 (2017): 349–58.

Bodin, Jean. *On Sovereignty: Four Chapters from Six Books of the Commonwealth.* Cambridge: Cambridge University Press, 1992.

Boehmer, Elleke. *Stories of Women: Gender and Narrative in the Postcolonial Nation.* Manchester: Manchester University Press, 2005.

Bowlby, John. "The Nature of the Child's Tie to His Mother." *International Journal of Psychoanalysis* 39 (1958): 350–73.

Boym, Svetlana. *The Future of Nostalgia.* New York: Basic Books, 2001.

Brightman, Sara. "Rights, Women, and the State of Pakistan." *Contemporary Justice Review* 18, no. 3 (2015): 334–51.

Brohi, Nazish, and Saba Gul Khattak. *Exploring Women's Voices: Women in Conflict Zones: The Pakistan Study: Community Conversations in Balochistan and Swat.* Pakistan: Women's Regional Network, 2014.

Brown, Katherine. "Violence and Gender Politics in the Proto-State 'Islamic State.'" In *Revisiting Gendered States,* edited by Swati Parashar, Ann Tickner, and Jacqui True, 174–90. Oxford: Oxford University Press, 2018.

Brown, Wendy. "Finding the Man in the State," *Feminist Studies* 18, no. 1 (1992): 7–34.

———. *Walled States, Waning Sovereignty.* Brooklyn: Zone Books, 2010.

Burki, Shireen. "The Politics of Misogyny: General Zia-ul-Haq's Islamization of Pakistan's Legal System." *Contemporary Justice Review* 19, no. 1 (2016): 103–19.

Bush, George W. *Decision Points.* New York: Broadway Books, 2011.

Butler, Judith. "Bodies and Power Revisited." In *Feminism and the Final Foucault,* edited by Diana Taylor and Karen Vintges, 183–94. Champaign: University of Illinois Press, 2004.

———. *Bodies That Matter: On the Discursive Limits of "Sex."* New York: Routledge, 1993.

———. *Frames of War.* New York: Verso, 2009.

———. *Notes toward a Performative Theory of Assembly.* Cambridge, MA: Harvard University Press, 2015.

———. "Performative Acts and Gender Constitution: An Essay in Phenomenology and Feminist Theory." *Theatre Journal* 40, no. 4 (1988): 519–31.

———. *The Psychic Life of Power.* Stanford, CA: Stanford University Press, 1997.

Center for Research and Security Studies. *The Cost of Conflict in Pakistan.* Islamabad: Center for Research and Security Studies, 2010.

Charania, Moon. *Will the Real Pakistani Woman Please Stand Up?* New York: McFarland, 2015.

Chaudhary, Muhammad Amjad. "Quam kay betay." In *Junoon-e-Rukhe Wafa,* 14–16. Rawalpindi: Hilal Publications, 2018.

Churchill, Winston. *The Story of the Malakand Field Force: An Episode of Frontier War.* London: Longmans, Green and Co., 1898 (repr. 2010).

Connell, R. W. *Masculinities.* Berkeley: University of California Press, 1995.

Connell, R. W., and James Messerschmidt, "Hegemonic Masculinity: Rethinking the Concept." *Gender and Society* 19, no. 6 (2005): 829–59.

Cvetkovich, Ann. *An Archive of Feelings: Trauma, Sexuality, and Lesbian Public Cultures.* Durham, NC: Duke University Press, 2003.

Czarniawska, Barbara. *A Tale of Three Cities.* Oxford: Oxford University Press, 2002.

Das, Veena. "Time, Self, and Community: Features of the Sikh Militant Discourse." *Contributions to Indian Sociology* 26, no. 2 (1992): 245–59.

De Sondy, Amanullah. *The Crisis of Islamic Masculinities.* London: Bloomsbury, 2014.

Devgan, Shruti. "Making the Disappeared Appear." *Sikh Research Journal* 5, no. 1 (2020): 73–81.

Devji, Faisal. "Red Mosque." In *Under the Drones: Modern Lives in the Afghanistan-Pakistan Borderlands,* edited by Shahzad Bashir and Robert Crews, 153–61. Cambridge, MA: Harvard University Press, 2012.

———. *The Terrorist in Search of Humanity: Militant Islam and Global Politics.* London: Hurst Publishers, 2009.

de Volo, Lorraine. "Drafting Motherhood: Maternal Imagery and Organizations in the United States and Nicaragua." In *The Women and War Reader*, edited by Lois Ann Lorentzen and Jennifer Turpin, 240–53. New York: New York University Press, 1998.

———. "Mobilizing Mothers for War: Cross-National Framing Strategies in Nicaragua's Contra War." *Gender and Society* 18, no. 6 (2004): 715–34.

Dowler, Lorraine. "Gender, Militarization and Sovereignty." *Geography Compass* 6, no. 8 (2012): 490–99.

Duschinsky, Robbie. "Sexualization: A State of Injury." *Theory and Psychology* 23, no. 3 (2013): 351–70.

Duschinsky, Robbie, Monica Greco, and Judith Solomon, "Wait Up!: Attachment and Sovereign Power." *International Journal of Politics, Culture, and Society* 28, no. 3 (2015): 223–42.

Edwards, David. *The Caravan of Martyrs: Sacrifice and Suicide Bombing in Afghanistan*. Oakland: University of California Press, 2017.

Eng, David, and David Kazanjian, eds. *Loss: The Politics of Mourning*. Berkeley: University of California Press, 2003.

Enloe, Cynthia. *Maneuvers: The Militarization of Women's Lives*. Berkeley: University of California Press, 2000.

Euben, Roxanne. "Humiliation and the Political Mobilization of Masculinity." *Political Theory* 43, no. 4 (2015): 500–32.

———. "Jihad and Political Violence." *Current History* 101, no. 658 (2002): 365–76.

———. "Spectacles of Sovereignty in Digital Time." *Perspectives on Politics* 15, no. 4 (2017): 1007–33.

Ferguson, Ann. "Cowboy Masculinity, Globalization, and the US War on Terror." *Center for Global Justice*, October 1, 2017, https://www.globaljusticecenter.org /papers/cowboy-masculinity-globalization-and-us-war-terror.

Flatley, Jonathan. *Affective Mapping*. Cambridge, MA: Harvard University Press, 2008.

Foucault, Michel. *The History of Sexuality*, Vol. 1, *The Will to Knowledge*. Translated by R. Hurley. New York: Pantheon Books, 1976.

———. *Power/Knowledge: Selected Interviews and Other Writings, 1972–1977*. Edited by Colin Gordon. New York: Pantheon Books, 1980.

———. *Society Must Be Defended: Lecture Series at the Collège de France, 1975–76*, Translated by D. Macey. New York: Picador, 2003.

Freud, Sigmund. *Beyond the Pleasure Principle*. Translated by C.J.M. Hubback. London: The International Psycho-analytic press, 1922.

———. "Mourning and Melancholia." *A General Selection from the Works of Sigmund Freud*. Edited by John Richman. New York: Anchor Books, 1989.

Galvan-Alvarez, Enrique. "Performing Sovereignty: War Documentaries and Documentary Wars in Syria." *European Journal of English Studies* 22, no. 2 (2018): 204–16.

Ghafoor, Asif. "Preface." In *Junoon-e-Rukhe Wafa*, 6–7. Pakistan: Hilal Publications, 2018.

Gilmartin, David. "Introduction." In *South Asian Sovereignty: The Conundrum of Worldly Power*, edited by David Gilmartin, Pamela Price, and Arild Ruud, 1–34. New York: Routledge, 2020.

Gilmartin, David, Pamela Price, and Arild Ruud, eds. *South Asian Sovereignty: The Conundrum of Worldly Power*. New York: Routledge, 2020.

Glanville, Luke. "The Myth of 'Traditional' Sovereignty." *International Studies Quarterly* 57, no. 1 (2013): 79–90.

Gould, Deborah. "Affect and Protest." In *Political Emotions*, edited by Janet Staiger, Ann Cvetkovich, and Ann Reynolds, 18–45. New York: Routledge, 2010.

Grewal, Inderpal. *Saving the Security State*. Durham, NC: Duke University Press, 2017.

Gullette, David, and John Heathershaw, "The Affective Politics of Sovereignty: Reflecting on the 2010 Conflict in Kyrgyzstan." *Nationalities Papers* 43, no. 1 (2015): 122–39.

"Hafiz Abdul Waheed (Petitioner) versus Miss Asma Jehangir and Another (Respondents), Criminal Miscellaneous, no. 425-H of 1996, Decided on March 10, 1997." In *The All Pakistan Legal Decisions*, 301–84. Lahore: PLD Publishers, 1997.

Halberstam, Jack. *Female Masculinity*. Durham, NC: Duke University Press, 2019.

Hall, Stuart. *Policing the Crisis: Mugging, the State, and Law and Order*. London: Macmillan Press, 1978.

Hall, Stuart, and Paddy Whannel. *The Popular Arts*. Durham, NC: Duke University Press, 2018.

Hansen, Thomas, and Finn Stepputat. *Sovereign Bodies: Citizens, Migrants, and States in the Postcolonial World*. Princeton, NJ: Princeton University Press, 2005.

———. "Sovereignty Revisited." *Annual Review of Anthropology* 35 (2005): 295–315.

Haq, Farhat. "Militarism and Motherhood." *Signs* 32, no. 4 (2007): 1023–46.

Haraway, Donna J. *Modest_Witness@Second_Millennium.FemaleMan©_Meets_OncoMouse: Feminism and Technoscience*. New York: Routledge, 1997.

Hariman, Robert. "Public Culture." In *Oxford Research Encyclopedia of Communication*, edited Jon Nussbaum, 1–16. Oxford: Oxford University Press, 2017.

Hassan, Riffat. "Iqbal's Concept of *Mard-e-momin* and Rumi's Influence." *Journal of the Regional Cultural Institute* 5, no. 2–3 (1972): 61–83.

Hayat, Maira. "Empire's Accidents: Law, Lies, and Sovereignty in the 'War on Terror' in Pakistan." *Critique of Anthropology* 40, no. 1 (2020): 49–80.

Higate, Paul. *Military Masculinities: Identity and the State*. Westport, CT: Praeger, 2003.

Hirschkind, Charles, and Saba Mahmood. "Feminism, the Taliban, and Politics of Counter-Insurgency." *Anthropological Quarterly* 75, no. 2 (2002): 339–54.

Hochschild, Arlie. *The Managed Heart*. Berkeley: University of California Press, 2012.

Hoodbhoy, Pervez. "Jinnah and the Islamic State: Setting the Record Straight." *Economic and Political Weekly* 42, no. 32 (Aug. 11–17, 2007): 3,300–3.

Human Terrain Team AF-6. "Research Update and Findings: Pashtun Sexuality." Human Terrain Team AF-6. https://info.publicintelligence.net/HTT-Pashtun-Sexuality.pdf. Accessed June 3, 2018.

Humphrey, Caroline. "Sovereignty." In *A Companion to the Anthropology of Politics,* edited by David Nugent and Joan Vincent, 418–36. Oxford: Blackwell Publishing, 2007.

Hussain, Neelam, Samlya Mumtaz, and Rubina Saigol, eds. *Engendering the Nation-State.* Lahore: Simorgh, 1997.

Hyde, Alexandra. "The Civilian Wives of Military Personnel: Mobile Subjects or Agents of Militarisation?" In *The Palgrave International Handbook of Gender and the Military,* edited by Rachel Woodward and Claire Duncanson, 195–210. London: Palgrave, 2017.

Ingram, Haroro. "An Analysis of the Taliban in Khurasan's *Azan* (Issues 1–5)." *Studies in Conflict and Terrorism* 38, no. 7 (2015): 560–79.

Islamabad Policy Research Institute. "Text of Swat Peace Accord." https://peacemaker.un.org/sites/peacemaker.un.org/files/PA_090116_Swat%20Peace%20Accord.pdf. Accessed September 4, 2019.

ISPR. *Junoon-e-Rukh-e-Wafa.* Rawalpindi: Hilal Publishers, 2018.

———. *Moonglade.* Rawalpindi: Hilal Publishers, 2018.

ISPR, and Hafsa Rehan. *Dam-e-Lahoo.* Islamabad: Pakistan Post Foundation, 2018.

Jadoon, Amira, and Sara Mahmood, "Fixing the Cracks in the Pakistani Taliban's Foundation." *CTC Sentinel* 11, no. 11 (December 2018):, 21–25.

Jalal, Ayesha. "The Convenience of Subservience: Women and the State of Pakistan." In *Women, Islam, and the State,* edited by Deniz Kandiyoti, 77–114. London: Palgrave Macmillan, 1991.

———. *The Sole Spokesman: Jinnah, the Muslim League and the Demand for Pakistan.* Cambridge: Cambridge University Press, 1985.

Jamal, Amina. "Feminism and 'Fundamentalism' in Pakistan." In *Dispatches from Pakistan,* edited by Madiha Tahir, 104–20. Minneapolis: University of Minnesota Press, 2014.

———. "Gender, Citizenship, and the Nation-State in Pakistan: Willful Daughters or Free Citizens?" *Signs* 31, no. 2 (2006): 283–304.

James, Alan. "The Practice of Sovereign Statehood in Contemporary International Society," *Political Studies* 47, no. 3 (1999): 457–73.

Jan, Faizullah. "Representing the Self and the Other: Discourse of Pakistan-Based Militant Organizations." PhD diss., American University, 2014.

Jan, Najeeb. *The Metacolonial State: Pakistan, Critical Ontology, and the Biopolitical Horizons of Political Islam.* Hoboken, NJ: Wiley, 2019.

Jervis, Sue. *Relocation, Gender, and Emotion: A Psycho-Social Perspective on the Experiences of Military Wives.* London: Karnac Books, 2011.

Jinnah, Muhammad Ali. *Jinnah: Speeches and Statements 1947–1948.* Karachi: Oxford University Press.

Johnson, Thomas. *Taliban Narratives: The Use and Power of Stories in the Afghanistan Conflict.* Oxford: Oxford University Press, 2018.

Kalyvas, Stathis. *The Logic of Violence in Civil War.* Cambridge: Cambridge University Press, 2006.

Kandiyoti, Deniz. *Women, Islam and the State.* Basingstoke: Macmillan, 1991.

Kapur, Anuradha. "Deity to Crusader: The Changing Iconography of Ram." In *Hindus and Others: The Question of Identity in India Today,* edited by Gyanendra Pandey, 74–109. New Delhi, Viking Publishers, 1993.

Kaviraj, Sudipo. "The Myth of Praxis. The Construction of the Figure of Krishna in Krishnacharitra." *Nehru Memorial Museum and Library Occasional Papers on History and Society,* no. 50 (1987): 72–106.

Keddie, Nikki. "The New Religious Politics and Women Worldwide: A Comparative Study." *Journal of Women's History* 10, no. 4 (1999): 11–34.

Khalili, Laleh. "Gendered Practices of Counterinsurgency." *Review of International Studies* 37, no. 4 (2010): 1471–91.

———. *Heroes and Martyrs of Palestine: The Politics of National Commemoration.* Cambridge: Cambridge University Press, 2009.

Khan, Arsalan. "Islam and Pious Sociality." *Social Analysis* 60, no. 4 (2016): 96–113.

———. "Pious Masculinity, Ethical Reflexivity, and Moral Order in an Islamic Piety Movement in Pakistan." *Anthropological Quarterly* 91, no. 1 (2018): 53–78.

Khan, Imran. *Pakistan: A Personal History.* London: Bantam, 2011.

Khan, Mukhtar. "The FM Mullah's and the Taliban's Propaganda War in Pakistan." *Terrorism Monitor* 7, no. 14 (2009).

Khattak, Saba Gul. "The Right to Life and Compensation in Pakistan's Tribal Areas." In *Violence and the Quest for Justice in South Asia,* edited by Deepak Mehta and Rahul Roy, 90–126. London: SAGE Publications, 2018.

Khoja-Moolji, Shenila. *Forging the Ideal Educated Girl: The Production of Desirable Subjects in Muslim South Asia.* Oakland: University of California Press, 2018.

———. "Patriarchal Assemblages." *South Asia: Journal of South Asian Studies,* forthcoming.

———. "The Making of Humans and Their Others in and through Transnational Human Rights Advocacy: Exploring the Cases of Mukhtar Mai and Malala Yousafzai." *Signs: Journal of Women in Culture and Society* 42, no. 2 (2017): 377–402.

———. "The Politics of Legislating 'Honor Crime' in Contemporary Pakistan." In *Gender-Based Violence,* edited by Lila Abu-Lughod, forthcoming.

———. "Reading Malala: (De)(Re)Territorialization of Muslim Collectivities." *Comparative Studies of South Asia, Africa and the Middle East* 35, no. 3 (2015): 539–56.

Krasner, Stephen. *Sovereignty: Organized Hypocrisy.* Princeton, NJ: Princeton University Press, 1999.

Kuntsman, Adi. "The Soldier and the Terrorist: Sexy Nationalism, Queer Violence." *Sexualities* 11, no. 1–2 (2008): 142–70.

Lal, Ruby. *Coming of Age in Nineteenth-Century India: The Girl-Child and the Art of Playfulness.* Cambridge: Cambridge University Press, 2012.

Laplanche, Jean, and Jean-Bertrand Pontalis, *Language of Psychoanalysis.* London: Abingdon, 1988.

Lehane, Orla, David Mair, Saffron Lee, and Jodie Parker. "Brides, Black Widows and Baby-Makers; or Not: An Analysis of the Portrayal of Women in English-Language Jihadi Magazine Image Content." *Critical Studies on Terrorism* 11, no. 3 (2018): 505–20.

Leigh, Darcy, and Cynthia Weber. "Gendered and Sexualized Figurations of Security." In *The Routledge Handbook of Gender and Security,* edited by Caron Gentry, Laura Shepherd, and Laura Sjoberg, 83–93. New York: Routledge, 2019.

Li, Darryl. "From Exception to Empire: Sovereignty, Carceral Circulation, and the 'Global War on Terror.'" In *Ethnographies of U.S. Empire,* edited by Carole McGranahan and John Collins, 456–75, Durham, NC: Duke University Press, 2018.

———. "Jihad in a World of Sovereigns: Law, Violence, and Islam in the Bosnia Crisis." *Law and Social Inquiry* 41, no. 2 (2016): 371–401.

Lutz, Catherine. "A Military History of the American Suburbs, the Discipline of Economics, and All Things Ordinary." *Antipode* 43, no. 3 (2011): 901–6.

Mahmood, Cynthia. *Fighting for Faith and Nation: Dialogues with Sikh Militants.* Philadelphia: University of Pennsylvania Press, 2010.

———. "Playing the Game of Love: Passion and Martyrdom among Khalistani Sikhs." In *Violence: A Reader,* edited by Catherine Besteman, 118–35. New York: New York University Press, 2002.

Malik, Anushay. "Public Authority and Local Resistance: Abdur Rehman and the Industrial Workers of Lahore, 1969–1974." *Modern Asian Studies* 52, no. 3 (2018): 815–48.

Manchanda, Nivi. "Queering the Pashtun: Afghan Sexuality in the Homo-Nationalist Imaginary." *Third World Quarterly* 36, no. 1 (2015): 130–46.

Mankekar, Purnima. *Screening Culture, Viewing Politics: An Ethnography of Television, Womanhood, and Nation in Postcolonial India.* Durham, NC: Duke University Press, 1999.

Mann, Bonnie. *Sovereign Masculinity: Gender Lessons from the War on Terror.* Oxford: Oxford University Press, 2014.

Maqsood, Ammara. "Mobility and Spatiality among Tribal Pashtuns." *Tanqeed,* no. 10 (January 2016).

Massumi, Brian. "Notes on the Translation and Acknowledgments." In *A Thousand Plateaus,* edited by Gilles Deleuze and Felix Guattari, xvi–xix. Minneapolis: University of Minnesota Press, 1987.

Mawdudi, Abul Ala. *Purdah and the Status of Women.* Translated by Al-Ashari. Lahore: Islamic Publications, 1972. First published 1938.

Mayer, Tamar, ed. *Gender Ironies of Nationalism: Sexing the Nation.* New York: Routledge, 2000.

Mbembe, Achille. "Necropolitics," *Public Culture* 15, no. 1 (2003): 11–40.

———. *Necropolitics.* Durham, NC: Duke University Press, 2019.

———. "Variations on the Beautiful in the Congolese World of Sounds." *Politique Africaine* 4, no. 100 (2005): 69–91.

McClintock, Anne. "Family Feuds: Gender, Nationalism and the Family." *Feminist Review* 44, no. 1 (1993): 61–81.

McLarney, Ellen Anne. *Soft Force: Women in Egypt's Islamic Awakening.* Princeton, NJ: Princeton University Press, 2015.

Melikoff, I. "Ghazi." In *Encyclopedia of Islam,* 2nd ed., edited by P. Bearman, Th. Bian- qghauis, C. E. Bosworth, E. van Donzel, and W. P. Heinrichs. Leiden: Brill, 2012.

Menon, Ritu, and Kamla Bhasin. *Borders and Boundaries: Women in India's Parti- tion.* New Brunswick, NJ: Rutgers University Press, 1998.

Michelutti, Lucia. *Mafia Raj: The Rule of Bosses in South Asia.* Stanford, CA: Stan- ford University Press, 2018.

Misri, Deepti. "The Violence of Memory: Renarrating Partition Violence in Shauna Singh Badwin's *What the Body Remembers.*" *Meridians* 11, no. 1 (2011): 1–25.

Mitchell, Timothy. *Colonising Egypt.* Cambridge Middle East Library. Cambridge: Cambridge University Press, 1988.

Moin, A. Azfar. "Messianism and the Constitution of Pakistan." In *South Asian Sovereignty: The Conundrum of Worldly Power,* edited by David Gilmartin, Pamela Price, and Arild Ruud, 175–95. New York: Routledge, 2020.

———. *The Millennial Sovereign: Sacred Kingship and Sainthood in Islam.* New York: Columbia University Press, 2010.

Morgenthau, Hans J. "The Problem of Sovereignty Reconsidered." *Columbia Law Review* 48, no. 3 (1948): 341–65.

Mortimer-Sandilands, Catriona. "Melancholy Natures, Queer Ecologies." In *Queer Ecologies: Sex, Nature, Politics, Desire,* edited by Catriona Mortimer-Sandilands and Bruce Erickson, 331–58. Bloomington: Indiana University Press: 2010.

Muñoz, José. "Feeling Brown: Ethnicity and Affect in Ricardo Bracho's *The Sweetest Hangover (and Other STDs).*" *Theatre Journal,* 52, no. 1 (2000): 67–79.

Musharraf, Pervez. *In the Line of Fire: A Memoir.* New York: Free Press, 2006.

Naeem, Major. "Blood's Tribute." In *Junoon-e-Rukhe Wafa,* 145–150. Rawalpindi: Hilal Publications, 2018.

Nagel, Joanne. "Masculinity and Nationalism: Gender and Sexuality in the Making of Nations." *Ethnic and Racial Studies* 21, no. 2 (1998): 242–69.

Najam-u-Din. "Pakistan—Media Landscape." *European Journalism Centre,* 2019, https://medialandscapes.org/country/pakistan.

Nasr, Seyyed Hossein, ed. *The Study Quran.* New York: HarperOne, 2015.

Ngai, Sianne. *Ugly Feelings.* Cambridge, MA: Harvard University Press, 2007.

O'Hanlon, Rosalind. "Issues of Masculinity in North Indian History." *Indian Jour- nal of Gender Studies* 4, no. 1 (1997): 1–19.

Palumbo-Liu, David. "Pre-emption, the Future, and the Imagination." In *America and the Misshaping of a New World Order,* edited by Giles Gunn and Carl Gutiér- rez-Jones, 59–78. Berkeley: University of California Press, 2010.

Parashar, Swati. "The Postcolonial/Emotional State." In *Revisiting Gendered States,* edited by Swati Parashar, Ann Tickner, and Jacqui True, 157–73. Oxford: Oxford University Press, 2018.

Parashar, Swati, Ann Tickner, and Jacqui True, eds. *Revisiting Gendered States: Feminist Imaginings of the State in International Relations.* Oxford: Oxford Uni- versity Press, 2018.

Philpott, Daniel. "Sovereignty: An Introduction and Brief History." *Journal of International Affairs* 48, no. 2 (1995): 353–68.

Puar, Jasbir, and Amit Rai. "Monster, Terrorist, Fag: The War on Terrorism and the Production of Docile Patriots." *Social Text* 20, no. 3 (2002): 117–48.

Puri, Jyoti. *Sexual States: Governance and the Decriminalization of Sodomy in India's Present.* Durham, NC: Duke University Press, 2016.

Quraishi, Asifa, and Frank Vogel. *The Islamic Marriage Contract.* Cambridge, MA: Harvard University Press, 2009.

Rahman, Tariq. *Interpretations of Jihad in South Asia: An Intellectual History.* Berlin: De Gruyter, 2018.

Rancière, Jacques. *The Future of Image.* London: Verso, 2007.

Rashid, Ahmed. *Taliban: Militant Islam, Oil and Fundamentalism in Central Asia.* New Haven, CT: Yale University Press, 2010.

Rashid, Maria. *Dying to Serve: Militarism, Affect, and the Politics of Sacrifice in the Pakistan Army.* Stanford, CA: Stanford University Press, 2020.

Reeser, Todd W. *Masculinities in Theory: An Introduction.* West Sussex: Wiley-Blackwell, 2010.

Rizvi, Hasan. *Military, State and Society in Pakistan.* Lahore: Sang-e-Meel Publications, 2003.

Robinson, Cabeiri deBergh. *Body of Victim, Body of Warrior: Refugee Families and the Making of Kashmiri Jihadists.* Berkeley: University of California Press, 2013.

Roe, Andrew. *Waging War in Waziristan: The British Struggle in the Land of bin Laden, 1849–1947.* Lawrence: University Press of Kansas, 2010.

Rouse, Shahnaz. "The Outsider(s) Within: Sovereignty and Citizenship in Pakistan." In *Appropriating Gender: Women's Activism and Politicized Religion in South Asia,* edited by Patricia Jeffrey and Amrita Basu, 52–70. Zones of Religion. New York: Routledge, 1998.

Roy, Kaushik. "Race and Recruitment in the Indian Army: 1880–1918." *Modern Asian Studies* 47, no. 4 (2013): 1310–47.

Roy, Olivier. *Jihad and Death: The Global Appeal of Islamic State.* New York: Oxford University Press, 2017.

Ruddick, Sara. *Maternal Thinking: Toward a Politics of Peace.* Boston: Beacon, 1989.

Rukh, Lala. "ImageNation: A Visual Text." In *Engendering the Nation-State,* edited by Neelam Hussain, Samiya Mumtaz, and Rubina Saigol, 75–101. Lahore: Simorg, 1997.

Saigol, Rubina. "His Rights/Her Duties: Citizen and Mother in the Civics Discourse." *Indian Journal of Gender Studies* 10, no. 3 (2003): 379–404.

———. "Militarization, Nation, and Gender: Women's Bodies as Arenas of Violent Conflict." In *Deconstructing Sexuality in the Middle East: Challenges and Discourses,* edited by Pinar Ilkkaracan, 165–75. London: Ashgate Publishing, 2008.

———. *The Pakistan Project: A Feminist Perspective on Nation and Identity.* Delhi: Women Unlimited, 2013.

Saikia, Yasmin. "Listening to the Enemy: The Pakistan Army, Violence and Memories of 1971." In *Beyond Crisis,* edited by Naveeda Khan, 177–209. New Delhi: Taylor and Francis, 2010.

Sassen, Saskia. *Territory, Authority, Rights: From Medieval to Global Assemblages.* Princeton, NJ: Princeton University Press, 2006.

Sayyid, Salman. *Recalling the Caliphate: Decolonisation and the World Order.* Oxford: Oxford University Press, 2014.

Schatzberg, Michael. *The Dialects of Oppression in Zaire.* Bloomington: Indiana University Press, 1991.

Sedgwick, Eve Kosofsky. *Touching Feeling: Affect, Pedagogy, Performativity.* Durham, NC: Duke University Press, 2003.

Sharjeel, Umm-e. "Without Whom the House Is Empty." In *Junoon-e-Rukhe Wafa*, 35–41. Pakistan: Hilal Publications, 2018.

Sheikh, Mona. *Guardians of God: Inside the Religious Mind of the Pakistani Taliban.* Oxford: Oxford University Press, 2016.

Siddiqa, Ayesha. *Military Inc.: Inside Pakistan's Military Economy.* Karachi: Oxford University, 2007.

———. "Pakistan Military: Ethnic Balance in the Armed Forces and Problems of Federalism." Manekshaw Paper, no. 39. New Delhi: Centre for Land Warfare Studies, 2013.

Siddique, Qandeel. *Tehrik-e-Taliban Pakistan.* Copenhagen: Danish Institute for International Studies, 2010.

Sinha, Mrinalini. *Colonial Masculinity: The 'Manly Englishman' and the 'Effeminate Bengali' in the Late Nineteenth Century.* New Delhi: Kali for Women, 1997.

———. "Giving Masculinity a History: Some Contributions from the Historiography of Colonial India." *Gender and History* 11, no. 3 (1999): 445–60.

Slater, Mark. "Places Everyone! Studying the Performativity of the Border." *Political Geography* 30, no. 2 (2011): 61–69.

Smyth, Lisa. "Narratives of Irishness and the Problem of Abortion: The X Case 1992." *Feminist Review* 60, no. 1 (1998): 61–83.

Spellman, Elizabeth. "Woman as Body: Ancient and Contemporary Views." *Feminist Studies* 8, no. 1 (1982): 109–31.

Stoler, Ann. "Affective States." In *A Companion to the Anthropology of Politics,* edited by David Nugent and Joan Vincent, 4–20. Oxford: Wiley-Blackwell, 2008.

———. "On Degrees of Imperial Sovereignty." *Public Culture* 18, no. 1 (2006): 125–46.

Tahir, Madiha. "The Ground Was Always in Play." *Public Culture* 29, no. 1 (2017): 5–16.

Tareen, SherAli. "Contesting Friendship in Colonial Muslim India." *South Asia: Journal of South Asian Studies* 38, no. 3 (2015): 419–34.

———. *Defending Muhammad in Modernity.* Notre Dame, IN: University of Notre Dame Press, 2020.

———. "Sayyid Abu'l-A'la Mawdudi." In *Oxford Bibliographies Online,* last modified May 25, 2011, https://www.oxfordbibliographies.com/view/document/obo-9780195390155/obo-9780195390155-0129.xml, accessed February 2021.

Tariq, Azam. *The Life of Baitullah Masood.* The Global Islamic Media Front, n.d.

Taussig-Rubbo, Mateo. "Sacrifice and Sovereignty." In *States of Violence: War, Capital Punishment, and Letting Die,* edited by Austin Sarat and Jennifer Culbert, 83–126. Cambridge: Cambridge University Press, 2009.

Taylor, Diana. *Disappearing Acts: Spectacles of Gender and Nationalism in Argentina's "Dirty War."* Durham, NC: Duke University Press, 1997.

Tickner, J. Ann. *Gender in International Relations.* New York: Columbia University Press, 1992.

Toor, Saadia. "Moral Regulation in a Postcolonial Nation-State." *Interventions* 9, no. 2 (2007): 255–75.

———. *The State of Islam: Culture and Cold War Politics in Pakistan.* London: Pluto Press, 2011.

Tyler, Imogen. "Class Disgust in Contemporary Britain." *Feminist Media Studies* 8, no. 1 (2008): 17–34.

USAID. "Department of State and USAID Joint Strategy on Countering Violent Extremism." May 2016. https://www.usaid.gov/countering-violent-extremism.

———. "Pakistan." Last modified March 27, 2019. https://www.usaid.gov/political-transition-initiatives/pakistan.

USAID, and Aurat Foundation. *Masculinity in Pakistan: A Formative Research Study.* Gender Equity Program, Aurat Foundation, September 2016.

US Department of State. "Country Reports on Terrorism 2015." https://2009–2017.state.gov/j/ct/rls/crt/2015/257522.htm. Accessed September 4, 2019.

US Institute of Peace. "Countering Violent Extremism in Pakistan." May 17, 2012. https://www.usip.org/publications/2012/05/countering-violent-extremism-pakistan.

US Office of the President. "Executive Order 13769: Executive Order Protecting the Nation from Foreign Terrorist Entry into the United States," January 27, 2017, https://www.federalregister.gov/documents/2017/02/01/2017–02281/protecting-the-nation-from-foreign-terrorist-entry-into-the-united-states.

Velleman, J. David. "The Genesis of Shame." *Philosophy and Public Affairs* 30, no. 1 (2001): 27–52.

Verdery, Katherine. *Political Lives of Dead Bodies.* New York: Columbia University Press, 1999.

Warner, Michael. "Publics and Counterpublics." *Public Culture* 14, no. 1 (2002): 49–90.

Weber, Cynthia. "Performative States." *Millennium* 27, no. 1 (1998): 77–95.

———. *Queer International Relations: Sovereignty, Sexuality and the Will to Knowledge.* Oxford: Oxford University Press, 2016.

Weber, Max. *The Vocation Lectures.* Edited by David Owen and Tracy Strong. Indianapolis: Hackett Publishing, 2004.

Weinstein, Laurie, and Christie White. *Wives and Warriors: Women and the Military in the United States and Canada.* Westport, CT: Bergin and Garvey, 1997.

Werbner, Pnina. "'The Lion of Lahore': Anthropology, Cultural Performance and Imran Khan." In *Anthropology and Cultural Studies,* edited by Stephen Nugent and Cris Shore, 34–67. London: Pluto Press, 1997.

Wheeler, Brannon. "Ummah." In *Encyclopedia of Religion,* vol. 14, edited by Lindsay Jones, 9446–48 (New York: Macmillan Reference, 2005).

Williams, Raymond. *The Long Revolution.* London: Hogarth Press, 1961.

Young, Iris Marion. "The Logic of Masculinist Protection: Reflections on the Current Security State." *Signs* 29, no.1 (2003): 1–25.

Yousafzai, Malala, and Christina Lamb. *I Am Malala: The Girl Who Stood Up for Education and Was Shot by the Taliban.* London: Little, Brown, 2013.

Yuval-Davis, Nira. *Gender and Nation.* London: SAGE Publications, 1997.

Zaman, Muhammad Qasim. *Islam in Pakistan: A History.* Princeton, NJ: Princeton University Press, 2018.

———. *Modern Islamic Thought in a Radical Age.* Cambridge: Cambridge University Press, 2012.

———. *The Ulama in Contemporary Islam: Custodians of Change.* Princeton, NJ: Princeton University Press, 2007.

Zarzycka, Marta. "The World Press Photo Contest and Visual Tropes." *Photographies* 6, no. 1 (2013): 177–84.

Zeiger, Susan. "She Didn't Raise Her Boy to Be a Slacker: Motherhood, Conscription, and the Culture of the First World War." *Feminist Studies* 22, no. 1 (1996): 7–39.

Zelizer, Barbie. *About to Die: How News Images Move the Public.* New York: Oxford University Press, 2010.

Zengin, Aslı. "The Afterlife of Gender: Sovereignty, Intimacy and Muslim Funerals of Transgender People in Turkey." *Cultural Anthropology* 34, no. 1 (2019): 78–102.

Zien, Katherine. *Sovereign Acts.* New Brunswick, NJ: Rutgers University Press, 2017.

INDEX

Aaj News, 188. *See also* media

Abbas, Hassan, 65, 209n53

Abdullah, Hamna, 132

Aciksoz, Salih, 36, 176

affect: as a dimension of sovereignty, 2–3, 7, 193; and emotional labor, 182–93; kinship and, 24–25; managing, 170–93; and memory, 4, 14, 19, 24; nationalist, 192; performance of, 190; and politics, 13–18; and publics, 2, 5, 7, 13–18; state-prescribed, 176–80, 200; studies of, 211n75; Taliban, 192; texts and, 7. *See also* affective residue; attachment; emotional labor; grief/grieving; hate; honor; humiliation; loss; love; melancholy; memory; mourning; nostalgia; shame; trust

affective residue, 24, 63, 147. *See also* affect

Afghanistan, 8–9, 50, 85; American invasion of, 9, 31, 62, 198; attempted assault of an American soldier in, 154; British defeat in, 64, 67; Soviet invasion of, 66, 99–100, 155

Agamben, Giorgio, 13, 66

Ahmed, Sara, 2, 56, 61, 186, 211n75

Akbar, Mughal ruler, 101–2

al-Ghazali, Zaynab, 23

Alimia, Sanaa, 13

al-Janabi, Abeer, 156

al-Muhajir, Abu Salamah, 191

al-Qaeda, 9–10, 50, 154–56. *See also* Taliban

alterity: in the cultural texts of the Pakistan Army, 54; and identity, 53–80. *See also* identity

Aman Chowk, 185*fig.*

ambivalence: in attachments, 15–16, 88–97, 143, 190; expressions of, 15

Amnesty International, 26

Anderson, Ben, 180

Anwar, Ikrimah, 98, 114, 116, 156

Arabian Peninsula, 97

Army Public School (APS), 1–2, 16, 20–21, 24–26, 55–58, 243n57; female student at a rally in Lahore condemning the attack on, 79*fig.*; mothers of attack victims of, 171, 182; students at a rally in Lahore condemning the attack on, 77, 77*fig.*; Taliban on the attack on, 81–84

ARY Digital, 189. *See also* media; television

Asad, Talal, 6

Asen, Robert, 119

attachment, 1, 15–16, 19, 24, 194; affective, 36, 96; ambivalent, 15–16, 88–97, 143; concept of, 15; familial, 196; kinship and, 1, 3, 194; militant, 203; to the military, 33–41; and *mujahid* masculinity, 101; nationalist, 203; political, 194, 200; relationships of, 195; religious, 196; sovereign, 15–16, 19–20, 24–25, 31–53, 77, 80, 84, 172, 194–95, 200; to the state, 16, 20, 172; stylizing ideal political, 139–41; to the Taliban, 192, 203. *See also* affect; kinship; Pakistani state; Taliban

Aurat Azadi marches, 161. *See also* women
autobiography, 31–52; as memory act, 32
azan (call to prayer), 104*fig.*, 105
Azan magazine, 22–23, 85–87, 91, 98, 101–5,
    104*fig.*, 107*fig.*, 109*fig.*, 110–16, 111*fig.*,
    112*fig.*, 129, 154–59, 191–92, 216n116. *See
    also* media
Aziz, Khaula Bint Abdul, 125–26, 128,
    160–61
Azmat, Ali, 75–77, 79

Babar, Aneela Zeb, 14
Bacha Khan University, 102, 186
bachi (child), 144–45
Badami, Waseem, 144
baighairat (men without honor), 188–89
Bajaur, 115. *See also* Pakistan
Banerjee, Milinda, 32
Barthes, Roland, 182
behan, 25, 142–43, 203. *See also* women
Benhabib, Seyla, 120
Berlant, Lauren, 5, 14–16, 244n1
Bernal, Victoria, 202
beti, 25, 73–74, 142–45, 147, 150, 203; kin-
    ship metaphor of, 153, 168. *See also*
    women
betrayal, 88–89
Bhutto, Prime Minister Benazir, 22, 32,
    37, 41–47, 44*fig.*, 52; gender play of,
    42–45; Works: *Daughter of Destiny*,
    42–44, 46; *Reconciliation: Islam,
    Democracy, and the West*, 42–43,
    45–46
Bhutto, Shah Nawaz Khan, 44
Bhutto, Zulfiqar Ali, 37, 40–41, 44–45
Bilal, Ummay, 130
bin Laden, Osama, 8–9, 51, 158
Bishara, Amahl, 167
bodies: of dead soldiers, 74; decimation of,
    27; gendered, 16, 33, 35, 43; hierarchizing
    of, 67; and statist sovereignty, 77, 80;
    and Taliban sovereignty, 103
Boehmer, Elleke, 32
Bolsonaro, President Jair, 47
Bowlby, John, 15
brothers: and fathers, 58, 72, 74, 83; as
    fraternal publics, 5, 25, 143, 153–61;
    humiliated, 153–58; in Islam, 83, 110;

and kinship, 75. *See also* fathers; kin-
    ship; mothers
Burma, 157
Bush, President George W., 116
Butler, Judith, 4, 15–16, 26, 143, 211n72

Carter, President Jimmy, 8
Central Intelligence Agency (CIA), 8, 50,
    66; drone attacks of the, 116; use of the
    terminology of *jihad* by the, 100. *See
    also* United States
Charsadda, 115, 186. *See also* Pakistan
Chaudhary, Muhammad Amjad: *Junoon-e-
    Rukh-e-Wafa*, 21
children: affective pedagogies and,
    176–80; dead APS, 1, 56–58, 176–93,
    200; disabled, 188–89; of militants, 59;
    as objects of love, 66, 190; sexual vio-
    lence against, 59–62. *See also* fathers;
    mothers
China, 7
Chirac, Jacques, 43, 44*fig.*
Christianity, 133. *See also* religion
Churchill, Winston: *The Story of the
    Malakand Field Force*, 64
civil war (1971): *Hilal* magazine writings
    on, 57, 69, 70, 100; Musharraf on, 51;
    Muslimness and, 199; songs about, 55;
    Taliban writings about, 115, 116
Cold War, 90
communism, 8
corruption, 37, 41, 47, 50; Taliban accusing
    army of, 115, 117; *fitna* as, 149; *kufr* as,
    226n34
counterinsurgency, 3, 76; affective
    landscape for, 171; operations of,
    171, 180
counterpublics: formation of, 15, 80, 194–
    95; of mothers, 189; politicized melan-
    cholia of, 171; Taliban as, 15, 80, 119–20,
    197. *See also* publics
coward, 1–2; and masculinity, 45, 54;
    mothers against being a, 137–38; the
    talib as, 56–59, 66, 76; the soldier as, 102
cricket, 48–49; and Imran Khan, 47
crying: of children, 60; of mothers, 173, 178,
    190. *See also* grief/grieving
Curzon, George, 64

Daesh, 10, 130–31, 207n26, 209n49; the Taliban in, 90

Daily Express Lahore, 182

dajjal (false messiah), 102, 110

Dam-e-Lahoo, 21

Dawn newspaper, 23

death: love of, 98, 100; martyrdom as liminal, 137; penalty of, 26; pursuit of, 99; Taliban discourse on, 99, 101. *See also* funeral; *jihad*; martyr; *shahadat*

democracy: Bhutto as symbol of, 45–47; Islam and, 45–47, 52; the Taliban against, 93

Deobandi: ideologues of, 96; interpretation of Islam of, 96–97, 201; madrasas of, 8, 96–97; and Salafi, 96; scholars of, 207n20. *See also* Taliban

Devji, Faisal, 6, 97

de Volo, Lorraine Bayaard, 181–82

dictatorship: Bhutto's views on, 45–46; and extremism, 46; of the military, 51

disgust: and relations of power, 67; staging love and, 54–75; *talib* as an object of, 54, 61, 66, 74

Dubai, 41

East India Company, 18

East Pakistan, 26; cyclone in, 40; killing of Muslims in, 115; secession of, 39, 55; surrender in, 51. *See also* Pakistan

Edelman, Lee, 5

Edwards, David, 99

Eid, 126, 128, 129*fig*. *See also* Islam

emotional labor, 16, 25, 172, 199, 201; affect and, 182–93; mothers performing, 137–38, 176–82; mourning as, 176; refusal of, 172; reproductive and, 124, 135; sovereign attachment and, 141. *See also* affect; gendered labor

Eng, David, 185

Enloe, Cynthia, 178

Euben, Roxanne, 98, 157, 206n11

Express Tribune, 23, 178

Express Urdu, 23

Farooq, Ayesha, 134, 135*fig*.

Faseel-e-Jaan se Agay (television drama series), 72. *See also* television

fathers: brothers and, 58, 72, 74, 83; *jawan* as, 74–75; of martyrs, 177, 189; mourning by, 180, 186, 189; of soldiers, 72, 133, 136–37, 180; state and, 147–51; of Taliban men and women, 83, 125–28. *See also* brothers; children; kinship; mothers

Fazlullah, Mullah, 11, 110, 125, 131, 155, 159, 209n53

Federally Administered Tribal Areas (FATA), 10, 63, 159. *See also* Pakistan

femininity: discourses of, 51; subordinate, 25, 123–41; vulnerable middle-class, 144. *See also* gender; women

feminist research, 3–4, 7, 13–17; in Pakistan, 14. *See also* women

First World War, 92

Foucault, Michel, 80

Freud, Sigmund, 88, 171, 240n5

Frontier Crimes Regulation (1901), 63

funeral: parents at their child's, 178–79, 182; of religious honor, 157; of transgender communities in Turkey, 235n5. *See also* death; grief/grieving

gender: Bhutto's play on, 42–45; hierarchies and norms of, 3–4, 36, 127–33, 140, 147; Islam and, 6, 131–33; performance of, 3, 42–45; roles of, 127–33, 160, 236n35. *See also* femininity; gendered figurations; gendered labor; masculinity; sexuality; women

gendered figurations, 4, 15, 194, 199; of army service, 137–38; of the female counterinsurgent, 224n85; of the female soldier, 138–39; as method, 23–26; subordination and, 124–25, 127–33, 140; violence and, 162. *See also* gender; gendered labor

gendered labor: in domestic life, 128–30, 132, 136–40; Islamo-masculinity and, 24, 123; in the Pakistani Army, 125, 137–38; political attachment and, 5, 199; in the project of *khilafat*, 127–33, 140; reproductive, 128. *See also* emotional labor; gendered figurations

Ghafoor, Asif, 21, 145–46, 150; *Junoon-e-Rukh-e-Wafa* of, 70. *See also* Inter Services Public Relations

partition of, 99; political sovereignty of, 18; racial politics of the British in colonial, 63; war of independence of, 65. *See also* South Asia

Indian Khilafat movement, 92

India-Pakistan War (1965), 57, 72; articulated as *jihad* by the Pakistani state, 99–100; *Hilal* magazine writings on the, 57, 71–72, 99–100, 137; songs about the, 55

India-Pakistan War (1971), 39, 57, 70, 116; *Hilal* magazine writings on the, 100

Insaf Student Federation (ISF), 162, 165. *See also* Pakistan Tehrik-e-Insaf

International Women's Day, 162, 178

Inter Services Public Relations (ISPR), 20–24, 53–61, 66–68, 72–73, 83, 112, 142–43, 179; films of the, 59–60, 75, 197; magazines of the, 123–24, 133, 136, 181; melodrama series of the, 138–39; music videos of the, 55–61, 67–68, 72–76, 102, 170, 179, 197, 241n31; televisual productions of the, 217n25. *See also* Ghafoor, Asif; *Hilal* magazine; media

Iqbal, Allama, 17, 67–68, 223n55; "War and Women," 135

Iran, 85

Islam: correct practice of, 90; defense of, 162; and democracy, 45–47, 52; esoteric interpretations of, 48–49; interpretations of, 8, 33–37, 40, 45–46, 52, 59; marriage and family in, 147; and modernity, 42; normative, 124, 194–95, 197–201; pietistic practices of, 114, 198; political concept of, 92; prayer rituals of, 69; Shia, 71, 157; Sufi, 47–49, 51–52; Sunni, 154, 157; women's status in, 43. *See also* Eid; hadith; *khilafat*; Mecca; Medina; Muslimness; Prophet Muhammad; Quran; religion; rituals; *sharia*; *sunnah*; *ummah*

Islamabad, 155–56, 162, 163*fig. See also* Pakistan

Islamic State, 10, 70, 187. *See also* Islamists

Islamists: interpretations of, 99; political parties of the, 84; "return to Islam" discourses of, 48; and the state, 5–6,

90–97, 110, 132, 198; as a term, 5–6. *See also* Islamic State

Islamo-masculinity, 17, 22, 24–25, 197, 200; performances of, 33, 51–53, 80, 84, 101–14, 111*fig.*, 120, 194–97. *See also* masculinity; Muslimness

Ismail, Khattab, 154

Jadoon, Amira, 12

Jaish-e-Muhammad, 84

Jamaat-e-Islami, 84, 93, 132, 165, 166*fig.*, 198, 228n91

Jamaat-ul-Ahrar, 81, 85, 87. *See also* Tehrik-e-Taliban Pakistan

Jami'a Hafsa, 155–56. *See also* Lal Masjid

Jan, Ammar Ali, 65

Jan, Najeeb, 32, 207n19

Jang Daily, 23

Jang Urdu, 176

jawan (soldier), 5, 24, 52–80, 158, 197; enchanted by the, 75–80, 77*fig.*, 78*fig.*; as fathers, 74–75; as *ghazi*, 67–70; Taliban texts about, 117–19; as object of love, 25, 54–75, 67, 197; as protector, 72–75, 137–38; as sacrificial blood, 70–72. *See also* masculinity; soldier

Jawzi, Allama Ibn, 157–58

Jehan, Madam Noor, 55

jihad (struggle), 5, 66, 87, 91–93, 98–99, 104*fig.*, 105, 110–12, 111*fig.*, 157; in Afghanistan, 215n114; discourse of, 99–101, 191, 198; ethics of, 100; and hardship, 130–31; as an individual responsibility, 192; justification of, 116–17; lands of, 191; martyrdom and, 98–99, 126; notions of, 195; in Pakistan, 215n114; in the Quran, 98, 100, 228n71; Taliban discourse on, 101–14, 198; terrorism and, 99; women's engagement in, 132–35; women writing for the cause of, 127, 135. *See also khilafat*; martyr; *mujahida*; *mujahidin*

Jinnah, Muhammad Ali, 17, 198

jirga (council of elders), 63

Johar, Major General Nigar, 133

Jordan, 115

Junoon-e-Rukhe Wafa, 133, 137

Kabul, 8. *See also* Afghanistan

kafir/kuffar (unbeliever), 103, 117, 114, 131, 153; imperial, 143, 158; state as, 143, 158; violation by the, 143, 153, 169; violence of the, 153–59; women against the, 131, 160

Kalyvas, Stathis, 6

Karachi, 78*fig.*, 115, 162, 163*fig.*, 165*fig.*, 174*fig.*, 181. *See also* Pakistan

Kashmir, 38, 99. *See also* India; Pakistan

Kayani, General Ashfaq, 20, 82, 116

Kazanjian, David, 185

Keddie, Nikki, 133

Khalique, Captain Ayesha, 134

Khan, General Ayub, 40

Khan, Prime Minister Imran, 22, 32, 47–52, 160, 182, 184*fig.*, 187; *Pakistan: A Personal History* of, 47–50

Khan, Sir Syed Ahmed, 64

khilafat (Islamic order), 11, 14, 23, 25, 86, 89, 196, 227n62; establishment of, 98–99, 133; land of, 124, 127, 142, 196; notions of, 97, 195; path of, 160; political apparatus of, 90–97; sacrifice for, 119, 127; *sharia* and, 92; in the Taliban magazines, 96–98; women in the land of, 140, 160. *See also* Islam; *jihad*

Khorasani, Muhammad Umar, 1–2, 10

Khudai Khidmatgar, 64

Khurasan, Umm, 157

Khurasani, Ibn Hassan, 103

Khurasani, Mukaram, 161

Khurasani, Omar Khalid, 119

Khyber Pakhtunkhwa, 35, 63–65, 181. *See also* Pakistan

kinship: and affect, 24–25, 123, 168; and attachment, 1, 3, 194; feelings of, 1, 3, 25, 142–69, 194, 199, 201; forging of new, 126; heterosexual relations of, 75; language of, 43, 118, 234n4; and memory, 24–25; metaphors of, 4–5, 42, 44–45, 123, 142–69, 196; to the Muslims of the past, 82; and permission for violence, 1–2; recourse to, 24–25; and soldiers, 53–55; and sovereign power, 36–37, 42–45; in Taliban productions, 103, 192. *See also* attachment; *behan*; *beti*; brothers; fathers; mothers

Kristof, Nicholas, 152

kufr (disbelief): declaration of, 117; definition of, 226n34; notions of, 195; as system of democratic governance, 89

Laghari, Naureen, 19, 142–54

Lahore, 77*fig.*, 79*fig.*, 126, 142–46, 162, 164*fig.*, 165–67, 166*fig.*, 167*fig.*, 173–74, 181. *See also* Pakistan

Lal Masjid, 115, 155; army siege of, 155–56; assault on Muslim women at, 156. *See also* Jami'a Hafsa

Lashkar-e-Taiba, 84

law: and discrimination towards women, 152; of God, 92–93; Islamic, 226n40; of the king, 92; as a legacy of the British colonial period, 200; Pakistani, 201. *See also sharia*

liberalism: and the rule of law, 32; and the state, 16

London, 41

loss: of the beloved, 186; betrayal and, 39, 88; of the children killed in the APS attack, 57, 180; grief and, 176, 180; of *khilafat*, 96; of life, 26; melancholy as an unhealthy response to, 185; mothers grieving a, 14, 170–71, 180; of an object of love, 88; of political sovereignty, 18. *See also* affect; mourning

love: for Allah, 177; and beloved objects, 171, 176; and the burial of loved ones, 186; children as objects of, 66; of death, 100; and disgust, 54–75; the *jawan* as object of, 25, 54–75, 197; for mothers, 177; for the nation, 55, 72, 89, 177; and publics, 36, 194; staging of, 54–75. *See also* affect; hate

love-hate relationship, 88. *See also* hate; love

madrasa (educational institution), 81, 96–97, 155

Mahenna, Tariq, 156

Mahmood, Captain Aijaz, 57

Mahmood, Cynthia, 6

Mahmood, Rafay, 6

Mahmood, Sara, 12

Mai, Mukhtar, 143, 151–53, 203

Majlis-i-Shura, 155

Malakand, 6, 11, 128, 195. *See also* Pakistan

Malik, Anushay, 13

Manchanda, Nivi, 62

Mankekar, Purnima, 139

Mann, Bonnie, 17

martial race ideology, 65, 222n43, 234n75

martyr: APS children as, 176–88; commemoration of, 84, 117; daughter of, 44; discourse of, 70, 99, 117, 137, 179; the *ghazi* as, 68; and *jihad*, 98–99, 126; mother of, 137, 176–93, 203; sister of, 44; soldier as, 55, 70–72. *See also* death; *jihad*; *shahadat*; widows of martyrs

masculinity: codes of honor of, 42, 99; English, 222n43; hierarchies of, 25, 44, 197, 202; Islamic warrior, 4, 53–54, 68, 98, 101–14, 157–58, 195, 197; military, 33–41, 79; and Muslimness, 4, 16–18, 25; of perfect men (*mard-e-momin*), 68, 223n57; performances of, 5, 33, 42–45, 99, 101–14, 158, 200–201; as a practice of power, 33, 42–45; in the process of nation-building, 245n8; redemptive, 47–51; softer, 103; sovereign, 41–45, 51; sovereign female, 41–45; study of, 213n88; tough, 34–35; traditional notions of, 114. *See also* gender; Islamomasculinity; *jawan*

Masud, Rahat, 173*fig.*

Mawdudi, Abul ʿala, 92–93, 97–98, 132; *Purdah and the Status of Women*, 132

Mbembe, Achille, 202

McLarney, Ellen, 133

Mecca, 82, 89. *See also* Islam

media: growth of Pakistani, 18–19, 34; Islamist print, 84; Pakistani Army and the, 20–21; politics and the, 2, 84–120; publishing, 217n5; and sexual violence, 60, 152; Western, 46, 237n43; world, 159. *See also Hilal* magazine; Inter Services Public Relations; newspaper; public culture; social media; television

Medina, 89. *See also* Islam

Meerawala, 151. *See also* Pakistan

Mehsud, Baitullah, 9, 22, 119, 155, 209n53

Mehsud, Hakimullah, 89–91

Mehsud, Khalid, 10

Mehsud, Noor Wali, 12

melancholy: creative potential of, 190; of mothers, 5, 16, 25, 171–72, 182–93, 203; mourning and, 171, 185–86, 192, 240n5; pathologization of, 171; politicized, 171; as resistance to forgetting, 185. *See also* affect; mourning

memory: affect and, 4, 14, 19, 24; autobiographies as acts of, 32; kinship and, 24–25; Muslim collective, 97, 114; national collective, 24, 55, 195; of past Muslim rule, 96; of past lives, 126; of past violence, 5, 114; politicized, 171; socially located embodied, 185–86; sovereign attachment and, 5, 7, 25. *See also* affect; memory work; nostalgia

memory work, 4, 123, 194, 198, 201. *See also* memory

messianism, 101–2, 227n56

militant women, 79–80, 79*fig.*, 124–33. *See also* women

militarism, 47, 75–80, 101, 120, 201; women's bodies as the terrain of, 240n103

military women, 124, 133–39, 233n73. *See also* women

Mitchell, Timothy, 19

modernity: discourses of, 4, 54; heteronormativity and, 17; Islam and, 42; and precarity, 96

Moin, Azfar, 101

momin (believer), 68, 117; mercy to, 103; pride of a, 100

Momin, Bilal, 102

Moonglade, 21

Mortimer-Sandilands, Catriona, 185, 190

mothers: of APS students, 16, 57, 172, 174, 176–93, 200, 203; counterpublic of, 189; emotional labor for the nation of, 172–93; love for, 177; of martyrs, 137, 176–93, 203; melancholic, 5, 16, 25, 171–72, 182–93, 203; militarization of, 179; mourning, 14, 16, 24–25, 170–93, 172*fig.*, 173*fig.*, 174*fig.*, 175*fig.*, 183*fig.*, 199, 242n36; of the *mujahidin*, 191–92; of soldiers, 74; and the Taliban, 119, 126, 128; in wartime, 27; women primarily as, 17, 128. *See also* children; fathers; kinship; women

of, 66. *See also* East Pakistan; Federally
Administered Tribal Areas; Pakistani
Army; Pakistani state; Pakistani Tali-
ban; South Asia
Pakistan Electronic Media Regulatory
Authority (PEMRA), 18–19
Pakistani Army, 2, 5, 19, 34–38, 51, 70, 114,
125, 213n99; coups of the, 20; cultural
productions of the, 20–24, 53–61,
66–68, 72–76, 83; as defender of Islam,
20; efforts to contain the Taliban of the,
12; and the media, 20–21; pride in the,
136–37; as a secularizing force, 126; and
state violence, 116, 155, 198. *See also*
Pakistani state; soldier
Pakistani Inter-Services Intelligence
Agency (ISI), 8
Pakistani state, 2–5, 7, 9, 211n75; apparatus
of the, 97; colonial legacies of the, 200;
Islamists and the, 5–6, 90–97, 110, 132,
198; *jihad* as articulated by the, 99–100;
khilafat as an alternative to the, 90–97;
as a modern nation-state, 196–97;
mourning mothers and the, 170, 179;
and the Pakistani Taliban, 11, 13–18, 24,
75–80, 88, 196–98; performances of
sovereignty of the, 1–2, 6–7, 16, 25–26,
151–53, 168, 181, 195; sovereign community of the nation for the, 196. *See also*
Pakistan; sovereignty
Pakistaniyat, 150, 168
Pakistan Muslim League, 37
Pakistan Peoples Party (PPP), 41, 47
Pakistan Tehrik-e-Insaf (PTI), 47–48, 160,
182; rally of the, 167; supporters of,
164*fig.*, 166*fig.*, 167*fig. See also* Insaf
Student Federation
Pakistan Telecommunications Authority,
18
Palumbo-Liu, David, 53
Parashar, Swati, 171
Pashtun: Afghanistan as the home of the,
50; death and war for the, 99; discrimination against, 62–67; in ISPR cultural
texts, 62; language of, 62–63; as a martial race, 66; mobility from tribal areas
to cities of, 65; in the Pakistani Army,
65–66, 117; sexuality of, 62; shared

ethnic code of the, 9; as terrorists, 65.
See also Pathan
Pathan, 43; the *talib* as, 62–67. *See also*
Pashtun
performativity, 200, 211
Peshawar, 1, 78*fig.*, 174, 185*fig. See also*
Pakistan
policing, 151; by the Taliban, 6, 11; of
women, 147, 153. *See also* protection
poverty, 119, 128
Powell, Secretary of State Colin, 31, 36
Prophet Muhammad, 69, 71, 90, 105; life of,
105. *See also* Islam
protection: attachment and, 15; of children,
149, 171; constitutional, 1; against
enemies, 53; kinship and, 45, 143–53;
relationships of, 3; of religion, 118; as a
sovereign function, 14, 17, 25, 51, 72, 77,
90, 142, 146; Taliban notions of, 6, 11,
89, 126, 154; of women, 61, 118, 128,
143–44, 167, 169, 171. *See also*
policing
protests: anti-American, 239n93; anti-Qadyani, 115; against the detention of Aafia
Siddiqui, 161–68, 163*fig.*, 164*fig.*, 165*fig.*,
166*fig.*; as sovereign actors, 143; and
sovereignty, 16, 143, 167–68; against
the Taliban, 174*fig.*, 176; by women,
79*fig.*, 157, 174*fig.*, 185*fig. See also* public
culture
public culture, 2, 13, 19, 80, 136, 146, 192;
the *jawan* in, 197; magazines and, 21, 53,
67, 69, 100, 123–24, 133–36, 141, 179, 181;
songs and, 55; sovereignty and, 7, 19, 24;
Taliban and, 10, 13, 54; women in, 161,
171, 176. *See also* media; protests
publics, 1, 4–5, 14, 203; affective, 5, 14–15,
194; allied, 14–15, 25, 143; claimants to
sovereignty and, 2, 17, 194; diverse, 24;
fraternal, 5, 25, 153–58, 161, 169, 199;
grieving, 180–82; making of, 4, 14–15;
masculine, 168–69; paternal, 5, 25,
144–53, 161, 169, 199, 237n47; and
public opinion, 14, 19–20; reading,
22–24, 31; masculine, 168–69. *See also*
counterpublics
Punjab, 35, 102. *See also* Pakistan
Punjab Murderous Outrages Act (1867), 63

Siddiqa, Ayesha, 12
Siddiqui, Aafia, 19, 143, 153–58, 161–69, 203, 239n93; kinship relations with, 200; portrait of, 165*fig.*
Sindh, 65, 71, 102. *See also* Pakistan
Sinha, Mrinalini, 16
social media, 145–47, 187. *See also* media
soldier, 5, 24, 52–80, 115; of Allah, 101–14; dead, 70; discrediting of the Pakistani and American, 102; enchanted by the, 75–80, 77*fig.*, 78*fig.*; the everyday female, 138–39; faith of a, 100; as fathers, 74–75; as *ghazi*, 67–70; imitation of the national, 120; and the *mujahidin*, 118–20; as object of love, 25, 54–75, 67, 197; profession of the, 100; as protector, 72–75; as sacrificial blood, 70–72; uniform of the, 113–14. See also *jawan*; Pakistani Army
South Asia, 17; Muslim, 17, 96–97, 101. *See also* India
sovereign: the military man as the ideal, 34–36; narrating the, 31–52; wrath of the, 152. *See also* heads of state; sovereignty
sovereignty: absolute, 2–4, 13, 26, 196, 201; affective dimensions of, 193–95; archives of, 18–27; and attachment, 15–16, 19–20, 24–25, 31–53, 77, 80, 84, 194–95; autonomy and, 196; claimants of, 124, 194, 200, 202; competing, 7–13; divine, 11, 26, 91, 96–97, 102–3, 119, 201; female masculinity and, 41–47; gestures of, 117; imbrications of, 3, 7, 25; imperial, 152, 201; through the institution of *khilafat*, 93–97; intensifying relations of, 199–201; mafia networks as localized systems of, 210n65; in Mawdudi's writings, 92; messianic, 101–2; performances of, 1–7, 16, 25–26, 151–53, 168, 181, 195, 200, 235n5; personifications of, 31–52; popular, 16, 161–62, 168; postcolonial, 195; practices of, 12, 147–49; public lives of, 1–27; redemption of, 50; relationships of, 4, 33; relinquishing of, 46; state, 13, 26, 77, 119, 152–53, 162, 205n6; transmutation of, 227n56; and violence, 1–2, 205n5; visible forms of, 32, 152. *See also* heads of state; Pakistani state; sovereign

Soviet Union, 8; invasion of Afghanistan by the, 66, 99–100, 155
Special Services Group, 40. *See also* Pakistani Army
Spellman, Elizabeth, 36
Stepputat, Finn, 7, 13, 19
Stoler, Ann, 14, 244n2
subjectivity: Islamic, 33; pious, 133
suffering: connecting to others in, 127; of the delay of justice, 188; of mothers, 171, 187–88; and the motives of *jihadis*, 127
suicide, 130; missions for women of, 131–32
sunnah (practices of the Prophet Muhammad), Islamic, 86–87, 105; Taliban and, 200. *See also* Islam
Sunnat-e-Khola magazine, 22–23, 85–87, 90, 123–28, 129*fig.*, 131, 160, 191–92
Swat, 6, 11, 26, 73, 115, 128, 150, 159, 195. *See also* Pakistan
Syria, 157, 192, 206n11

tafsir (interpretation), 97
taghut (tyrant, idolator), 114
talib (student), 54–67, 82–83, 197; as a coward, 56–59; as "Pathan," 62–67; as prisoner, 115–16; as sexually perverse, 59–62; slippage with the Pashtun and the, 63–66, 202
Taliban: Afghan, 8–10, 38, 88, 97, 225n8; attachment to the, 192, 203; backwardness of the, 80; campaign against girls' education of the, 159; cultural productions of the, 84–120; as a counterpublic, 15, 80, 119–20, 197–98; death in the ideology of the, 99, 101; flag of the, 93, 94*fig.*; history of the, 8; ideology of the, 6, 96–99, 110; loss of *khilafat* for the, 96; magazines of the, 84–88, 96–97, 101–14, 119–20, 124–33, 143, 153–56, 171, 198; mourning mother in archives of the, 191–92; occupation of territory by the, 3, 8, 139; operations of the Pakistani Army against the, 1, 26, 138–39; Pakistani state and the, 11, 13–18, 24, 75–80, 88, 196–98; performances of sovereignty of the, 22, 103, 195, 197–98; pledge of

Founded in 1893,
UNIVERSITY OF CALIFORNIA PRESS
publishes bold, progressive books and journals
on topics in the arts, humanities, social sciences,
and natural sciences—with a focus on social
justice issues—that inspire thought and action
among readers worldwide.

The UC PRESS FOUNDATION
raises funds to uphold the press's vital role
as an independent, nonprofit publisher, and
receives philanthropic support from a wide
range of individuals and institutions—and from
committed readers like you. To learn more, visit
ucpress.edu/supportus.